The Russian Revolution

The Russian Revolution

A View from the Third World

Walter Rodney

Edited and with an Introduction by
Robin D. G. Kelley and Jesse J. Benjamin
Foreword by Vijay Prashad

V
VERSO
London • New York

First published by Verso 2018
© Walter Rodney Foundation 2018
Introduction © Jesse J. Benjamin and Robin D. G. Kelley 2018
Foreword © Vijay Prashad 2018

Frontispiece, original art by Abbyssinian.
Redesigned by Aajay Murphy.

1 3 5 7 9 10 8 6 4 2

Verso
UK: 6 Meard Street, London W1F 0EG
US: 20 Jay Street, Suite 1010, Brooklyn, NY 11201
versobooks.com

Verso is the imprint of New Left Books

ISBN-13: 978-1-78663-530-3
ISBN-13: 978-1-78663-531-0 (UK EBK)
ISBN-13: 978-1-78663-532-7 (US EBK)

British Library Cataloguing in Publication Data
A catalogue record for this book is available from the British Library

Library of Congress Cataloging-in-Publication Data
A catalog record for this book is available
from the Library of Congress

Typeset in Sabon LT by Hewer Text UK Ltd, Edinburgh
Printed and bound by CPI Group (UK) Ltd, Croydon CR0 4YY

Most dedications are written by the author to someone or something that was important to the book's creation. Who or what Walter Rodney would have written here was taken from us when his life was violently snatched from us at the age of thirty-eight. It has taken us the sum of his lifetime, another thirty-eight years, to publish this book. So, given this task, I dedicate this book to Walter Rodney, who brilliantly penned these lectures; and to his immeasurable mind and thirst for knowledge that made this work possible.

This book is dedicated to you Daddy, the world's Walter Rodney. It is your first original work produced solely from your lecture notes that has been published posthumously, and we hope it does you justice. Most people speak. Fewer write. Fewer research. Even fewer are fastidious and prolific. Rare are those who do them all, and well. This book takes its place in your tradition of research, scholarship and radical analysis and in your ability to teach complex issues (of consciousness, self-activity, mass movements, class struggle) in an understandable way.

Asha T. Rodney

Contents

Foreword
Rodney and the Revolution
Vijay Prashad

Live Through a Revolution

In the first years of the 1960s, Walter Rodney went to the Soviet Union. He was in his early twenties, a young man from a working-class Guyanese family who had read history at the University of the West Indies in Jamaica. He arrived in the airport in Moscow and knew he had arrived somewhere different:

> When I travelled to the Soviet Union, I was struck on arrival at the airport by the physical demeanour and the social aspect of the people in the airport. They were workers and peasants, as far as I could see, who were flying on those TU-104's to Moscow, to Leningrad, etc., as though they were using a bus. And my understanding of an airport was that it was a very bourgeois institution. There were only certain of us who were supposed to be in an airport. But the Soviets seemed to have ascended beyond that. That was what one confronted going into the country. And then, having left the airport, one goes into the streets and one is amazed at the number of books they sell—in the streets, on the pavement, all over. In my society, you have to search for

a bookstore and be directed and told that *the* bookstore is down *that* street, as if it's an alien institution. And even in America, one can buy hot dogs and hamburgers on the sidewalks, a lot of nice things like that, but not books.[1]

Rodney had visited Cuba as a student, the year after the Cuban Revolution of 1959. Things were not settled in Cuba, as they had become in the Soviet Union—nearly fifty years after the October Revolution of 1917. The familiarity to him of Cuba as a Caribbean society and the actuality of its revolution pleased Rodney. "The Cubans were up and about, talking and bustling and running and jumping and really living the revolution in a way that was completely outside of anything that one could read anywhere or listen to or conceptualize in an island such as Jamaica," where Rodney was still a student. "One has to live with a revolution to get its full impact," Rodney said in 1975, "but the next best thing is to go there and see a people actually attempting to grapple with real problems of development." Rodney made this comment on April 30, the precise day that the Vietnamese people watched the US imperialists retreat from their country. Another revolution—in a different form—had triumphed.

Times of Transformation

Rodney taught at the University of Dar es Salaam (Tanzania) in 1967 and then again from 1969 to 1974. This was the high point of the country's experiment with self-reliance and non-alignment, with what was then called "African socialism" across the continent and "Ujamaa" in Tanzania. These were times of transformation.

In November 1967, not long after Rodney began to teach at the university, the radical students from across the region formed the University Students' African Revolutionary Front, led by Yoweri Museveni (the president of Uganda since 1986).

The students had been inspired by the February 1967 Arusha Declaration, which urged Tanzanian society to move in the direction of "socialism and self-reliance." "For a country to be socialist," the Declaration—drafted by Tanzania's president Julius Nyerere—noted, "it is essential that its government is chosen and led by the peasants and workers themselves." The centrality of the workers and peasants was a fact established not only by the Marxists at the university or the students, but also by the governing party in Tanzania. The energy toward serious transformation had become clear. As the Arusha Declaration pointed out,

> We have been oppressed a great deal, we have been exploited a great deal and we have been disregarded a great deal. It is our weakness that has led to our being oppressed, exploited and disregarded. Now we want a revolution—a revolution which brings to an end our weakness, so that we are never again exploited, oppressed or humiliated.[2]

A revolution against weakness was at the heart of the national liberation project. It is what the students also understood in their desire to produce a front that would not only consolidate their concerns but also provide an avenue for them to stimulate debate about the way forward. Students at the University of Dar es Salaam who came from Sudan, Zambia, Ethiopia and Rhodesia brought with them the energy of their anti-colonial movements—many far more radical than Nyerere's Tanganyika African National Union (TANU). Dar es Salaam was the headquarters of the Liberation Committee, a platform urged on by Nyerere within the Organisation of African Unity in 1963. One of the key players in the Liberation Committee was the anti-colonial Mozambican political movement FRELIMO (Mozambique Liberation Front), which was then based in Dar es Salaam. FRELIMO had begun to move from an inchoate national liberation ideology toward Marxism. The presence of FRELIMO revolutionaries such as Marcelino dos Santos and Samora Machel, alongside Marxist intellectuals such as A. M. Babu, John Saul, Issa Shivji and—for a brief period—Ruth First, provided an avenue for the students to read about and bend toward Marxism and Leninism.

Reflecting back on the formation of the students' Revolutionary Front in 1970, its president, Museveni, wrote, "We waged such a resolute struggle against the interests of imperialism that the reactionaries thought we were mad."[3] This essay appeared in *Cheche*, the magazine started in 1969 by the Revolutionary Front and the TANU Youth League. This magazine, edited by student radicals Karim Hirji, Henry Mapolu and Zakia Meghji, took its name from the Soviet newspaper *Iskra* (Spark). This gives one a sense of the times, where Marxism was the governing creed of the national liberation movements and of the radical students. Rodney not only contributed to the sharpening of this mood, but he was—in turn—deeply marked by it.

Africa Is on the Move

During his time in Tanzania, Rodney paid attention to the state of the African workers. In the first issue of *Cheche*, he wrote an essay entitled "African Labour Under Capitalism and Imperialism," which attempted to chart the current motion of the African working-class and revolutionary sections of the peasantry. Rodney was interested in the objective and subjective situation of the African workers: How was capitalism across the continent organized, what kind of labor organization was possible as a consequence, what was the general sensibility of the African workers (both the proletariat and the peasantry) and what was the relationship between African workers and the anti-imperialist national liberation movements and regimes that had taken hold across the continent? These were the kinds of questions raised by Rodney in this period—questions stimulated by his turn fully into Marxism, which was deeply inflected by his awareness of the situation in the Third World and its particular ground for a Marxist analysis.

This is why Rodney moved into the archives in Dar es Salaam, looking carefully at the long-history of the working people in the region. He was interested in how colonialism had divested the working people of the area of their skills and of their bodies—impoverishing the workers and peasants to the point that their dependency was coterminous with their survival. These studies resulted in few publications, but one of them—an essay on migrant labor in Tanzania during the colonial period for the sisal industry—was published after his death.[4] That volume included essays by Rodney's graduate students, Kapepwa Tambila—who was later head of the Department of History at Dar—and Laurent Sago. They were interested in looking for signs of labor quiescence and for labor unrest—for the potential within current realities for revolutionary transformation.

In an important text, published posthumously, entitled "Marxism in Africa," Rodney considered how Marxism had to be creatively applied by the major revolutions of the twentieth century. Lenin, he wrote, had to delve deeply into the situation of the Russian peasantry—the majority of the working people—to uncover the differentiation within it, so as to clarify who were the revolutionary classes. Much the same applied for Mao, who had to understand the "inner dynamics of Chinese society, relating to the question of the peasantry."[5] In his own time, Rodney looked at the work of Amílcar Cabral, who could not search for identifiable classes in colonial Guinea-Bissau but began his investigations with the production process, the people in that process, and the sharp edges of radicalism in that situation. Marxism, for Rodney, was a "revolutionary ideology" that required close attention to the facts on the ground in order to search for the revolutionary energy that made itself manifest in various ways. Here Rodney echoed Lenin, who wrote that "the living soul of Marxism" is the "concrete analysis of concrete conditions." These quiet studies of Tanzanian labor conditions and of the work of Cabral reveal an imagination gripped by the necessity of searching for motion in African societies.

It was this kind of attention to the working people that drew Rodney—like Frantz Fanon before him—to sharply criticize the limited positions of national liberation. In early December 1969, Rodney spoke at the Second Seminar of East and Central African Youth, a forum at the University of Dar es Salaam organized by the students.[6] His talk, on the second day, was entitled "The Ideology of the African Revolution." Rodney lit into the limitations of national liberation, pointing out that the African workers were not central to the project, which led these new states to compromise their integrity by making alliances with imperialism. Rodney had not included Tanzania in the list. But nonetheless, a few days later, the newspaper of the ruling party, the *Nationalist*, responded with a sharp editorial entitled "Revolutionary Hot Air." It suggested that Rodney and others were unrealistic hotheads who misjudged the moment. Rodney's move deeper into Marxism and into the imperative for worker-led communist politics resulted from having settled accounts with the limitations of national liberation and Pan-African politics. More was needed, as was reflected in Rodney's lecture at the university on "Marxism, Ujamaa and the Stages of Social Development" as well as in his 1972 critique for *African Review*.[7]

Taking History to the Streets

Rodney turned to the October Revolution while in Dar es Salaam not merely to discover what happened there, but also to teach his students—who were on the move—about that major revolutionary experience. Certainly Rodney was aware that the context of the October Revolution mattered a great deal.[8] But what mattered more was to teach a new generation of African revolutionaries about the importance of historical materialism and Marxism, of the necessity of studying the objective and subjective conditions of society toward revolutionary transformation, and of then looking carefully at the "actuality of revolution" and its own contradictions. This is what his lectures show us: rather than acting as an erudite scholar, teaching about the events of 1917 and their aftermath *for their own sake*, Rodney used the October Revolution to instruct the revolutionary students about the experience of 1917.

Rodney obviously had read a great deal about the October Revolution, mastering both the bourgeois and socialist scholarship to produce his own vision of October. There are indications everywhere of his training with C. L. R. James and Selma James, particularly in his insistence that the Russian workers and peasants led the way in the revolution. In *Notes on Dialectics* (1948), C. L. R. James wrote that the "workers did the theoretical work on the soviet. *They* thought over the soviet. They analysed it and remembered it."[9]

Rodney's perspective is alive, dazzling with the potential of the October Revolution for Africa, aware that a new generation—including himself—must learn of the possibility of breaking with the old hierarchies to produce a dynamic toward equality. It was not enough to be seized by anger and frustration, resentment and humiliation. These are what the Arusha Declaration warned against. What was needed was a precise assessment of the potential for working-class and peasant struggle as well as the possibility—after the October Revolution and the revolutions in China, Vietnam and Cuba—for the replication of the events of 1917 in Africa. Rodney took history to the streets to make sure that his students saw that the past had to guide them in their fights to build the future. It was not to happen in Tanzania nor in his native Guyana, where Rodney was assassinated in 1980 at the age of thirty-eight.

Editors' Note
Robin D. G. Kelley and
Jesse J. Benjamin

The organization, editing, and annotation of this book began over three decades ago. In the aftermath of Rodney's assassination in 1980, his papers were moved from Guyana to Barbados, where the Rodney family then resided, for safekeeping. Patricia Rodney, Walter's wife, subsequently asked Ned Alpers—a close family friend and colleague from Dar who was visiting Barbados—to secure the papers temporarily at the University of California, Los Angeles, where he was a professor of African history.

In 1984, Alpers hired Robin D. G. Kelley, then a second-year graduate student in African history, to help catalog some of the material. In particular, Kelley was assigned the task of organizing, transcribing and annotating Rodney's lectures on the Russian Revolution. The lectures, twenty in all, were numbered and almost entirely typed, with some handwritten notes scrawled in between and in the margins. Some of them had been written out as prose, while others were simply in outline form or cryptic notes. The files also contained a handwritten preface bearing the title "Two World Views of the Russian

Revolution: Reflections from Africa." The preface was evidence that Rodney had planned to turn his lectures into a book, but what was found in those files in 1984 was still a long way from becoming the current book.

Kelley "digitized" each lecture by retyping everything onto a computer disc. There were no scanners in those days, and personal computers did not have hard drives. Everything was stored on floppy disks using software that is now defunct. In addition to transcribing everything, Kelley performed some light editing—eliminating repetition, fixing minor grammatical, spelling and punctuation errors, and correcting small mistakes (inaccurate dates, misidentified individuals, and so forth). Rodney's work was still largely in the form of lecture notes, and he had not yet transformed all the lectures into book-ready chapters. For example, the lectures had no footnotes, and when there were references, these typically consisted of an author's name and maybe a title. The lectures were rich with quotations, statistics, and critiques of scholars, often without full references, leading Kelley to spend the better part of a year tracking down sources and citations. Rodney quoted liberally, but his lecture notes did not always record the quote precisely; sometimes a word was missing or he cut out portions of an excerpt without replacing the excision with ellipses. In his review, in a few cases, Kelley decided to include the complete quote rather than ellipses if it provided greater clarity. In other instances, the issue had to do with translation: quotes translated from Russian and German were not always from the same edition, so Kelley made a determined effort to source the exact edition Rodney used; where this was impossible, he revised the quote to correspond with the latest or most respected translation. Occasionally Rodney included a parenthetical reference to a particular book; in these instances, the reference has been moved to a footnote with an indication that the citation came from Rodney, and we have explained how it appeared in the original text.

Sometime in 1985, Patricia Rodney decided to remove the papers from UCLA, both to secure Rodney's intellectual property and to find them a permanent home. By the time the papers left UCLA, all of the lectures had been transcribed, most had been lightly edited, and about half of them had been sourced with citations. These early manuscripts were printed and archived. Kelley retained a copy for his own records, and over the years shared copies with two other scholars—Rupert Lewis, a professor at the University of the West Indies, Mona who was working on a biography of Rodney, and Marxist historian David Roediger. Unfortunately, the floppy disks eventually deteriorated, and the digitized lectures were never saved to a hard drive. Nevertheless, over the years, researchers have been able to access both the original lectures and the slightly edited, sourced versions of the Rodney papers at the Atlanta University Center Robert W. Woodruff Library, where they were deposited by the Rodney family in 2003.

Fast-forward to a chance meeting in October 2011, when historian David Roediger met Jesse Benjamin after presenting at a Kennesaw State University conference on post–World War II workplace integration. When Benjamin mentioned some of his work as a board member of the Walter Rodney Foundation in Atlanta, Roediger brought up the exciting manuscript that had been in his possession and related that he'd always hoped to confer with the Rodney family before making any decision about publishing. The existence of the manuscript, outside of the Rodney papers at the AUC Woodruff archives, was a revelation to Benjamin, who shared it with the Rodney family when Roediger promptly sent a copy; it was soon confirmed that this edited copy was the same as the one deposited in the archives. More importantly, this jump-started a discussion about publication. Roediger later returned a copy of the uncompleted manuscript to Kelley with a note mentioning that the Rodney family was considering publishing the Russian Revolution lectures as a book. Thus began a series of conversations about moving the project forward, as well as an invitation from Benjamin, coordinator of the annual Walter Rodney Speakers Series, for Kelley to deliver a lecture on Rodney and the Russian

Revolution in April 2015. Out of those conversations and meetings in Atlanta, Kelley and Benjamin agreed to team up as coeditors to complete the work Kelley had advanced thirty years earlier, and that Rodney had created almost half a century prior.

With help from four research assistants, Shamell Bell, Amber Withers, Kristen Glasgow, and Kela Caldwell, Kelley re-digitized the hard copies of the sourced lectures, and Benjamin helped scrub and proof them into more-final copy. Kelley then rearranged the lectures into coherent chapters and spent the next eighteen months tracking down the remaining citations, as well as adding additional footnotes that explain and contextualize the revolution, outlining pertinent debates, organizations, personalities, historiographical controversies, and so forth. The editors then collaboratively revised the final version of the manuscript and cowrote an introduction, with Benjamin focusing on Rodney's life and theoretical contributions, and Kelley on the history of the Russian Revolution and Rodney's interpretation.

We can only imagine what sort of creative process Rodney would have used to turn these lectures into a book, and what he may have added or cut out in the process. Instead, the reader encounters here an unfinished work, interrupted at the height of Rodney's power as a thinker and as an agent of liberation, and at a moment when anti-capitalist and anti-colonial struggles were at a crossroads. It is a testament to his brilliance that his lecture notes constitute a nearly fully formed book, worthy of publication and careful consideration almost fifty years later.

We have endeavored to make the present volume available to the public in a way that mirrors as closely as possible what we think Walter Rodney would have wanted under these unusual circumstances. We were especially fortunate to have his family working closely with us throughout the entire process, in particular Patricia Rodney and his daughter Asha Rodney.

Introduction
An "African Perspective" on the Russian Revolution
Jesse J. Benjamin and Robin D. G. Kelley

During the 1970–71 academic year, Walter Rodney, the renowned Marxist historian of Africa and the Caribbean, taught an advanced graduate course at the University of Dar es Salaam titled "Historians and Revolutions," focusing entirely on the historiographies of the French and Russian Revolutions. This wasn't your run-of-the-mill European historiography course. Rodney's objectives were to introduce students to dialectical materialism as a methodology for interpreting the history of revolutionary movements, to critique bourgeois histories and their liberal conceits of objectivity, and to draw political lessons for the Third World. Russia, having experienced the first successful socialist revolution in the world, figured prominently in the course.[1]

To prepare, he underwent a thorough review of Russian history in the years prior to the course, reading on the emancipation of the serfs, the rise of the Russian left intelligentsia, the 1905 Revolution, the February Revolution of 1917, the Bolshevik seizure of power in October, Lenin's New Economic

Policy, Trotsky's interpretation of history, and the rise of Stalinism and "socialism in one country." He read voraciously and systematically, critically absorbing virtually everything available to him in the English language—from US and British Cold War scholarship to translations of Soviet historiography. The result was a series of original lectures that revisited key economic and political developments, the challenges of socialist transformation in a "backwards" empire, the consolidation of state power, debates within Marxist circles over the character of Russia's revolution, and the ideological bases of historical interpretation. Rather than simply re-narrate well-known events, Rodney took up the more challenging task of interrogating the meaning, representation, and significance of the Russian Revolution as a world-historical event whose reverberations profoundly shaped Marxist thought, Third World liberation movements, and theories of socialist transformation.

Probably before the course ended, Rodney had begun to turn these lectures into a book. In 1971, he wrote his friend Ewart Thomas, a professor of psychology at the University of Michigan who was visiting Stanford University, that while he had been teaching courses on Cuba and China,

> my main teaching field has been Russia. My publications obviously do not provide evidence of expertise in European History, but I really have done a great deal of work on the Russian Revolution. This year I was about to start a monograph covering the 1917 Revolution and the period up to World War 2 and I put it aside only because the African material had to be given higher priority.[2]

Of course, the "African material" turned out to be *How Europe Underdeveloped Africa* (1972).

He did start writing the book but was unable to complete it due to other constraints, including several years of travel and the intense political struggle in Guyana in the late 1970s. Walter's wife Patricia Rodney notes that he always worked on many projects at the same time, advancing them whenever time allowed or opportunity arose. Many of the Russian lectures were typed out in essay form, and Rodney's personal papers and writings, now located at the Atlanta University Center Robert W. Woodruff Library, contained a hand-written preface to what he called *Two World Views of the Russian Revolution: Reflections from Africa*.[3] Preparation of these lectures overlapped, in fact, with the writing of *How Europe Underdeveloped Africa*, and with other projects Rodney completed during the Tanzania (1969–74) and Guyana (1974–80) years.[4] *How Europe Underdeveloped Africa* (*HEUA*) not only argued for a socialist path of development as the only viable future for the continent, but adopted a favorable stance toward the Soviet Union. Rodney praised the Soviet command economy as a bulwark against fascism and hailed Lenin's work on imperialism as "prophetic" and the "most thorough and best-known analysis."[5] Partly because they were delivered as lectures, the intended book was crafted with a broad audience in mind, as was the case with *HEUA*. It is direct, witty, and occasionally biting; it is also daringly original, honest, and brazenly willing to deploy an anti-colonial perspective that resonated with politicized readers across the world. On the other hand, this is a very different sort of book from *HEUA*, focusing more on historiography than history, and on the political stakes involved in the interpretation of revolution. Rodney charts a new direction for Black Studies and African studies—one bold enough to examine the entire world. Thus, consistent with all of his work, this volume exhibits the same sort of truth telling and rigorous intellectual commitment to solving, rather than just studying, pressing problems in the society and its social movements.

The lectures provided a fresh analysis of the Russian Revolution at the height of the Cold War. Rodney's "Two World Views" framing clarified (1) that bourgeois perspectives writ large are simply particular, biased perspectives among others; and (2) that these are distinct from Soviet perspectives, which are themselves worthy of engagement despite being dismissed by bourgeois scholarship. In the same way that Edward Said's *Orientalism* analytic exposed the occidental and imperial nexus of modern thought, Rodney's framing and circumscription of Western thought *as bourgeois* named it as a located interpretive agent in the world, aligned with the interests of bourgeois capitalism. By drawing attention to the material conditions underwriting divergent historiographies, the "two world views" concept relativizes bourgeois thought while legitimizing Soviet and other Marxist thought, even as it criticizes the latter. Therefore, the concept provides the theoretical ground for an alternative: that of Third World, non-aligned Marxism, which Rodney refers to here as "an African perspective"—an explicitly global viewpoint from an African position.

During Rodney's time at the University of Dar es Salaam, Tanzania was experimenting with a socialist ideology. The university attracted radical scholars—those who were looking for a different approach and place in which to solve Africa's underdevelopment. In an era characterized by armed struggles for decolonization, the emergence of the Non-Aligned Movement, socialist revolutions in the Third World, and a deepening of Sino-Soviet rifts, Rodney examined the Russian Revolution for inspiration and lessons for the continent and the Diaspora as it struggled to overcome the forces of colonial and capitalist history. Tanzania had become the base for several anti-colonial and liberation movements in exile, and the competing models of Soviet and Chinese societies were common topics of discussion and debate. Professor Issa Shivji, one of Rodney's former students, recalled the sectarian splits that emerged—partly as a reaction to the split in international socialism—between China and the Soviet Union: "The Dar es Salaam campus followed very closely that debate of the Communist Party of China and the Communist Party of the Soviet Union: the rising socialist imperialism. We had lots of discussions on that. But many of them were internal splits within our groups."[6] Dar was a miniature global community, and one could be in the same room with radical, bourgeois or reactionary intellectuals from many regions and countries, including South Africa, East Africa, Nigeria, Ghana, Vietnam, Britain, Canada and the United States—as rich a cast of characters as the world knew at that time.[7]

Rodney was uniquely allergic to sectarian politics. Understanding the Russian Revolution and its consequences required deep study and reflection if it was to provide useful lessons for the Third World. As he explains in the first chapter, one of his primary objectives was to demonstrate the value of historical materialism in apprehending the processes of revolution and socialist transformation. Rodney set out to defend both the achievements of the Russian Revolution and a Marxist interpretation of history from the distortions of bourgeois historians—namely, those Western European and American scholars motivated by Cold War imperatives and neocolonial designs. But this was not merely a defensive exercise, a desperate search and rescue mission for a "discredited" ideology; writing in the afterglow of the fiftieth anniversary of the October Revolution in 1917, Rodney surmised that the Masters of the Universe and their historians were now themselves on the defensive, if not running for their lives.

As we engage this text in 2018, just after the centennial of the October Revolution, and some three decades after the *collapse* of the Soviet Union, the idea that the global bourgeoisie was on the verge of defeat may come across as overly optimistic or a terrible miscalculation. However, this work needs to be examined in the context of the world as it existed at that time. In the late 1960s and early '70s, as Vijay Prashad discusses in the preface to this book, the political winds had shifted toward Marxism-Leninism, not only in the Third World but within social movements in the Global North. The question of a socialist path for Africa was hardly settled; in fact, it seemed to be the winning position given the direction of anti-colonial struggles in Mozambique, Guinea-Bissau, Angola, South Africa, Zimbabwe, Namibia, People's Republic of the Congo and Tanzania. Unlike Russia's dominant role as the backer of most of Africa's Marxist parties and left-leaning guerrilla movements, China's role as an international player was not so clear. Although the general public had yet to learn of the state repression that accompanied the Cultural Revolution, few observers could miss the rise of *socialist* China as an economic power willing to invest in and engage with Africa. Like Rodney, much of the Third World Left believed the momentum of history was on their side.

Rodney was not clairvoyant, so he could not have predicted how the next half century would turn out. And unlike our generation, he did not have access to the Soviet archives, nor to the deluge of new revisionist scholarship. Indeed, historians of Russia will immediately note that recent research calls into question some of Rodney's assertions and begins to complicate a Manichean view of historians as either bourgeois or Marxist. These lectures have to be read instead as a historical document produced in a particular conjuncture: before the defeat of socialism, before China's neoliberal turn, before the rollback of Third World socialist revolutions, and at the exact moment when the Global South's proposal for a New International Economic Order contested neoliberalism to shape the world's future—and lost.[8] And yet, Rodney's insights into the historical dynamics of revolution, state power, peasant rebellion, war, and the dialectics of class and nationalism are nonetheless profound and prescient.

But before we can critically assess the value and significance of this book, we proceed by briefly examining the life of Walter Rodney and then the history of the Russian Revolution.

The Life of Walter Rodney: The Making of a Black Radical Intellectual

Walter Anthony Rodney was a foremost Pan-Africanist, historian, Marxist scholar, activist and leader, born March 23, 1942, and assassinated in his native Guyana on June 13, 1980.[9]

During his lifetime, he interacted with many leaders of the Black world, becoming one of the most important activists and thinkers of his generation, particularly in relation to Pan-African, anti-colonial, anti-neocolonial, Black Power, non-aligned, and other revolutionary movements of the 1960s and '70s. He is perhaps the most recognizable face of the Black Power and Pan-African movements to emerge from the Caribbean in the post-independence era of neocolonialism and US empire, where he had a broad impact, especially in the histories of two countries. In Jamaica, he was arguably the most significant figure in its Black Power period, which catalyzed the 1968 "Rodney Riots," the impacts of which are still felt today. In Guyana, he helped lead its most effective multiracial party to date, the Working People's Alliance, directly opposing the divisive politics of racial polarization and challenging an increasingly repressive dictatorship. And while his work continues to have its strongest and widest reception within the African continent, his legacy is notable throughout the Americas, Europe and the Caribbean.

Much of Rodney's work remains in continuous print, having achieved renowned status in Black and radical communities throughout the world, especially *How Europe Underdeveloped Africa* and *The Groundings with My Brothers*. Rodney has therefore been associated with several overlapping circles of great twentieth-century thinkers, including W. E. B. Du Bois, C. L. R. James, Claudia Jones, Kwame Nkrumah, Julius Nyerere, Frantz Fanon, Amílcar Cabral, Aimé Césaire, Angela Davis, Cedric Robinson, Bob Marley and others in the Pan-African tradition; Paulo Freire, Ngũgĩ wa Thiong'o, Nyerere and others working on anti-colonial education and decolonizing the mind; Celso Furtado, Paul Sweezy, Paul Baran, Andre Gunder Frank, Samir Amin, Immanuel Wallerstein and others in the dependency, underdevelopment, and world systems schools of thought; Lenin, Trotsky, Nkrumah, Cabral, James, Jones, Davis and many others in the Marxist traditions; and Malcolm X, Huey Newton, Kathleen Cleaver, Stokely Carmichael, Steve Biko, Peter Tosh and A. M. Babu in the Black Power traditions.

It is therefore a unique honor to introduce this "new" work of Walter Rodney to the general public. It is rare to discover original work by a scholar of this stature, much less an entire book, and this is amplified in the case of an author who was murdered because of his convictions. Its publication marks an exceptional moment, officially expanding the catalog of books by Walter Rodney. In addition to *How Europe Underdeveloped Africa* (1972) and *The Groundings with My Brothers* (1969), Rodney's other well-known texts include the *History of the Upper Guinea Coast, 1545–1800* (1970), *A History of the Guyanese Working People, 1885–1905* (1981), and *Walter Rodney Speaks: The Making of an African Intellectual* (1990).

Walter Rodney was born into a working-class family influenced by and participating in the major political movements of that period in Guyana, including the national independence movement and the afterlives of Garveyism, at a time when Guyana was at the forefront of anti-colonial movements in the Caribbean. When he was eleven years old, Guyana became the first Caribbean nation to elect a multiracial socialist government, but only months after its election, the government would be suspended by the British for its anti-colonial ambitions. In these tumultuous times of decolonization and practical engagement of socialist thought by both his family and the wider society, Rodney showed himself to be an outstanding student, winning scholarships at every level of his education, from primary to high school and then university. He also developed his skills as a debater in team competitions, often securing victories against more-senior teams, which earned him national exposure.[10]

Rodney earned a first-class honors degree in history at the University of the West Indies at Mona, Jamaica in 1963, and then a PhD in African history at the School of Oriental and African Studies (SOAS), University of London, in 1966, both of which were formative educational experiences. In 1966, at age twenty-four, he completed his dissertation (*A History of the*

Upper Guinea Coast, 1545–1800), defending his thesis a few hours after his son Shaka was born. His thesis was published in 1970 and remains foundational in the study of West Africa.

Rodney was part of one of the earliest student cohorts from the former and recently liberated colonies to enter and challenge the conservative, Eurocentric, racist institutional context of imperial higher education. In graduate school, he heightened his disciplinary training and skills, enabling him to argue from *within* the academy radical positions that had previously been kept outside it. To ensure that he researched and reviewed all historical records for his dissertation, Rodney, who was already fluent in Spanish, learned both Portuguese and Italian in order to interrogate the original historical documents and records that were only available in the colonial archives.

At the same time, his political education and involvement continued mostly outside the university, where he became a noted orator in Hyde Park, London and a member of C. L. R. and Selma James's study group with fellow West Indian graduate students. It was probably here, as much as in Guyana, that his engagement of the complexities of both race and class deepened and cohered; certainly, he was already concerned with the complex historical specificity of any given community of oppressed people and their struggles for liberation. A scholar of Marxist theory and a fiercely independent thinker, he was one of the few willing to challenge and debate C. L. R. James, and rarer still in his ability to hold his own.

Rodney might be thought of as part of the first wave of Black Power professors in the predominantly white institutions (PWIs) of the academy. Whereas W. E. B. Du Bois, C. L. R. James, Claudia Jones, John Henrik Clarke, and many other great Pan-African thinkers generally operated from Historically Black Colleges and Universities or from institutional environments altogether outside the academy, Rodney consistently worked from both inside and outside the ivory tower. Rodney was the archetypal scholar-activist. He asserted a conscious Black presence within the academy while always maintaining ties and involvements outside it, working in the community and among the working class. At the same time that Rodney was completing his dissertation and taking up his first full-time academic appointment at the University of Dar es Salaam, Tanzania in 1966, the Black Power movement in the United States was already asserting its presence and escalating demands for Black Studies programs that finally erupted into widespread movements in 1968.

Rodney returned to his alma mater, UWI Mona, as a lecturer in history in January 1968, at the age of twenty-six. Unlike other professors at UWI, he chose to live with his young family outside the insular university compound housing. Rodney encountered a Black Power movement in Jamaica that was already well underway. He provided a framework that critically examined the impact of slavery and colonialism and that gave a foundation for interpreting the current situation of Black and oppressed peoples in these newly independent countries, who continued to be marginalized. He shared his scholarly and firsthand knowledge of Africa, its history and culture, and its social and political conditions with students as well as working-class, marginalized, and oppressed communities. Rodney was asked to give speeches on Black Power at the University Student Union. He spent time learning from and connecting with disenfranchised Jamaicans, in particular the Rastafarian communities, and actively engaged with anyone with a thirst for knowledge of African history. Although he was a university lecturer from another country, Rodney's acceptance in these spaces speaks volumes about both his scholarly knowledge and his ability to connect with people. In Jamaica, Rodney informed the people, but also simultaneously exemplified their process of *grounding*—learning from and listening to the people and their communal wisdom, learning the local history and cultural dynamics, and reasoning together.

The way Rodney engaged society as a university lecturer was considered so "strange" and even dangerous that it was interpreted as a challenge to the establishment. Less than ten months after his return to Jamaica, during his attendance of the 1968 Montreal Congress of Black Writers, the government declared Rodney persona non grata and banned him from reentering the country. What began as an off-campus student protest escalated into an outpouring of disdain for and frustration with the system. This set off the "Rodney Riots," or Rodney Rebellion, one of the three major mass uprisings in Jamaican history. Though Rodney was removed, the impact of this work with students and the community persisted. A year after his ban, Rodney's speeches in Jamaica were published in London as *The Groundings with My Brothers* (1969), and they have become a classic of the Caribbean Black Power period.

Walter Rodney's path in Jamaica serves as a kind of parallel case in the global trajectory of the Black Power intervention in institutional higher learning, often referred to as the academic industrial complex. His experiences, and his ultimate rejection and ban from Jamaica by the state, were contemporaneous to the explosion of Black Studies in the United States. The parallels are significant, as they rode the same global anti-colonial wave seeking radical transformation of society. They also exemplified the potential of the relationships between working people and their advocates in the academy.

After a short period of introspection that included travel to the UK and Cuba, Rodney returned to Tanzania, this time as a senior lecturer at the University of Dar es Salaam, from 1969 to 1974.[11] Here too, Rodney endeavored to engage with groups outside of the university, although his experience differed from that of grassroots Jamaica in that he was more often invited to speak and contribute to various formal groups such as high school students, adult education classes and the Tanganyika African National Union (TANU) Youth League. During his time at the University of Dar es Salaam, Rodney worked on and published his best-known work, *How Europe Underdeveloped Africa* (1972). Rodney simultaneously worked on numerous projects, including the Russian Revolution lectures he developed and delivered to his university students, which are now published as this book. During these years, he also traveled widely, including to Egypt, Ghana, Mauritius, Nigeria, Uganda, and the Institute of the Black World in Atlanta, Georgia.

In both *How Europe Underdeveloped Africa* (*HEUA*) and in this book, Rodney was more explicit in his radical Marxist analysis than in his earlier work. *HEUA* described the complex relationship between Europe and its colonies with historical accuracy across a 500-year period, providing a much-needed antidote to Eurocentric histories in which Africa "had no history" and Europe's rise was treated as entirely independent of its exploitation of Africa and its other colonies. The book has been described as a Black Power economic history of Africa and a major work of Black Marxism, with implications for all societies emerging from centuries of direct colonial rule.

How Europe Underdeveloped Africa should be seen as in direct dialogue with Lenin's *Imperialism: The Highest Stage of Capitalism* (1917), and Nkrumah's *Neo-Colonialism: The Last Stage of Imperialism* (1965), forming a third volume in what constitutes a trilogy of studies of modern capitalism and imperialism on a world-systemic scale. Like *Groundings*, these books were written in an accessible style intended to reach a wide audience, both inside and outside the academy. *Groundings* and *HEUA* were widely sold on the streets of major cities throughout the Black world, from Harlem and Dakar to Havana and Nairobi. In the pattern common to many of our greatest Pan-African scholars, many establishment scholars—including those on the left—discounted *HEUA*'s academic merits. However, its popularity was undeniable, and its theoretical and scholarly worth has only grown over time.

In the late 1960s and early '70s, Dar es Salaam was the most important hub of radical thought and organizing activity in Africa, perhaps in the world. Many leading thinkers, underground movements and students gravitated toward this radical, intellectual, culturally open society, flourishing under the progressive, revolutionary influence of Julius Nyerere's African socialist government. Rodney quickly became one of the most dynamic and leading thinkers on the scene, and he continued to engage not just within the walls of the ivory tower but also among the people of Tanzania during their historic Ujamaa socialist experiment and at the peak of activity by Frontline States against apartheid South Africa and Portuguese colonialism. Walter was active in many of the revolutionary movements at that time, while also finding time to both teach courses for high school students and to engage with peasants in Ujamaa villages and members of the TANU Youth League. Some of Rodney's most important work was produced during these years—on Tanzania, Mozambique, development theory, and radical pedagogy—as he engaged deeply and sincerely with the non-aligned "Third World" revolution underway at that time.

Though supportive of the intent of Nyerere's socialism, he was also willing to critique the government, particularly as its contradictions deepened over the years. He helped launch the journal *Cheche*, Ki-Swahili for "Spark" and named after the organ of the Russian Social Democrats edited by Lenin. *Cheche* was mildly critical of Ujamaa and the bourgeois character of university education. Always principled on the limited role he could play as a non-national, even though he was perhaps the most deeply engaged expatriate at that time, Rodney argued that Nyerere's Ujamaa project was in fact a form of scientific socialism, worthy of respect by the international Left.[12] But he also spoke in favor of the rights and arguments of the student radicals on his campus when they clashed with the government, and he raised questions about the ability of Tanzanian society to practically engage Ujamaa theory at the regional and local levels, given existing structures and social systems.[13] He remained the epitome of the public intellectual, famously debating his friend Issa Shivji on Ujamaa policy in Tanzania, and memorably defeating the more conservative senior scholar Ali Mazrui in debates at Makerere University in Kampala, Uganda on the subject of African colonialism and neocolonialism. In 1974, Tanzania was suffering external political and economic pressure and domestic political challenges, and Rodney realized that he could not adequately engage in the struggle as a non-Tanzanian; nor were his criticisms, however accurate, always welcome in the one-party state and its nationalist environment. His decision to return to Guyana was both professional—to take the position of head of the Department of History at the University of Guyana—and for family reasons—to raise his children in his natal home. Rodney's desire was to serve his homeland, Guyana, where he felt a certain obligation to the working class that had funded his education, and where he could also directly engage with them in study and action. This book was one of several unfinished projects that he took with him when the family relocated.

Despite his renown as an academic, global thinker and leader, Rodney was nevertheless denied the right to take up his post in Guyana by the openly hostile and repressive government of Forbes Burnham. The premise was that this would force him to seek employment elsewhere and not return to Guyana. Undeterred, Rodney remained in Guyana, taking up speaking engagements and various visiting professorships in the United States, Canada and Europe to provide for his family. Rodney engaged deeply in Guyana, becoming a coleader of the Working People's Alliance as they confronted a society purposefully divided on the basis of race, and held down by an increasingly brazen dictatorship. His historical analysis of African enslavement and Indian indenture helped these divided majority communities to respect their own histories and their shared colonial experiences, and to develop shared aspirations—not for a color-blind society, but for a just context in which different communities could all benefit from development, the economy, and civil society. He spoke publicly about these histories, and about their misrepresentation, mostly at "bottom house" gatherings, at meetings and at rallies that were increasingly attacked by government forces. In addition to his political work, Rodney conscientiously engaged in research and writing, penning a number of academic and political texts, some of which were published posthumously. These include *A History of the Guyanese Working People, 1881–1905* (1981), *People's Power, No Dictator (1979)*, and a series of children's books about the origins and history of each major ethno-racial community in Guyana, starting with *Kofi Baadu Out of Africa* (1980), and *Lakshmi Out of India* (2000). Unfortunately, the multi-volume children's series, volumes II and III of the *History of the Guyanese Working People*, and other works in progress, such as the present volume, were cut short or lost entirely in the aftermath of his assassination.[14]

This was the high point globally of the Non-Aligned Movement, and Rodney, both as a thinker and as a participant in the struggle in Guyana, was a major player in its unfolding. Some conjecture existed that he was destined to become head of state in Guyana, had not the forces of imperialism and national dictatorship intervened. Though we can never be sure, we do know that Guyana would likely have gone a different route under his leadership, and since his death the country has reverted to the neocolonial racial divide that enables inequality, corruption and exploitation to continue unabated. Rodney's trajectory toward non-aligned national, regional and Pan-African leadership puts him in the company of Patrice Lumumba, Maurice Bishop, Martin Luther King Jr., Malcolm X, Stokely Carmichael, Huey Newton, Angela Davis, Amílcar Cabral and Thomas Sankara. That each of these figures was so heavily repressed and targeted speaks to the power of the movements they led, and to their potential to transform global systems and bring about a new, more socialist, less racially divided world.

Rodney was a coleader of the Working People's Alliance, one of the main opposition parties, and emerged as a popular leader in the resistance movement against Prime Minister Burnham and his People's National Congress (PNC) administration. Rodney and other civil society and social movement leaders were targeted by the Burnham PNC, in an escalating campaign of repression that included street violence, harassment and surveillance, false arrests and accusations, including politically motivated, trumped-up arson charges against Rodney and his associates in the period leading up to the assassination. Then, on June 13, 1980, a car bomb exploded in Georgetown, Guyana, killing Walter Rodney. He was thirty-eight years old. The Government of Guyana contended that Walter Rodney was responsible for his own death—that Rodney planned to use a bomb concealed in a walkie-talkie to blow up the prison, but that it accidentally exploded. The Rodney family, including Walter Rodney's brother Donald Rodney, who was in the car but survived the explosion, vehemently denied the government's claim. People and organizations around the world protested the assassination, and over 30,000 attended his funeral.

Calls for a commission of inquiry sprung up in the immediate aftermath of the 1980 assassination, even as that general period of violence and repression by the dictatorship persisted.[15] Years later, in 1993, Walter Rodney's son Shaka held a protest to demand a parliamentary commission; but only in 2014, after decades of struggle and demands for investigation and justice by his immediate family and activists around the world, did the government of Guyana initiate the first official international commission of inquiry (COI) into his assassination. The final Commission Report (2016) revealed new details about not only his political murder, but those of other activists at the hands of the dictatorship at that time.

The COI report concluded that Walter Rodney's death was an act of violence for political purposes—an act of state terrorism—and that the assassin Gregory Smith was an agent of the state. Without Walter Rodney's knowledge, Smith placed the bomb in the walkie-talkie and remotely triggered it, resulting in his death. The report further concluded that Smith acted under the direction of the highest echelons of the PNC government, and it specifically identified officials at the highest levels of government and public office who played major roles in the conspiracy to kill Walter Rodney.

However, the COI process was truncated and the final report rejected by the next government in office, ostensibly on grounds of technicality and expenditure. The government of Guyana has acknowledged receipt of the report from the Rodney Commission but, as of this writing, has rejected its findings and recommendations. Their official position reflects more so the fact that the report heavily and directly implicated the former PNC Burnham regime as well as the highest ranks of the police force and army. The fight for justice for Walter Rodney, his brother Donald Rodney, the Rodney family, the truth for all Guyanese people, and for Pan-Africanists and people of conscience everywhere has therefore been deferred and requires continued agitation—notwithstanding the preponderance of definitive and damning evidence that was revealed and/or confirmed in the COI report.[16]

In the years since 1980, Rodney's work has only increased in its significance, in part because it continues to resonate with contemporary conditions, but a proper assessment of the range and power of Rodney's scholastic work is beyond the scope of this introduction. His work exemplified a political economy that was literally grounded in the specificities and complexities of the communities and peoples he lived with and researched. Some interpret Rodney as having begun his life with Black Power and racial politics, before progressing toward a more orthodox Marxist analysis as he matured and became a scholar. Rodney was indeed a strong proponent of Black consciousness, pride and power, and, as this volume attests, a powerful Marxist thinker as well. However, such falsely dichotomous race/class readings of Rodney ignore his praxis, where theory was always historically grounded and attentive to the complexity of lived experience. Rodney deepened his early exposure to socialism through engaged study of Marxism and the Russian, Cuban, Tanzanian and other socialist revolutions, always using a critical, dialectical approach. This attention to history and cultural specificity makes his work an unacknowledged precursor of the "cultural turn" in which the power/knowledge relationship is made explicit. He always advocated for nuanced readings of the presence and agency of Africans, on the continent and abroad, and as a sophisticated Marxist scholar, he remained attentive to the specificity of material conditions and was adept at engaging major works of theory and historiography.

Indeed, Rodney interrogates the Russian Revolution primarily as a problem of Marxist theory and historiography. Rather than attempt to write a new "history" of the revolution, Rodney examines, among other things, the self-activity of workers and peasants in advancing (and arresting) socialist transformation; the theoretical contributions and historical choices of figures such as Lenin, Trotsky and Stalin; and the particular shape of class struggle in Russia (a so-called "backward" country) and the lessons it may offer for the Black world. Rodney's interventions assume a basic knowledge of the Russian Revolution. We do not assume such knowledge, especially now that the collapse of the Soviet bloc is over a quarter-century old. For this reason, we've included a brief sketch of Russia during the era of revolution.

A Brief History of the Russian Revolution

We generally think of the revolution as the Bolshevik seizure of power in October 1917, or date its origins to the spontaneous workers rebellions of February 1917. Still others invoke the failed 1905 Revolution as a sort of rehearsal for October 1917. But the Russian Revolution was a long, protracted struggle whose origins can be traced back to the late nineteenth century. It involved the overthrow of an imperial monarchy by peasants, workers, soldiers, left-wing intellectuals, and liberal forces; ushered in the modern world's first attempt to create a socialist state; and set in motion Marxist-inspired movements on a global scale that fundamentally shaped the ideas, ideologies, strategies, direction, and aesthetics of the Left in the twentieth century.[17]

The collapse of the Tsarist Empire was rooted in a series of political and economic crises. In the decades following the abolition of serfdom in 1861, the state set out to rapidly modernize Russia's economy in order to compete militarily and economically with the major European powers. By 1913, Russia had become the fifth-largest industrial power in the world. Consequently, like European and American workers at the turn of the century, the Russian working class was subject to extremely exploitative, dangerous and even fatal working conditions. Workplace injuries and deaths were commonplace; a ten-hour day, let alone an eight-hour day, was not.

Contrary to the pronouncements of Western Marxists, Russian workers were hardly "backward." Rather, they were among the most organized and militant in Europe. In 1905, the year of the first revolution, about 75 percent of the workforce went out on strike or participated in some form of militant action. A large proportion of the unskilled workers were drawn directly from the countryside and turned to forms of resistance associated with peasants—looting, machine breaking, and physically removing or assaulting managers they disliked. The most disciplined of industrial workers gravitated to underground Marxist political organizations, especially since the tsarist state banned formal trade unions. Indeed, the repressive nature of the Russian state largely determined the revolutionary character of the working class. As historian Orlando Figes writes, "Had they been able to develop their own legal trade unions, the workers might have gone down the path of moderate reform taken by the European labour movements."[18]

At the time of the Revolution, Russia was still largely a country of peasants: 75 percent of its population worked in agriculture. Similar to the emancipation of enslaved people in the Western Hemisphere, the emancipation of the serfs in 1861 did not result in land reform or greater economic or political power. On the contrary, the newly "freed" peasants were forced to buy land for more than its market value, enabling the old landed gentry to hold on to the best-quality land. Railway expansion and market growth allowed peasants to supplement their meager income from farming with wage labor in mining, in industry, or on larger farms, as well as through trade and handicrafts. By 1913, the Russian Empire had become the world's leading grain exporter, although the average peasant continued to endure a life of extreme poverty and hardship.

Capitalist expansion coincided with tsarist imperialist expansion and the consolidation of Russian settler colonialism. Beginning in the 1880s, the state launched a campaign to centralize its rule by creating a more uniform system of governance and introducing policies of "Russification." Efforts to impose the Russian language and the Orthodox Church on the peoples of the western borderlands and the Baltic littoral—notably Ukraine and Poland—were met with resistance. Poles and Jews, in particular, were targets of the most discriminatory legislation. In the Volga–Ural region, where a pan-Muslim identity had emerged, Russification proceeded with less vigor. In Central Asia and the Caucasus, however, the tsarist state had only recently consolidated its rule after a series of brutal military campaigns. Consistent with virtually every other modern European colonial project, Russian settlers were tasked with establishing viable economic outposts and "civilizing" the Muslims.

By the turn of the twentieth century, the costs of imperialist expansion and the unprecedented exploitation of labor and resources had begun to take its toll on the tsarist state. The Russian capitalist class was politically weak, divided by region and industry (notably mining, metallurgy, and engineering), and almost completely dependent on the state to buy its products and provide subsidies in order to stay competitive. But the more immediate crisis facing the tsarist state wasn't economic; it was political.

The first stirrings of the modern revolutionary movement begin in the mid 1870s, when a small group of radical intellectuals attempted to launch a populist movement among the peasantry. Known as the Narodniks or the Narodniki, they saw in the peasant commune (the *mir*) collectivist and egalitarian values upon which to build a socialist society and challenge both tsarist rule and industrial capitalism. Their initial efforts were met by swift state repression and skepticism among many peasants. In 1879, in response to state violence, a segment of the Narodniks founded the People's Will—an armed underground movement that used terror to provoke popular insurgency in the countryside. The People's Will did gain a militant following, but the anticipated revolt never materialized. Instead, many of its members were jailed, executed, or sent to Siberia. Some supporters of the People's Will turned to Marxism, Georgii Plekhanov being among the first. A founder of the first Russian Marxist organization (the Emancipation of Labour group) in 1883, Plekhanov abandoned the Narodnik vision of peasant revolution, arguing that the penetration of capitalist relations in the countryside had strengthened the rural bourgeoisie at the expense of the poor peasantry. Exploitation had eroded the peasants' collective social base and driven a significant portion of the agrarian poor into the cities and industrial centers, thus expanding the proletariat. The proletariat, Plekhanov concluded, was the only class capable of ushering in revolution. As a delegate to the founding of the Second International in Paris in 1889, he famously announced, "The task of our revolutionary intelligentsia therefore comes, in the opinion of the Russian Social-Democrats, to the following: they must adopt the views of modern scientific socialism, spread them among the workers, and, with the help of the workers, storm the stronghold of autocracy. The revolutionary movement in Russia can triumph only as the revolutionary movement of the workers."[19]

An early follower of Plekhanov was a brilliant student at Kazan University named Vladimir Il'ich—after 1903 known as V. I. Lenin. In 1887, his brother, A. I. Ul'ianov, a member of the People's Will, was hanged for participating in an assassination plot against the tsar. Vladimir reacted by intensifying his own political work, for which he was expelled from the university.

He became a professional revolutionary, cofounding with Lulii Martov the Union of Struggle for the Emancipation of the Working Class in St. Petersburg, whose propaganda work among workers resulted in their arrest in 1897. Lenin and his wife, the dynamic revolutionary Nadezhda Krupskaya, were exiled to Siberia for three years. In fact, Lenin's exile kept him from attending the founding congress of the Russian Social-Democratic Labour Party (RSDLP) in 1898. Nevertheless, within five years he would be at the center of the famous split that produced the Bolshevik and Menshevik factions of the party. In the meantime, Lenin devoted his time to researching and writing his first major work, *The Development of Capitalism in Russia*, published in 1899. The book empirically proved Plekhanov's assertion that the penetration of capitalism in the countryside produced sharp class differentiation among the peasantry, although he came to a slightly different conclusion. For Lenin, the deepening exploitation of the rural poor made them potentially revolutionary allies of the industrial working class and put them in a unique position to help bring about a bourgeois democratic revolution. In 1899, most Marxists still held on to the idea that the bourgeois revolution must precede the socialist revolution.

The publication of Lenin's pamphlet *What Is to Be Done?* (1902) took aim at the "economistic" tendencies dominant among European Marxists and social democrats—notably figures such as Eduard Bernstein, a leading member of the German Social Democratic Party (SPD). Bernstein believed that as industrialization created the conditions for the expansion and consolidation of working-class organization through trade unions and labor parties, socialist transformation was possible without dissolving the modern state system. The "dictatorship of the proletariat" Marx once predicted was now obsolete; Bernstein imagined socialist transformation through the spread of parliamentary democracy and the embrace of "liberalism." Concluding that capitalism's periodic crises were a thing of the past, he believed that working-class organizations were strong enough to control the economy through electoral means. Karl Kautsky, the SPD's main theorist, dissented. He did not think capitalism could be reformed out of existence, nor that social revolution was necessary. Nevertheless, he concurred with Bernstein that the socialist revolution would come about through the inevitable growth of the socialist vote. Eventually the party would have an electoral majority and legitimacy. The sole dissenting voice within the German SPD who anticipated Lenin's main arguments in *What Is to Be Done?* was Rosa Luxemburg, then only twenty-eight years old. In 1900 she published the pamphlet *Social Reform or Revolution*, which argued unequivocally that socialism cannot be voted into power, that revolution is unavoidable, and that capitalism's illusory stability was the result of imperialist expansion.[20] Lenin agreed with Luxemburg but went further, arguing that while workers are capable of achieving a "trade union consciousness," a genuine revolution requires a qualitative leap, which for him meant creating a vanguard organization of professional revolutionaries fully conversant in Marxist theory and praxis. Lenin rejected the strategy of building alliances with liberals, insisting instead that the bourgeois-democratic revolution would be brought about by the proletariat in alliance with poor peasants.

What Is to Be Done? caused a rift at the RSDLP's Second Congress in 1903. A significant minority took issue with Lenin's proposal to transform the party into a highly disciplined, conspiratorial and restrictive organization, worrying that such a vanguard party would become a substitute for the working class itself. The minority, or "Mensheviks," included some of Lenin's closest collaborators—among them Martov and, later, Plekhanov. Leon Trotsky, a leading Social Democrat who had been exiled to Siberia in 1900 and initially allied with Lenin, surprised many of his comrades by siding with the Mensheviks. The majority, or the "Bolsheviks," supported Lenin's position. Although the split would continue to be a feature of Russian Marxism throughout the revolution, neither faction acted or voted entirely as distinct, unified entities. Many comrades, notably Trotsky, switched sides more than once. Over the course of the next decade and a half, Bolsheviks and Mensheviks experienced splits within their own ranks, moments of unity across the divide, periods of indecision and reversal, and many instances in which Bolsheviks and Mensheviks scrambled to catch up with the masses.

The RSDLP was certainly Russia's largest proletarian party, but it was not the largest political movement. That distinction belonged to the peasant-based Socialist Revolutionary Party (SR). Founded in 1902 by Viktor Chernov, the SRs wedded populist ideology with Marxism, arguing for unity among industrial workers and peasants to resist the advance of capitalism in the countryside through the radical redistribution of land to the tiller. Expropriating big landowners would not only create the conditions for rural socialism but also have the effect of arresting, or at least retarding, industrial capitalism. A political descendant of the People's Will, the SRs resuscitated terrorist tactics such as assassinations, thus remaining a small organization during its first few years. Indeed, the 1905 Revolution provided the boost both the SRs and the RSDLPs needed to become mass organizations and significant players in Russian politics.

The revolution was sparked by a peaceful workers' march on the Winter Palace on January 9, 1905.[21] Led by liberal priest Father G. A. Gapon, 150,000 workers sought to deliver a petition to Tsar Nicholas II demanding a number of social and political reforms. The protests began several weeks earlier when workers at the Putilov metallurgical and machine-building factory in St. Petersburg went on strike to protest the firing of fellow workers. The company's recalcitrance only escalated the conflict, drawing more workers from across the city as well as liberal groups such as the Union of Liberation, whose raison d'être had been to establish a constitutional monarchy. The petition included the right to vote; freedom of speech, the press, and association; freedom of conscience; separation of Church and state; equality before the law; freedom to form trade unions; the right to strike; an eight-hour working day; insurance benefits; and improved wages. They also demanded an end to the Russo-Japanese War, especially after Russia's humiliating defeat at the hands of the Japanese in 1904. It was the first time in modern history that an Asian nation had militarily defeated a "European" power. The war not only weakened the economy but generated a crisis of confidence in tsarist rule. But Tsar Nicholas II was not fazed; the Imperial Guards fired on unarmed protesters, provoking what would be known as "Bloody Sunday." About 200 protesters were gunned down and some 800 wounded in the initial battle, and scores of others were injured or trampled to death in the ensuing melee. Bloody Sunday was the spark that set in motion a year of worker insurrections, general strikes, urban and agrarian unrest, and military mutinies that spread from St. Petersburg to Moscow, Warsaw, Vilna, Kovno, Baku, the Baltic region, and other parts of the empire. Altogether, about half of Russia's industrial working class went out on strike in 1905, and in Poland the figure exceeded 90 percent.

Peasants organized rent strikes, cut trees and hay from the gentry's land, attacked estates, seized property, and even physically assaulted the big landowners and burned down their manors. During the first ten months of 1905, the army was deployed at least 2,700 times to put down peasant uprisings, though sometimes these counterinsurgency efforts were half-hearted because many of the soldiers had themselves been peasants and knew the grievances well. Entire units refused to carry out orders, mutinied, or simply deserted rather than suppress the peasants. Besides, military discipline had already begun to spiral out of control as Russian soldiers faced defeat by the better-prepared and better-equipped Japanese troops in Manchuria. Mutinies dogged the Russian navy, occurring at Sevastopol, Vladivostok, and Kronstadt during the first half of 1905, with the most famous insurrection taking place aboard the battleship *Potemkin*. Indeed, the prospect of mutiny within the military as well as rebellion at home left the tsar with no choice but to sue for peace.

Meanwhile, the tsar and his acolytes responded with a policy of repression and limited reform. With Nicholas's blessing and backing, the Right formed the Union of the Russian People and paramilitary groups known as the Black Hundreds that attacked revolutionaries and carried out pogroms against Jews.[22] The tsar's attempts at piecemeal reform went nowhere. Ignoring calls for a constitutional monarchy, adult suffrage, and an independent legislature with sovereign rights, the tsar was only willing to allow a duma (a legislative body) whose role would be purely consultative. Given the terms of the franchise, less than 1 percent of St. Petersburg's adult residents were qualified to vote. The RSDLP and SRs called it a sham and chose to boycott the elections, instead backing the workers who launched a general strike in September that proved to be something of a dress rehearsal for 1917. Initiated by the Moscow printers who struck for better pay and working conditions, they were soon followed by railway workers affiliated with the Union of Unions, a liberal organization that had begun planning a general strike in order to win basic political reforms. By October 10, a national strike was underway involving millions of workers and professionals. Coordinating the strike was a new organization, the St. Petersburg Soviet of Workers' Deputies, which was formed during the strike and directed by Leon Trotsky. ("Soviet" simply means "council" in Russian.) The Soviet proved to be the only functioning democracy in St. Petersburg and a source of workers' power: it elected representatives, organized self-defense, distributed food and supplies, and served as the model for similar workers' councils in fifty other cities. Trotsky edited its newspaper, *Isvestia*, and was responsible for drafting its major resolutions.

Fearing the end of tsarist rule, on October 17 Nicholas's advisers compelled him to sign a manifesto drafted by Count Witte that would grant civil liberties and permit a legislative duma to be elected on a wide franchise. In short, the tsar acceded to a constitutional monarchy. While liberals rejoiced, workers and peasants saw very little in the manifesto that addressed their grievances. The next day, the Soviet adopted a resolution stating, "The struggling revolutionary proletariat cannot lay down its arms until the political rights of the Russian people are put on a solid footing, until a democratic republic is established." At minimum, the Soviet insisted on the withdrawal of the military and police from the city, full amnesty to all political prisoners, an end to the state of emergency in Russia, and a constituent assembly on equal suffrage for all based on direct and secret ballot. Insurrections and mutinies continued from October through December. Social Democrats in St. Petersburg and Moscow armed the workers and prepared for class war. However, the rebellions were poorly organized and uncoordinated; neither the RSDLP nor the SRs were strong enough to lead a national movement, and sectarian squabbles did not help matters; nationalist and anti-Semitic sentiment sometimes undercut class solidarity; and the concessions in the manifesto divided liberals from most of the working class. Ultimately, the empire salvaged enough loyalty from the army to suppress the rebellion.

Liberals hoped the October Manifesto would usher in a new era of democracy in Russia. They were mistaken. The decade leading up to the First World War was instead characterized by political repression, militarization, and imperial expansion. Still reeling from Japan's victory over Russia, the tsar and his elite backers commenced a massive military buildup that drained one-third of the country's national budget between 1909 and 1913. The colonization of Central Asia also intensified, especially in the Kazakh steppes where the building of the Orenburg to Tashkent railway enabled 1.5 million Russians to settle there between 1906 and 1912. Tashkent, Turkestan's largest city, was already a major hub for Russian settlers. But as the new wave of settlers turned to commercial cotton production, conflicts erupted between natives and settlers over land and water rights in the Fergana Valley. State policies of restricting non-Russian nationalism only exacerbated tensions. The Duma not only supported settlers in Central Asia but they in turn dispossessed nomadic herders from their customary grazing land. This further radicalized the Muslim population in Central Asia, though their grievances generally found expression in anti-colonialism and pan-Islamism rather than the language of class struggle.

Meanwhile, working-class unrest never ceased, intensifying on the eve of the war. In 1912, Russia was wracked by 2,032 strikes involving 725,491 workers. The following year, 2,404 strikes occurred involving 887,096 workers. And in the first half of 1914 alone, the country experienced an unprecedented 3,534 strikes with over 1.3 million workers participating.[23] The state responded to the strike wave with immediate force. In 1912, soldiers put down a miners' strike in Siberia, killing at least 200 workers and sparking protests across the empire reminiscent of "Bloody Sunday." The spark that turned the strike wave into a workers' insurrection occurred on July 3, 1914, after soldiers killed two workers on strike from the Putilov plant in St. Petersburg. The workers called a general strike and swiftly erected barricades in the streets.

It was under such conditions of mass worker unrest, peasant rebellion, anti-colonial resistance, industrial expansion, growing income inequality, and political instability that Russia entered World War I. Russia, an ally of France and supporter of Serbian nationalism, considered Germany its main territorial threat. Having built the largest military force in Europe, if not the world, the tsarist regime was anxious to go to war—especially since the declaration of war stoked the flames of Russian nationalism, temporarily dampening the fires of working-class revolt. Anti-German sentiment prevailed over proletarian internationalism. Even the capital city of St. Petersburg was renamed Petrograd, or "Peter's City," removing all vestiges of German. And despite rhetorical claims that the European powers were defending their sovereignty, all parties were looking to expand their imperial holdings. Once the Ottoman Empire entered the war, in fact, the tsarist regime had designs on the Bosporus Straits, Austrian-ruled Galicia, and a large portion of Anatolia. The war turned out to be a disaster for Russia. It ultimately brought about the downfall of the tsar and became the cauldron for the revolutions of 1917. Four months into the fighting, the Russian army had ballooned to just over 6.5 million men, equipped with only 4,652,000 rifles. Poorly trained troops were sent into battle without adequate equipment, arms or ammunition, resulting in over 2 million casualties in 1915 alone. All told, some 14 million men were mobilized to fight, and 67 million people in the western provinces came under enemy occupation. The mobilization of men and loss of territory resulted in a decline in agricultural production, food shortages, and a deepening of rural unrest. The government financed the war by raising taxes, borrowing heavily from foreign banks, and increasing the amount of paper currency in circulation. Consequently, inflation wiped out hard-fought wage increases, provoking a new strike wave beginning in 1916.

The February Revolution began most unexpectedly. On February 23, 1917, thousands of female textile workers and housewives took to the streets of Petrograd to protest the bread shortage and to mark International Women's Day. The following day, more than 200,000 workers went on strike and some 400,000 participated in demonstrations. They fought police and carried placards proclaiming "Down with the War" and "Down with the Tsarist Government." Tsar Nicholas II, who was away at the war front, dispatched thousands of troops who had been waiting in Petrograd's barracks preparing to go to war, but by the fourth day of the uprising even the soldiers had mutinied and switched sides. Suddenly the world turned upside down; workers and soldiers intermingled, called each other comrade, brandished guns and red flags, and performed citizens' arrests of police and government officials. When the tsar sent a trainload of troops to restore order to the city, they too joined the insurgents. Nicholas II had lost all authority. Even as he tried to return to the city, he was blocked by a group of railway workers. His generals finally informed him that order could not be restored unless he agreed to abdicate. Revolution had broken out, but where was the vanguard party? Initially, no political party had given leadership to the revolution—at least not at first. Many of the main leaders of the RSDLP were in exile. Lenin was in hiding in Zurich, Trotsky in New York City. There were Mensheviks, Bolsheviks and Socialist Revolutionaries on the ground, circulating among the masses. Four days into the general strike, the Petrograd Soviet of Workers' and Soldiers' Deputies was formed, its executive committee comprised primarily of Mensheviks. Like the Soviet of 1905, it did much of the actual administration of the city, meting out justice, organizing militias, producing and distributing a workers' press, and creating a model for worker self-organization. Soviets popped up in factories, as well, where they set about dismantling "autocracy" on the shop floor, driving out foremen, and implementing the practice of workers' control. They demanded an eight-hour working day and wage increases to compensate for wartime inflation. Workers regarded the soviet as an organ of "revolutionary democracy" comprised not only of workers and soldiers, but peasants, ethnic minorities, teachers, journalists, lawyers, and doctors—including men and women. Soviets spread throughout the country; by October there were at least 1,429 soviets, 455 of which were peasant soviets.

Meanwhile, the overthrow of the tsar paved the way for the old state-sanctioned Duma to assume responsibility for the state. To become a legitimate democratic institution, however, it had to do away with property requirements for voting, eliminate rampant corruption, and represent the interests of all the people—not just those of the bourgeoisie and middle-class liberals. In February, under the new prime minister, Georgii Lvov, leader of the liberal Constitutional Democratic (Cadet) Party, the Duma was transformed into the Russian Provisional Government. Distrustful of the new government, the Petrograd Soviet refused to disband. Instead, they proposed a system of shared governance known as "dual power." What it meant in practice, however, was not entirely clear. For many moderate socialist intellectuals who understood the character of the revolution as "bourgeois"—which is to say, advancing democracy and capitalist development in Russia rather than socialism—joining the Provisional Government made sense. And within the soviets there were socialists who feared that any attempt to assert their authority might provoke counterrevolution. Nevertheless, the dominant position on the left was to support the Provisional Government in principle without *joining* it—the one exception being Alexander Kerensky, a popular leader of the February Revolution and vice-chair of the Petrograd Soviet. Bolshevik leaders Lev Kamenev and Josef Stalin, having returned from exile in Siberia just days after the start of the February Revolution, pledged conditional support for the Provisional Government, called for negotiations with the Mensheviks in order to reunify the RSDLP, and promoted "revolutionary defensism" in support of the war. Revolutionary defensism argued for continuing the war in order to defend the gains of the revolution from foreign powers. It was essentially patriotism dressed up in proletarian language.

Lenin returned from exile in April 1917 and promptly issued his April Theses, criticizing the positions adopted by Kamenev and Stalin and pushing the Bolsheviks to the left. He called on the party to abandon the Provisional Government and transfer *all* power to the soviets; for immediate withdrawal from the "imperialist war" (he dismissed revolutionary defensism as misguided); the nationalization of land and redistribution to the peasantry; abolition of the police, the army and the bureaucracy; soviet control of production and distribution of goods; a central bank; the organization of peasants and soldiers (at the front); and the creation of a new Socialist International. In place of a parliamentary republic he called for a "republic of Soviets of Workers', Agricultural Labourers' and Peasants' Deputies throughout the country."[24] Concluding that the revolution had passed through its bourgeois stage and that socialism was on the horizon, Lenin had moved much closer to Trotsky's position. When Lenin presented his theses to Social Democrats and to a Bolshevik committee, they were roundly rejected, although the newspaper *Pravda* did publish them. A few weeks later, however, delegates to the larger Seventh Congress of the RSDLP adopted the theses as well as the slogan "All Power to the Soviets."

By July of 1917, disgruntled soldiers, sailors, and workers organized a series of militant demonstrations against the government, demanding an end to war and the transfer of power to the soviets. The Bolshevik Central Committee believed a seizure of power was premature and tried to rein in the revolt, but when this proved impossible, the Bolsheviks agreed to assume leadership. What began as a peaceful march ultimately erupted in a general strike and a contest for power, and the inability of Prime Minister Lvov to address strikers' demands soon led him and the entire Cadet Party to resign. The socialist Alexander Kerensky replaced Lvov, but this did not satisfy the rebels. Kerensky mercilessly crushed the revolt and vowed to destroy the Bolsheviks, whom he had accused of being German spies. Kerensky issued arrest warrants for Lenin and Trotsky, forcing them, once again, to go into hiding.

The Bolsheviks had become the target of attacks by the state and elements of the Right as well as some on the left, largely for their opposition to the Provisional Government and unequivocal opposition to the war. The attacks didn't stick, however, because the war was genuinely unpopular. Desertions became commonplace, and reports of heroic Russian victories at the front proved apocryphal. Indeed, the Bolshevik slogan of "Peace, Land and Bread" earned them popular support among workers, peasants and war-weary soldiers. Their popularity also grew at the ballot box. In Petrograd, the Bolshevik vote in municipal and parliamentary elections rose from 20 percent in May, 33 percent in August, and 45 percent in November. In Moscow it rose from 11.5 percent in June to a whopping 51 percent in late September. During the First All-Russia Soviet

Congress in June, Bolsheviks made up only 13 percent of the delegates; by the Second Congress in October, they dominated the proceedings with 53 percent of the delegates and the Left Socialist Revolutionaries, now allied with the Bolsheviks, making up another 21 percent.

Meanwhile, not only did the Provisional Government continue to throw its full support behind the war, but Alexander Kerensky took over as minister of war and in turn appointed the right-wing General Lavr Kornilov as supreme commander of the Russian army in July 1917. Kornilov hated the Left and blamed the Petrograd Soviet for the breakdown in military discipline. In September, Kornilov attempted to crush the Petrograd Soviet and overthrow the Provisional Government, ironically forcing Kerensky to turn to the Bolsheviks for help. The Bolsheviks mobilized an army of workers and soldiers to defend the city, but they defeated Kornilov's forces without firing a single shot. Railway workers redirected away from the city the trains carrying troops, and Soviet delegates persuaded a Cossack battalion to retreat. Kornilov was arrested, but he would go on to play a leading role in the White Army assault on the Bolsheviks during the Civil War.

Ironically, the Bolsheviks had not become the kind of tightly knit, underground organization Lenin had proposed in *What Is to be Done?* fourteen years earlier. While their numbers never matched that of the SRs, they had grown from 10,000 in March to over 400,000 in October. Having now essentially abandoned the slogan "All Power to the Soviets," Lenin convinced the party that the time was right to seize state power. Historians are sharply divided over whether the October Revolution was a coup or a mass uprising, but we do know that the party could not have succeeded without significant support from workers and soldiers, despite denunciations from Menshevik and SR leaders. The Red Guards—the Bolshevik-organized workers' militias—were decisive in securing state power. And since the Bolshevik-led Military Revolutionary Committee was part of the democratically run Petrograd Soviet, it had far more authority and legitimacy than the Provisional Government—especially in the aftermath of Kornilov's failed attack. Kerensky, after all, had appointed Kornilov in the first place. No wonder the vast majority of troops ignored Kerensky's commands, forcing him to flee the city.

Once in power, the Bolsheviks moved swiftly to pull out of the war and implement its program. On October 26, within hours of taking over the Winter Palace, Lenin issued statements promising massive land reform, democratization of the military, workers' control over production, bread and other necessities to the cities, immediate peace negotiations on the basis of no annexations or indemnities, and the right of self-determination for national minorities. Lenin also promised to expose the secret treaties of the Allies as evidence of the war's imperialist character and pledged "the unconditional and immediate annulment of everything contained in these secret treaties insofar as it is aimed, as is mostly the case, at securing advantages and privileges for the Russian landowners and capitalists."[25] (A few weeks later, Trotsky would publish all of the treaties, correspondence, and diplomatic cables between the Allies.)

The Allies were unwilling to end the war. Peace proved costly. Lenin had no choice but to sign an armistice agreement with Germany in 1918 that forced Russia to cede the Baltic provinces and a large part of Belorussia and Ukraine, depriving Russia access to one-third of its agricultural land and railways, virtually all of its oil, and three-quarters of its coal and iron deposits. The Bolsheviks tried to buttress the failing economy by nationalizing some industries and the banks, but after the money economy had practically collapsed, the state ultimately began to provide free housing, clothing, food rations, and transportation. Production levels and wages fell to a fraction of what they were four years earlier. The Bolsheviks now had to reorganize industrial production and persuade peasants to provide the towns with food.

The Bolsheviks also had to contend with a series of crises. The new regime was immediately beset by war from multiple forces: the White Army (former tsarists, right-wingers, and representatives of the ancien régime); foreign powers, including former Allies, concerned about a Russian-German alliance (France, England, the United States, Japan, et cetera); and Ukrainian and other nationalists and anti-colonial movements, hostile to Bolshevik rule. The civil wars lasted for at least three years. And as war broke out, the regime faced an internal crisis, partly of its own making. Prior to the October Revolution, the Provisional Government was to be replaced by a Constituent Assembly and elections were scheduled for September, but, faced with the Kornilov affair, Kerensky put off the elections until November. Lenin preferred the soviet model—direct elections of workers, by workers—over parliamentary democracy, which he viewed as an instrument of bourgeois rule.[26]

But the Bolsheviks decided to proceed with elections knowing that they probably would not get a national majority. Of the over 48 million men and women who went to the polls, 19.1 million cast their votes for the SRs, while the Bolsheviks won 10.9 million, the Cadets 2.2 million, and the Mensheviks a mere 1.5 million; the remaining 7 million votes went to non-Russian socialist parties (mostly in Ukraine). The SR tally makes sense because they represented the peasantry and Russia was still an overwhelmingly rural country. However, the Bolsheviks managed to gain the majority of workers and at least 42 percent of the soldiers' votes.[27] When the Constituent Assembly held its opening session on January 5, 1918, tensions were high. Even before delegates sat down, Red Guards fired on a group of demonstrators outside, killing twelve people. The Bolsheviks insisted that the assembly recognize soviet power and its political program. When SR leader Viktor Chernov, the assembly's elected chair, put forward his own agenda instead, the Bolshevik delegates walked out. The next day Lenin dissolved the Constituent Assembly for good. His version of a "dictatorship of the proletariat" based on the direct democracy of the soviets prevailed—at least for a time.

Although Trotsky is generally credited with arguing that the success of the Soviet Union depended on world revolution, in 1917 this was a common position among Marxists in Russia and across the Western world. Indeed, in his "Report on Peace" issued immediately after the seizure of power, Lenin made a direct appeal "to the class-conscious workers" of Great Britain, France, and Germany to join the revolution and resist the war, implying that the fate of the Russian Revolution depended on their "comprehensive, determined, and supremely vigorous action." Lenin looked to the proletariat in the "advanced" countries "to help us to conclude peace successfully, and at the same time emancipate the labouring and exploited masses of our population from all forms of slavery and all forms of exploitation."[28] A few months later, Lenin put it more succinctly: "without the German revolution we shall perish."[29]

At the time, the Bolsheviks had reason to be optimistic. In 1917 alone, mutinies occurred in the French and British armies as well as the German navy; some 200,000 German metal workers struck against cuts in bread rations; fighting between workers and soldiers erupted in the Italian industrial city of Turin. In January 1918, a wave of strikes swept through Austria-Hungary and Germany, involving half a million metal workers in Vienna and Berlin. Opposition to the war was now widespread across the continent. In Germany, the Social Democratic Party (SPD)—supporters of the war since 1914— had expelled members of its own parliamentary party for anti-war activism, leading them to form a new party, the Independent Social Democrats. In January of 1919, huge demonstrations of workers and soldiers seized control of Bremen, Hamburg, Hanover, Cologne, Leipzig, Dresden, Munich—even Berlin, where armed demonstrators carrying red flags gathered to hear German revolutionary socialist Karl Liebknecht proclaim a "socialist republic" and the "world revolution" from the balcony of the imperial palace. But the revolution was crushed with the help of the SPD. Liebknecht and Rosa Luxemburg, cofounders of the Spartacus League and the German Communist Party, were assassinated in 1919.

The smashing of the German Revolution opened the door for the liberal, though short-lived, Weimar Republic, but it also set the stage for the rise of fascism. Still, the Russian Revolution did not perish—not exactly. The revolution survived civil war, international isolation, and the near collapse of its economy, but only as a result of extraordinary measures. In 1918, the Bolsheviks introduced "War Communism"—emergency policies based on a centralized system of economic administration, including the nationalization of industry, a state monopoly on grain and other agricultural commodities, and a "food dictatorship," whereby all surpluses above a fixed consumption norm would be subject to confiscation. They also reversed their commitment to workers' control, integrated factory committees into the more centralized apparatus of the trade unions, restored the hated practices of paying workers by piece rate, and required the appointment of individuals (foremen, directors, managers) to oversee each enterprise—a policy that undercut workers' self-management.

The regime's ability to weather the crisis using coercion and militarization convinced many Bolshevik leaders that the draconian methods of War Communism could be deployed in the service of building socialism. Lenin, by contrast, grew skeptical of coercive measures, especially since popular uprisings, strikes, and work stoppages continued throughout the Civil War and were not the result of counterrevolutionary conspiracies. Thus, in 1921, he introduced his New Economic Policy (NEP), which relaxed state controls and allowed for limited free market activity. The policies were aimed at encouraging the peasantry to increase production for the cities. By conceding to market forces, the Bolsheviks were forced to make major policy reversals, including the denationalization of small-scale industry and services, the establishment of trusts to finance and market the products of large-scale industry, and the granting of concessions to foreign investors. NEP succeeded in stimulating the Soviet economy, but at a price. Class differentiation and inequality sharpened in the countryside, a new class of capitalists emerged in the cities ("NEP men," as they were derisively called), and persistent unemployment became a problem. Stalin's ascent to power and adoption of the first Five-Year Plan for industrialization in 1929 effectively marked the end of NEP. Yet, even prior to the consolidation of Stalinism, both Lenin and Trotsky recognized that a creeping state bureaucracy had begun to eclipse the revolutionary vision of the soviet. During an inner-party debate in the winter of 1920–21, Lenin warned: "Ours is a workers' state with bureaucratic distortions." In the end, what appeared to be a workers' state concealed a party-state bureaucracy headed by Stalin. The military bureaucracy improvised to weather the postrevolutionary storm and became permanent. The state, not the workers, effectively controlled the means of production. Difficult questions have since dogged and divided Marxists of every ideological current: Was Stalinism a distorted form of state socialism, or bureaucratic state capitalism? Is socialism in one country possible, or will it die on the vine without the global overthrow of capitalism? Is the state inherently an instrument of repression and subjugation, and does human liberation require its dismantling? Or can the state be harnessed to create the conditions for a just and economically secure life for all—that is to say, a genuine socialist society? Was Stalinism an aberration or a divergence from the revolution's original vision and trajectory, or was it a logical manifestation of its history?

Finally, perhaps the most important legacy of the Russian Revolution is the creation of the Third International or the Communist International (Comintern). Founded in March of 1919, the Comintern played a pivotal role in promoting revolution and Communist parties not only throughout Europe and the United States, but around the world. Unlike the First International (the International Workingmen's Association, 1864–72) and the Second International (the Socialist International, 1889–1916), the Third International included "colonial and semi-colonial" people in its ranks and helped to promote and coordinate anti-imperialist movements. Indeed, at the Second Congress of the Communist International (1920), Lenin submitted his famous "Theses on the National and Colonial Questions." While holding on to the idea that the colonies must first undergo a bourgeois revolution before a socialist one, Lenin insisted that the "communist parties must give direct support to the revolutionary movements among the dependent nations and those without equal rights (e.g. Ireland, and among American Negroes), and in the colonies."[30] During those early years of internationalism, colonial subjects were not just the object of revolutionary theory; they were its authors. Indian Communist leader M. N. Roy submitted his own theses that were sharply critical of Lenin's original draft. Roy argued that the bourgeoisie in the colonies was often reactionary and could not be counted on to lead a revolution, and while he agreed that proletarian revolution was out of the question, he did insist that a struggle of workers and peasants under the guidance of a disciplined Communist party would invariably take on a revolutionary character. Whereas Lenin was willing to support nearly all anti-colonial movements, Roy feared that the petty-bourgeois leadership of the respective nationalist movements "would compromise with Imperialism in return for some economic and political concessions to their class."[31]

Prominent radicals from Africa, Asia, and Latin America spoke at subsequent meetings of the Comintern, some playing a role in drafting language on self-determination for Africans in South Africa and African Americans in the US South. In 1926, it helped form the League Against Colonial Oppression, which combatted pro-imperialist sentiment in Germany and elsewhere, and in 1930 the Comintern launched the International Trade Union Congress of Negro Workers, under the leadership of George Padmore (Malcolm Nurse). Moscow attracted many of the world's leading Third World revolutionaries, who trained at the Communist University of the Toilers of the East or simply visited at the behest of the Comintern—most notably, Ho Chi Minh of Vietnam, China's Deng Xiaoping, George Padmore, I. T. A. Wallace-Johnson from Sierra Leone, Jomo Kenyatta from

Kenya, and South African Communists Moses Kotane, Edwin Mofutsanyana, James and Alex LaGuma, and Albert Nzula, not to mention Black American Communists such as Harry Haywood, Otto Huiswoud, Lovett Fort-Whiteman, William L. Patterson, and Mack Coad. Of course, not all of these figures found the Comintern or the Soviet Union to be inviting, supportive, safe, democratic spaces, and not long after its founding the Soviet came to dominate the Third International, even to the point of stifling dissent.

Walter Rodney on the Russian Revolution

Remarkably, given Rodney's stated task to glean the lessons of February and October for the incipient revolutionary movements in Africa and Asia, he has nothing to say about the Third International in the lectures and notes that have come down to us. Rodney's silence on the significance of the Comintern is surprising since it is the one institution that directly influenced anti-colonial and national liberation movements throughout the Third World. Not to mention the fact that his friend and teacher C. L. R. James wrote one of the earliest book-length histories of the Third International.[32] While bearing in mind that Rodney never had the opportunity to finish the book, leaving us to speculate as to what he might have eventually included or excised, it is hard to believe that Rodney never intended to include it. And to be fair, the deluge of new books commemorating the revolution's centennial have had very little to say about the Third International, even as they acknowledge the revolution's impact in Central Asia and other parts of the empire.[33]

The course from which this project developed, "Historians and Revolution," was designed to focus on the *interpretation* of the internal dynamics of revolution. Therefore, the opening lectures frame the basic antagonism in historical interpretation (between "idealism and materialism"), identify what is at stake in the study of the Russian Revolution and the political economy of the Soviet state, and present what Rodney calls a "preliminary categorization of writers" on the revolution. He then sweeps through the history of the revolution, from nineteenth-century resistance to the tsar to the February and October Revolutions of 1917, taking several detours to compare mainstream Cold War historians' interpretations of events to those of Soviet and some independent Marxist scholars (for instance, Maurice Dobb). The subsequent lectures examine the critical debates in Western Marxist circles over the capacity for, and nature of, socialist revolution in Russia; the contributions of Russia's "pre-Marxist" Left prior to the 1905 Revolution; and the question that dogged Marx, Engels, and many late-nineteenth-century Russian Marxists: whether a "backward" state (empire) like Tsarist Russia could make the leap to socialism without first establishing a strong bourgeois democratic state. For Rodney this was never an issue of leaping from feudalism to socialism, because the Russian economy was indisputably capitalist, already in the throes of rapid industrialization and "modernization."

Rodney is particularly interested in the historiography of 1917. He asks whether the events between February and October were inevitable, or instead the results of bad judgment, unforeseen circumstances, and happenstance. Here he takes a more expansive view of the terrain covered in the preceding chapters, juxtaposing bourgeois and Soviet interpretations of events with Trotsky's historical analysis, notably his epic three-volume *History of the Russian Revolution*, which he called a "monumental work [of] history at the highest level of analysis." Rodney praises Trotsky for the way he stresses specific historical conditions rather than simply quoting Marx, chapter and verse (something he admires in Lenin, as well). Although he criticizes Trotsky's later assessments of the devolution of the Soviet state, Rodney takes from his dynamic notion of combined and uneven development an explanation for how skipping over the vaunted "stages" of history could be a way of promoting a socialist path for Africa.

Whereas the first five chapters focus on the path to the Bolshevik seizure of power, the second half of the book examines the consolidation of power, the tension between workers' democracy and dictatorship, and the efforts to build a socialist state. And it is precisely in his reflections on socialist transformation, democracy and the state that Rodney makes his most original contributions and links the revolution more directly to post-colonial Africa.

First, the role of the peasantry in socialist revolution was an unavoidable issue for Rodney since this was the fundamental question for post-independence Africa, especially in Tanzania where Ujamaa entailed the creation of collective villages. Likewise, the "peasant question" had long been a central issue in Russian revolutionary politics. The Socialist Revolutionaries had rejected the Marxist view of the peasantry as petty bourgeois, believing that the principles of collectivism inherent in the peasant commune made Russia peculiarly fitted for socialism. (Interestingly, Rodney almost never mentions the SRs, but does talk about the Narodnik view that the peasant commune can be the basis for socialism.) Instead, like most Marxists debating the peasant question at that time, Rodney returned to Marx, whom he argued did not consider peasants "a revolutionary force," because he believed they were disappearing. As Rodney explains in chapter 6, according to Marx, "Peasants were becoming capitalists through their slow accumulation of capital and the improvement of techniques since the Middle Ages." Most other peasants were dispossessed and became a proletariat. But, as Rodney also acknowledges in chapter 3, Marx had begun to move away from an interpretation of the peasantry modeled on England and France when he and Engels turned their attention to Russia. Indeed, Rodney reminds his readers that Marx and Engels not only predicted that revolution might break out in Russia before Western Europe, but that "the present Russian common ownership of land may serve as the starting point for a communist development."[34]

Lenin, he felt, had it right: based on his studies of

nineteenth-century agriculture in Russia, Lenin envisaged an alliance of workers and peasants constituting the dictatorship of the proletariat; he recognized that there were contradictions between the two classes, but that these were not antagonistic, since their basic interests were the same. Rodney recognized three phases in Lenin's incorporation of the peasantry in the revolution: (1) land redistribution; (2) contribution to the Civil War and feeding the Red Army (War Communism); and (3) the New Economic Policy (NEP).

Of course, the fourth phase, for which Lenin bore no responsibility, was collectivization of agriculture. Without going into detail, Rodney generally accepts the characterization of kulaks as a rural exploiting class and even suggests that Stalin's directive to "liquidate the kulaks" was never intended to mean direct fatal acts of violence. Instead, Rodney suggested that the terror was largely organic—an opportunity for poor peasants to settle scores and to retaliate against hated landholders. He also accepted the argument that because the sale of surplus grain was needed to accumulate capital for industrialization, the fact that the kulaks controlled 20 percent of the marketable surplus of grain but chose to hoard or cut back production "was one reason why the kulaks had to be crushed and agriculture collectivised."

At the same time, Rodney summarily rejected the use of force by a socialist state to impose socialist or collectivist policies. For him this was "a matter of principle." Revolutionary violence "is the social violence that is necessary for the change-over of power from the hands of the bourgeoisie into the hands of the workers and the peasants. Once they have the power, a workers' government has to carry out the Revolution by transforming society, and that is not done through violence." Rodney not only critiques Soviet policies of collectivization, but takes Soviet historians to task (in the post-Stalin period) for *only* criticizing Stalin, the individual, rather than the party and the state apparatus as a whole.

Thus, rather than dwell on Stalin or the Soviet Union, a

central theme of his lectures is the treatment of peasants under *capitalism*. The question alone should cause anyone who regards Stalinist collectivization as especially more brutal than enclosure in Europe and colonialism to rethink the premise, especially given their attendant processes: dispossession, forced taxation, forced labor, and outright genocide. And it makes sense, since Rodney had been wrestling with the question of collectivization, especially in Tanzania at the time. He wrote a provocative essay that argued President Julius Nyerere's concept of Ujamaa was not "African socialism," as the latter described it, but an expression of scientific socialism, in that it called for forms of collectivization that challenged (severed) the relationship with the bourgeoisie in the metropoles and challenged the formation of a kulak class (African farmers who hired other rural Africans as wage laborers) and local bourgeoisie (in the form of Indian merchants, et cetera). The parallel he drew with Russia was not one of forced collectivization, but a vision of direct peasant socialism promoted by the Narodniks—specifically, the idea that the *mir* (village communes) and *artel* (artisans cooperatives) might lay the foundations for "a socialist society that was qualitatively different from that envisaged by their counterparts in industrialized Western Europe." His point was that stages of development are not fixed; Africa, notably Tanzania, could leap over the capitalist stage and move directly to socialism through Ujamaa villages. He did not advocate a return to communalism; instead, collective ownership and production in the countryside would benefit from the technological advances of industrial socialist (and even capitalist) countries. He thus tied Ujamaa to the international socialist movement.[35]

In chapter 8, Rodney takes special interest in Russia's transition from empire to Soviet Federalism. He begins by describing Russian imperialism as a form of settler colonialism. "As in all colonial states," he writes, "there was a legal distinction between the citizen (Russian) and the colonial subject. The Constitution of Tsarist Russia explicitly based discriminatory measures on the racial or national origin or religion of those affected. It was in some ways like the distinctions made under Portuguese and Belgian colonialism, and South African and Rhodesian apartheid"(p. 154). He draws stark parallels with Western European imperialism as well as US imperial expansion across the continent (Manifest Destiny), expressing the problem succinctly in a particularly memorable line: "The British sent warships—the Russians sent the Cossacks." He describes economic exploitation and investments across the empire (grain production in European Russia and Siberia; cotton production and oil in Soviet Central Asia; railroads and ports in the Far East, notably the Trans-Siberian Railway). And he briefly discusses cultural domination (the oppression and persecution of Catholics, Jews, Muslims, Yakuts, Afghans, et cetera), making frequent comparisons with Africans under colonial domination. "If someone saw a school somewhere in Soviet Central Asia, one could be quite sure that it was for the children of the Russian settlers, and quite naturally it taught in Russian, which was unintelligible to the local people. Incidentally, this cultural superiority readily gave way to *racism*. Inherent superiority is a good excuse for suppression"(p. 156).

As rule under the tsar took colonial form—moving from direct rule to settler colonialism, and the rise of extractive industries (such as mining and timber), one-crop economies, and so forth—resistance was less proletarian and more anti-colonial (which is to say, they drew together labor as well as propertied classes, religious leaders, and intellectuals). He writes, "The main conclusion that one could draw from all this is that for non-Russian peoples, the struggle against Tsarism was often indistinguishable from the struggle [against] Russia and Russian settlers in their country"(p. 159).

Rodney saw Soviet Federalism as a *potential* model for decolonization, but ultimately a failed model since—in his view—Russian imperialism persisted. He surmised from a critical reading of Frederick C. Barghoorn's *Soviet Russian Nationalism* (1956) that the Soviets were promoting one kind of nationalism under Stalinism while denying the validity of nationalist sentiments in Central Asia. Specifically, he noted a shift in Soviet historiography, where, initially, the revolts in Central Asia were characterized as twofold: masses resisting tsarist oppression, and indigenous ruling classes resisting the imposition of colonial rule. This meant the Bolsheviks initially treated these revolts sympathetically, as national liberation movements. But in the 1930s, as the USSR stressed national unity and patriotism, any evidence of Russian domination over non-Russian peoples was simply erased, along with the history of anti-colonial resistance. Not that national minorities were erased; they, too, were celebrated in an early expression of multicultural pluralism, and they often reached some of the highest posts in the party and state. But the analysis of antagonisms emanating from the afterlives of the tsar's colonial policies was practically eliminated, replaced with another narrative: that *the native ruling classes* were the most immediate source of oppression. The penetration of capitalism under the tsar deepened those contradictions, creating the conditions for class unity between non-Russian and Russian toilers. As Rodney put it, "Soviet historians began to stress that along with the tsarist soldiers and officials came Russian workers, scientists, doctors and teachers who played a great cultural and revolutionary role in the life of the peoples of Asia. By 1951, the Russian 'annexation' became a positive good"(p. 160).

Finally, his last lectures are brief reflections on Stalinism, beginning with an assessment of Trotsky's critique of Stalin. Trotsky, after all, was Stalin's most visible adversary, silenced only by an assassin at the behest of Stalin himself. Rodney addresses Trotsky's four main criticisms:

(1) Stalin encouraged socialism in one country instead of international socialism.

(2) The state did not wither away but became more oppressive and bureaucratic.

(3) Social and economic inequalities were fostered under Stalinism.

(4) There was an inadmissible element of force in building Socialism.

On the first point, Rodney disagrees, arguing that it was not Stalin's policy to promote socialism in one country but that he had no choice given the failure of socialist revolutions in Western European nations. Why? Imperialism undercut revolutions, propping up capitalism and a white working class. Rodney sharply criticizes Trotsky, saying that his *History of the Russian Revolution* promoted Russia's rapid industrialization and transition to socialism, and implying that Trotsky himself was open to building socialism in one country: "One can only conclude that Trotsky's stand is conditioned by bitterness through having been defeated in the struggle for power"(p. 174).

On the rise of the bureaucratic state, Rodney again absolves Stalin of responsibility and suggests that it was "a consequence of Russian backwardness," established when Lenin and Trotsky were leading the nascent state. On the other hand, he agrees that under Stalinism there were distortions and problems, and while he gives credit to the Communist Party of the Soviet Union (CPSU) for exposing some of the crimes and to Soviet historians for revising history to reflect this, he is not convinced. Rodney finds it hypocritical on the part of Soviet historians to claim that the USSR was on the right path and celebrate the revolution's great achievements by 1938, but then to place the responsibility for the regime's problems (bureaucratic state, persecutions, et cetera) solely on Stalin. He argues that the whole of Soviet society, including its leaders and the party, was responsible for its successes and failures. And yet, he recognizes that the Soviet Union in this period was undergoing a crisis of leadership as a result of the rapid loss of ideologically sophisticated revolutionaries and the growing number of sycophants surrounding Stalin. However, Rodney never actually accuses Stalin himself of having opponents liquidated, nor of grooming those who would become his lackeys.

The final lectures acknowledge the post-1956 Soviet critique of Stalin, the cult of personality, his dismantling of autonomous worker and peasant organizations, the devolution of power from the Central Committee to his hands, and so forth. However, Rodney takes Soviet historians to task for holding on to the idea that the party never strayed from the path toward socialist development. He insisted that this was impossible because Stalinism distorted socialist society, weakening its ideology and the political culture. Indeed, in the final section he echoes C. L. R. James, Raya Dunayevskaya, and Grace Lee Boggs's *State Capitalism and World Revolution* (1950) when he suggests that the contemporary Soviet Union, especially following the invasion of Czechoslovakia and its treatment of China, "is behaving so much like a capitalist state"(p. 186).[36] Although both Rodney and James take issue with Trotsky's critique of Stalin's theory that the Soviet Union is building "socialism in one country," their positions diverge sharply. Whereas Rodney treats Stalin's turn to socialism in one country as a pragmatic choice given the absence of world revolution, James insists that the very question is flawed. "Does anyone believe that Stalin or any of his people believe that what is in Russia is socialism?" asks James. "Only an utter fool can think so. What the debate was about was whether the state-property system would be maintained without a revolution sooner or later in the West."[37]

Or in the Soviet Union itself. Here again, Rodney breaks sharply with James. In the chapter on Stalinism, Rodney makes a case for directing the internal security apparatus against counterrevolution. "The Soviet experience demonstrated the various ways in which counterrevolution could manifest itself in modern socialist society. It was not just the person who aimed at killing a party official who was dangerous, but the economic saboteur, who tried to undermine economic administration by black market practices or by deliberately slowing down production. To root out such individuals required an extension of the secret police machinery"(p. 182). Given the external threat of counterrevolution from capitalist forces in Western countries, Rodney sees the security apparatus as flawed, but necessary to defend the gains of Soviet socialism. James, by contrast, saw worker slow-downs and sabotage as acts of *worker self-activity*—not crimes against the state. After all, worker resistance to the Stalinist regimes, whether in Hungary or the Soviet Union, was resistance to state capitalism.[38]

James and Rodney's differences have much to do with the contexts in which they lived and worked. Rodney's perspective was shaped profoundly by his location in an African country that was attempting to build something that resembled social-ism, in an era when the "one-party state" was regarded as a vehicle for national economic and social development. Because Rodney witnessed firsthand the enormous constraints placed on the Tanzanian state as it launched Ujamaa villages, attempted to build an expansive welfare state, and sought to govern in the face of internal and external enemies, his sympathetic assess-ment of Lenin's critique of parliamentary democracy makes a great deal of sense. James, on the other hand, never had the experience of living in a country attempting to actively build socialism. Besides, James submitted his most cogent indict-ments of the Soviet Union and the Eastern bloc countries during the 1950s, between fifteen and twenty years before Rodney delivered his lectures. Rodney, therefore, has a significantly different perspective on the difficulty of establishing and sustaining socialism in the era of US empire. He doesn't say this exactly, but he is considering what it means to build socialism in the era of global depression, world war, the ascendance of the Keynesian welfare-warfare state (and the consolidation of US political and economic hegemony), the reconfiguration of empires, and US/NATO militarism as a permanent condition (not to mention a main economic driver) forcing the Soviet bloc into a perpetual state of military readiness.

C. L. R. James is present throughout this book, despite the absence of references or citations to his work. Again, this is perhaps a liability of an unfinished manuscript. James was not only one of Rodney's most important teachers and friends, but possessed the most thorough knowledge of both the French and Russian revolutions of anyone else in Rodney's vast circle. Rodney's essay "The African Revolution," published in *Urgent Tasks*, explicitly credits James's "detailed knowledge of the Russian Revolution" for revealing the parallels between the problems confronting the post-colonial regimes of Kwame Nkrumah and Julius Nyerere, and those faced by Lenin and the Soviet state. "James isolated the two matters on which Lenin placed absolute priority in his last years," Rodney explained. "The first was the break-up of the old state machinery and the second was educational work among the peasants. Marxism-Leninism was not Nyerere's point of reference, but he decided upon these same two priorities for Tanzania after the experience gained from several years in office as head of state."[39] James and Rodney concurred that after the Bolsheviks seized state power, Lenin was a democratizing force, as seen in his tireless promotion of literacy campaigns, workers' control and participation in planning, peasant cooperatives, and the emancipation of women. Lenin had become the model for the new wave of Third World revolutionary leadership.[40] But whereas James's image of Lenin sometimes clashed with the historical Lenin, who was willing to deploy the coercive arm of the state to suppress popular councils and dissent from workers and peasants, Rodney tended to be less utopian. Not that Rodney was particularly critical of Lenin, but he subtly parts company with James by hinting that the suppression of dissent preceded Stalin and, as we've seen, finds it justified in some instances.[41]

In the end, Rodney was impressed with the Soviet economy and its emphasis on growth, investment, rising incomes, its focus on heavy industry, and its ability to avoid periodic crises and depressions. While he has nothing to say about the consequences of rapid mass production, speed-ups, alienation caused by the division of labor, and lack of workers' control—the sorts of problems that occupied young Marx—he makes a case for the command economy's role in solving the problem of poverty and hunger. Pushing back against bourgeois historians, Rodney argues that the Soviet economy demonstrated a capacity to at least maintain a humane standard of living and to improve aspects of the quality of life for the broad masses of people. This for him is the critical lesson for the colonized world: that they must resist bourgeois historians and economists who claim that Soviet planning slows growth, suppresses scientific developments, reduces worker productivity, and produces little more than immiseration for the masses. For the present generation, even being able to *conceive* of a socialist society is no small matter. Can we speak of socialist revolution anymore and, if so, what does that look like? Most of the former socialist countries are now models of neoliberalism (except perhaps for Cuba, and its future is hardly settled). The Bolivarian revolutions perhaps come close, but these are, more or less, left social democratic experiments with weak democratic foundations—and they are now being dismantled before our eyes.

And yet, the point of this book is not to write socialism's epitaph, nor to reminisce in the glory of October. To study the Russian Revolution, Rodney insists, is not to emulate it. There are lessons to be learned, and the principle of socialism must be defended, but African and Third World revolutionaries cannot slavishly adopt it as a model. Or as Rupert Lewis put it, "The most important aspect of Rodney's approach to the Russian Revolution was that its experience and lessons could not be mechanically applied to the African continent."[42] Third World revolutionaries needed Marxism, but Rodney wisely counsels that we need to be wary of either a "Marxist view through [a] distorted bourgeois lens" or the Soviet view despite being "very close because of the similarity of our present and past with their past in the period under study." He ends on a profoundly reflective note: "Assuming a view springing from some Socialist variant is not necessarily Marxist but anti-capitalist, assuming a view that is at least radical humanist—then the Soviet Revolution of 1917 and the subsequent construction of Socialism emerges as a very positive historical experience from which we ourselves can derive a great deal as we move to confront similar problems"(p. 186).

The Theoretical Significance of Rodney's Work: Traditions and Genealogies

Rodney's work exemplifies a kind of non-Western double consciousness of the West; a consciousness of the West from within, but also from a distinctly and even defiantly non-Western perspective. The concept of his working title, "Two World Views of the Russian Revolution," exemplifies this returning of the gaze, this making-visible of the West and of bourgeois thought, from outside but also from within. In some ways akin to subaltern studies,[43] in terms of shifting which voices and traces are listened to in the writing of history, Rodney's work is simultaneously akin to indigenous studies,[44] in foregrounding the relationality of the writer to historical and ongoing processes of colonization. It also overlaps and engages with African studies, Caribbean studies, Black Studies and Pan-African studies, but their inclusion in the academy *as theory* remains problematic, as they are often seen as peripheral and are still associated with activism, politics, and anti-Western protest. However, if we situate the rise of the Western academy within historical processes of white settler colonialism and imperialism,[45] the political and epistemic volatility of Black radical thought *as theory* can be more deeply understood as a direct challenge to prevailing systems of Eurocentric knowledge and power. Too little has changed since Rodney opened his introduction to this book with a similar argument about the need to decolonize Africana studies, to make "African history and society ... a legitimate field of enquiry," to "counter the racist, colonialist orientation" that prevailed under colonialism, and to give "primacy to interpretations by Africans themselves"(p. 1). While US Black Studies would generally be repressed and scaled back in the years since Rodney's statement, and is generally held to have crested in terms of growth and overall size around 1980, the discipline persists in smaller but formidable numbers, continuing to resist—with ever greater theoretical, epistemic and political strength, and with broader social consequences.

What does it mean that Rodney is writing from both inside and outside the academic industrial complex, in direct critique of Western bourgeois thought? Or that he directly confronts the politics of academic knowledge production and embodies the kind of internationalist, community-committed scholarship that was then being pioneered, as exemplified by US Black Studies in general and the Institute of the Black World in particular?[46] What does it mean that he names and demarcates the scholarly arena in this way, and how does this relate to Foucault's concept of discourse, which emerged around this time, in the context of a dying colonialism?[47] And how does Rodney's "two world views" concept relate to Said's more politicized intervention in *Orientalism*, which extended the application of discourse to the non-Western world, but also (as *How Europe Underdeveloped Africa* had done in 1972) to the West/non-West *relationship*?[48] In short, how do we situate Rodney's theoretical practice, so clearly stamped by the experience of anti-colonial revolution, in the annals of the late twentieth century's revolt in academic thought?

On the one hand, the Marxist concept of ideology provided foundations for ideological and proto-discursive analyses since the mid nineteenth century; on the other, Pan-African theory exemplifies the state of "double consciousness," the simultaneously inside/outside perspective critical to anti-colonial scholarship and consciousness. More than with post-colonial and post-structuralist scholarship in recent decades, this deeper epistemological duality forged around contested relations of power reflects, and potentially connects with, anti-colonial and decolonial theory, including the works of scholar-activists like Angela Davis, Cedric Robinson, Ngũgĩ wa Thiong'o and Sylvia Wynter—all contemporaries of Rodney whose work continues into the present. Davis and Robinson represent some of the best work within the US Black Left tradition in the 1960s and '70s;[49] Ngũgĩ famously engaged a radical anti-colonial praxis during Kenyan dictatorships;[50] and Wynter deployed Marxism within her Caribbean epistemological framework.[51] Throughout the 1970s, theories of coloniality and the coloniality of power had their origins in the racially conscious Marxisms of Latin America, before being reframed as decolonial theory.[52] Rodney was grounded in precisely these kinds of praxis-based, anti-colonial, Third World Marxist struggles of body and mind that represented the cutting edge of social revolutionary consciousness in the international 1960s and '70s.

Rodney emerged as part of the first generation of post-colonial scholars to establish a presence in the nearly all-white metropolitan academy and its classrooms, where they had to confront leading colonial scholars like Hugh Trevor-Roper on the very presence and details of African cultures and history. But Rodney also challenged Trevor-Roper and his bourgeois colleagues within the core fields of Western and European history—and in the case of this volume, Russian historiography. Rodney needed neither approval nor sanction. As he noted, "In initiating a study of the world at large, the African scholar or student can exercise choice—something that was impossible under colonialism . . . There is no need to justify the selection; understanding the Soviet Union is a priority that is self-evident"(p. 3).

We can only speculate on the directions Rodney's thinking would have taken, but the confluence of Pan-African theory, Third World Marxism and cutting-edge critical theories inside the academic industrial complex seem to typify his trajectory. His "two views" perspective allowed him to see the West from outside, with double consciousness, and to seek a third path at the height of the Cold War—an alternative heralded by the signal fires of the Non-Aligned Movement and Third World Marxism. In the wake of its centennial, Rodney reminds us of the relevance of the Russian Revolution and shows us some of the way forward, both in terms of engaging the most significant socialist revolution in world history, and in terms of the broader theory we will need in any context of interpretation and struggle. The Soviet system, the Non-Aligned movement, and the optimism of his time in Dar es Salaam have all passed. But the most fundamental impulse of Rodney's work remains our most urgent task: to join grounded revolutionary theory and history with the people in motion, in whatever form this takes.

1

The Two World Views of the Russian Revolution

> Throughout the history of human knowledge, there have been two conceptions concerning the law of development of the universe, the metaphysical conception and the dialectical conception, which form two opposing world outlooks.
>
> —Chairman Mao Zedong, "On Contradiction" (1937)[1]

In the era from the confrontation with colonial rule in the 1950s and 1960s through the process of decolonization, African scholars have resolved a number of issues. First, African history and society became a legitimate field of inquiry. Second, they have emphasized the need to counter the racist, colonialist orientation that predominated within the little that had been previously written. Third, they have given primacy to interpretations by Africans themselves. A similar and even more determined effort to overturn racist interpretations of history was made by African descendants in the New World, notably in the United States. This work is the basis for the proliferation of Black Studies programs and is responsible for the demand that, as far as black people are concerned, white people are historically disqualified from interpreting black folks *to* black folks. Consequently, the terms "African perspective," and/or "black perspective" have emerged from both the continent and the Diaspora.

The concept of an "African perspective" is much broader than those of "African history," "African society," and African culture." An African scholar naturally designates activity by Africans as his primary field of study, but it does not take very long to discover that he/she is obligated to arrive at his/her own interpretation of human societies outside of Africa. At the University of the West Indies, Ibadan, Dar es Salaam, for example, the normal demands of teaching led rapidly to the decision that local staff should not merely master local affairs, but should replace Europeans presenting and interpreting Europe to Africa, and initiate the study of Asia, so as to provide our own people with a global perspective.

It was not so long ago that "we" in textbooks designed for Africans meant "we the British" or "we the French." Conversely, "they" referred to Africans, which posed a crisis of identity, even when "they the Africans" are not referred to as savages or natives. This point hardly needs discussion with regard to studies of Africa itself, where the battle for an African identity has already been fought and won in principle. But looking at the outside world is necessary to underscore the new realization that Africans are "we," and that we have to interpret the totality of human existence.

At the simplest level, an African account of, say, Australia or Switzerland written for Africans would demonstrate the characteristics of relating the foreign and unknown phenomenon to what is familiar in Africa. That is a very normal procedure. When the Dutch went to Benin in the seventeenth century, they exclaimed that Benin City was comparable to the best that Holland had to offer. Similarly, all Europeans compare Shaka to Napoleon, Dahomey to Sparta, and so on. Of course, for the present generation of educated Africans, a European parallel comes to mind more quickly than an African one. Nevertheless, the time will probably come when African teachers will make seventeenth-century European feudalism more readily comprehensible to African students by pointing to similarities and contrasts in fourteenth-century Ethiopia.

In initiating a study of the world at large, the African scholar or student can exercise choice—something that was impossible under colonialism. The colonized African did not merely study Europe; he concentrated heavily, sometimes exclusively on the "mother country." The opening of the options allows for the establishment of priorities of relevance. In any event, the history of Europe or of a given European country from the fifteenth century to the present has had to give way to courses on African history. Therefore, what remains outside of African consciousness has to be rigorously studied.

There is no need to justify the selection; understanding the Soviet Union is a priority that is self-evident. Some awareness of the Soviet Union has seeped into the African consciousness, occasionally through direct tutoring among the educated, and more usually by inference and occasional references in different contexts. Both the books and the indirect references come from the colonizer to the colonized. The colonizer had national and ideological conflicts with the Soviet Union. Indeed, they were self-declared enemies. Therefore, "A" was interpreting his enemy, "B," to a third party, "C," which happens to be comprised of Africans. In the best of circumstances, such a procedure would be questionable, unless Africans had already agreed that our interests and basic outlooks coincided with those of Europe. As it is, we know for a fact how prejudiced and distorted Europe's view of Africa has been. We know that European capitalism and imperialism continue to have our exploitation as their main objective. There is, therefore, every reason to be suspicious of the Western European (and American) view of the Soviet Revolution, and there is every reason to seek an African view.

In society, there are a variety of options within systems. To understand a system requires that we analyze both its national expressions and the social forces that shape the environment.

The lives of Africans over the last five centuries have been affected to varying degrees by forces originating in Europe. Increasingly, Africa became enmeshed in the web of relations that constitute international capitalism—imperialism.[2] The Russian Revolution was the first decisive break away from international capitalism, affecting thereby the subsequent course of events around the world, including Africa.

To a certain extent, this inquiry has as a premise that there is such a thing as "an African perspective," and hopefully it will be demonstrated that the literature on the Russian Revolution bears out such an assumption. However, it is also possible to test the limits of the assumption by penetrating more deeply into the process of consciousness, the process by which individuals in society come to rationalize their social relations and external environment. Hence, it is necessary to introduce at a very early stage the concept of the two world views—idealism and materialism—representing fundamentally opposed aspects of consciousness.

There is an area of potential conflict that arises by trying to reconcile an African view with the two world views. It can be argued that aspects of ideology coming from Europe are irrelevant to the African perspective or the black world view. Conversely, it can and has been said that a world view is either idealist or materialist and that the label "African" conveys no meaning and probably mystifies. That issue can only be resolved in the forces of discussion, and it is my intention to try and avoid prejudgment. However, the very title of this chapter should indicate to the reader that whatever uniqueness one may attach to any given African view, it does not dispense with the necessity to recognize (1) the superiority of materialism over idealism, and (2) that materialist views are partial and do not take African perspectives into account.

A Preliminary Categorization of Writers
on the Russian Revolution

Every piece of scholarship is implicitly and explicitly a review of previous work on a given subject. But, from time to time, it is also illuminating to direct attention specifically to the nature of existing studies on a particular theme. Historians often resort to this approach, as part of a tradition of assessing the scope and limitations of their own discipline. When this is done, the problem that immediately arises is one of categorization. Into what slot can this or that writer be fitted as a basis for further discussion? Not surprisingly, for the historian the answer is often to make use of a chronological scale. Assuming that the discussion concerns a set of events that took place at least a century or two ago, then it is a relatively simple matter to follow changing patterns of interpretation—starting with contemporaries of the events and moving toward the present. However, when the events are close to the present, a more synchronic approach is unavoidable. This is the situation with regard to the Russian Revolution.

The contrast implied above can best be seen by comparing writings on the Russian Revolution with those on the French Revolution. The mass of material produced by French historians on the central event in their national history falls fairly neatly into chronological eras. In the nineteenth century, it is possible to distinguish the Restoration from the rest of what was essentially a Republican era. The purposes and preoccupations of historians under the monarchy were quite different from those writers of a later date, even though liberal and conservative tendencies could be discerned in both periods. By the turn of the twentieth century, the nature of the debate among French historians on the French Revolution changed under the impact of socialist perceptions, which had been developing during the nineteenth century. After the First World War, the debate became more and more a clear-cut confrontation between socialists and non-socialists.[3] This latter is the only framework that is meaningful as far as the Russian Revolution is concerned.

A chronological categorization to a great extent obscures the emergence of fundamental ideological differences in the interpretations of major historical events. The English Civil War of the seventeenth century, which often competes for the title of Revolution, is a case in point. It is entirely justifiable to distinguish between the predominantly "religious," "constitutional," and "economic" interpretations that have arisen at various times since the seventeenth century among historians reconstructing the English Civil War. In doing so, however, one or two Marxist views are brought in on the fringe as exhibits of how wide and exotic historical interpretations can be.[4] But Marxist conclusions start from such different premises that they constitute a camp apart from all other interpretations, which share much more in common. From a Marxist viewpoint, in effect, there are only two world views that enter the picture. In the case of the historiography of the French Revolution, in spite of the more recent evolution, there is still confusion as to the order of difference between several interpretations. That is to say, it is still fashionable to list the "Liberal" Thiers, the "Conservative" Taine, the "Social Democrat" Jaurès and Marx himself (or the "Marxist" Soboul) as though the difference of degree and kind are more or less constant as one takes each of these writers in turn.[5] That is the equivalent of a taxonomy which presumed the same order of difference between sheepdog, wolf, cat and lion!

The Russian Revolution, which broke out in 1917, is virtually a contemporary event. The sorts of changes that took place in the manner in which this event has been presented over time are not yet very significant. Any overview of the literature on the topic must use compartments based on differences of approach among historians and other social scientists, viewed virtually as a single generation of writers. This compartmentalization can be done on a purely subjective basis, as evidenced by James Billington's article "Six Views of the Russian Revolution," in which he is solely concerned with subjective attitudes such as nostalgia, regret and notions of glory.[6] However, the division reflecting the social reality of the contemporary world is that between Marxist and bourgeois views. When this is overlooked, it suggests an extreme case of mental confusion, since the Russian Revolution itself did more than any other historical event to bring about ideological polarization on a world scale between the two world views of the socialist and capitalist systems.

Before the Russian Revolution, the world at large shared the "metaphysical conception" of which Chairman Mao Zedong speaks in the opening epigraph. In Europe, the metaphysical conception took the form of bourgeois idealism, which had largely superseded the more overtly metaphysical views that had dominated Europe's perception of man and nature during the feudal epoch. Outside of Europe, metaphysical views with a highly religious and anti-scientific content predominated. In such a context, the materialist conception was partially and inadequately grasped. Nevertheless, in the form clarified by Marx and Engels, the materialist world view was accepted by a number of *individuals* in the latter part of the nineteenth century. With the rise of the Soviet Union, Marxism was to acquire a *class base* and the support of a state power. Later, other states were to follow this lead through revolution.

The rise of states governed by Marxism sharpened the contradictions between socialist and bourgeois ideologies, producing an ideological war for the possession of the whole world. The writing of history has been a facet of, and a weapon in, that war, and historians interpreting the Russian Revolution itself have been active combatants. In analyzing the alignment of different historians, it is easier to start with the Marxist camp, which is the more readily recognizable because it is self-declared. Foremost in that camp are the Soviet historians. To the outside world, and especially to the non-specialist, the names of individual Soviet scholars of the revolution are not well known. Their works in foreign languages were almost invariably joint productions under the aegis of the Communist Party of the Soviet Union or the Soviet Academy of Sciences. However, it does not in the least defeat our purpose to recognize the collective personality that Soviet writers have assumed. Any history of the Communist Party of the Soviet Union, any text on the Russian Revolution, any biography of Lenin or Stalin produced at any time in the Soviet Union, can be fairly regarded as the official Soviet view at that particular time, rather than a purely personal and perhaps eccentric expression by a single writer.[7] It is only reasonable that Soviet historians should receive priority in a study of the historiography of the Russian Revolution, because they are interpreting national history. They have been closest to the most-relevant source materials, and they are trying to make sense of a reality that they themselves have experienced and are still experiencing.

Outside of the Soviet Union, a number of Marxists have also produced conclusions substantially in accord with those in vogue in the Soviet Union. Most supporting interpretations were written not by professional scholars but people who had ideological affinities with those who had firsthand knowledge of the revolution. One of the most famous contemporary accounts was that of John Reed, whose memoir *Ten Days that Shook the World* received the imprimatur of Lenin himself.[8] The publication by the American labor unionist William Z. Foster was also in the same vein; and it was written after a visit to the Soviet Union in 1922.[9] However, in the Western world, much of the early enthusiasm for the Russian Revolution died out within a short time. That seems to be one of the key reasons why few major scholarly Marxist studies have been carried out in the West on the Russian Revolution from an entirely sympathetic viewpoint. A well-known example is Christopher Hill's biography of Lenin, written as long ago as 1947.[10] Since then, a number of articles and monographs by the English Marxian economist Maurice Dobb have had a virtual monopoly of the role of the pro-Soviet interpretations in the Anglophone world.[11] Most Western Marxist interpretations of the Russian Revolution and the Soviet regime range from mild criticism to bitter denunciation. This started at the period contemporaneous with the outbreak of the Revolution of 1917, as part of the debate among European Marxists concerning tactics, strategy and the fundamentals of Marxism. Inside of Russia, the Mensheviks provided the major dissident Marxist force. Their later writings constitute a self-declared Marxist interpretation that is often diametrically opposed to the equally self-declared Marxist position of officially endorsed Soviet historians. One acceptable piece of Menshevik historical writing is that of Raphael Abramovitch, a prominent figure in the Menshevik hierarchy in the period before 1917.[12] Karl Kautsky and Rosa Luxemburg, two of the most prominent Marxists on the European scene at the time of the 1917 Revolution, took issue with the Bolsheviks. Their disagreements are in fact part of the history of that period, but they must be considered within the context of Marxist scholars commenting on the Russian Revolution. In the first place, one of the crucial issues of the historiography is that concerning the application of Marxism as theory to the program of revolution and reconstruction in Russia. Both Kautsky and Luxemburg have a contribution to make in that respect. Secondly, their works have been republished and integrated into subsequent debate on the nature of the Russian Revolution.[13]

With regard to Leon Trotsky, there is a similar situation of contemporary debate leading directly to subsequent historical controversy. Trotsky began writing historical and polemical accounts before his departure from the Soviet Union. That part of his work written at that time, and even subsequently, which dealt with the period before 1924 does bear a considerable resemblance to the official Soviet versions.[14] But, of course, when Trotsky writes of the period when he was Stalin' s foremost antagonist, the gap between his interpretation and that of Soviet historians is virtually unbridgeable. Trotsky was not just a participant at the center of the Russian Revolution, but a historian in his own right. He was also the founder of the Fourth International and attracted a considerable intellectual following.[15] The work of the "Trotskyites," both in the form of pamphlets and full-length historical interpretations, constitutes a body of literature that is distinctive and has to be dealt with separately in a study such as this.

Apart from Trotsky and Trotskyites, many other Marxists fell out with the government and the Party of the Soviet Union. There has been a common thread uniting the published work of a larger number of defectors from the Soviet Union and Eastern Europe as well as ex-members of the Communist parties in the West. Their shared disillusionment is well brought out in the oft-cited compilation *The God That Failed*.[16] In some instances, these ex-members of Communist parties have become apostates ideologically, but in other instances they claim to continue to make their criticism of the Russian Revolution from a committed, initially Marxist standpoint. This is to group them with all others with sufficient reason to profess to share the materialist world outlook; and the scant attention which will actually be paid to that particular approach in this study is due solely to the fact that most of their literature relates to the period following upon the second great war started by the capitalist powers, while the limit of the Russian Revolution is here taken to be the eve of that war.

To the extent that doubt may be cast upon the Marxist authenticity of any one of the writers or groups referred to above, their categorization remains provisional at this stage. There are many popes in the Marxist world who ordain and excommunicate this or that person or organization as true or false Marxists. Hopefully, that attitude will be avoided in this study, but it may be that in the final analysis a self-professed Marxist interpretation of the Russian Revolution will appear to have ignored all the principles of analysis based on the materialist/dialectical mode of perception. With regard to bourgeois interpretations, there is no such likelihood of having to deny the claims of self-declared supporters of capitalism. On the contrary, their modus operandi is such that they seldom declare their initial position in unequivocal terms; therefore one of the first tasks is weighing up the terms; and non-Marxist scholarship is to bring to the fore its idealist subjective bourgeois premises.

It is quite justifiable to treat the bourgeois writers as falling into a residual category of non-Marxists. All writers who do not claim to be Marxist, or at least some form of socialist, are solidly in the bourgeois camp. One reason that they are very coy in declaring themselves as such is that the word "bourgeois" carries powerful condemnatory overtones, which they would not readily accept. A second reason is that bourgeois scholarship always pretends to hold a monopoly of truth and reason; and most bourgeois writers fall over themselves to stress that they approach issues open-mindedly and dispassionately. According to that line of argument, the Marxist has prejudged issues, has a closed mind and is partisan. It would therefore be unwise for the bourgeois scholar to expose his own set of assumptions—thereby revealing that he and the Marxist are following the same pattern of arguing from established premises, but that the premises are different and the very methodology of analysis is different. Such an exposure and revelation would force one to reconsider the relative premises and methodologies; and it is clear that the bourgeois scholar is afraid of just that.

In a situation in which bourgeois scholars have a monopoly, their differing conclusions are considered as the complete sample of reasoned inquiry into that particular subject, with a Marxist view occasionally thrown in to illustrate that men are sometimes bereft of reason. For all practical purposes, the historiography of the Russian Revolution in a standard Western institution means the several opinions expressed by orthodox Western scholars on the subject. A useful illustration of that fact is seen in the selections produced in the series "Problems in European History." That series ostensibly sets out to demonstrate significant interpretations on various subjects, and it includes three volumes relevant to the Russian Revolution.[17] In none of them is there any serious presentation of the Soviet view—a view that is significant if for no reason other than the fact that it is the common understanding of Soviet citizens and millions of other residents in socialist countries. In none of the said volumes is there any balancing in terms of space of the various Marxist views alongside of various bourgeois positions.

The Bourgeois Overview

The bourgeois view has the following characteristics: (1) claims to be concerned with humanity rather than a given class; (2) high level of subjectivism; (3) refuses to recognize contradictions, except at a superficial level. As an example of the first, one can take the work of the English historian, Hugh Seton-Watson of Oxford, one of the leading English historians of Russia and Communist Europe. Seton-Watson is solidly in the bourgeois camp, as seen when he refers skeptically to communism as "a theory which professes to explain philosophy, religion, history, economics and society." He then goes on to say bluntly that "Communism is a science of conspiracy, a technique of wrecking and subversion."[18] While decrying the Bolsheviks for crushing democracy, he constantly makes statements such as the "simple and guileless workers and peasants," the "politically ignorant and gullible masses," the "simple peasants."[19] However much as he might pretend to be speaking in the name of democracy, he gives himself away by those terms in two ways. He indirectly admits of the fundamental class gulf between his class and the working class; and he shows that at bottom he has little regard for the workers and peasants and their political capacities.

It should be noted that within revolutionary historiography, the conservative historians always expose themselves by their contemptuous attitude to the common people. Burke, Barruel, Taine and to some extent de Tocqueville writing on the French Revolution can be found constantly referring to the "mob" and the "rabble." They claim that these people have no right or capacity to rule and merely give way to blind passions. There are other historians who are even less discreet than Seton-Watson in hiding their bourgeois snobbery toward the workers and peasants.

An extreme example is Jacob Walkin's *The Rise of Democracy in Pre-Revolutionary Russia*. By the very title, he lays claim to be speaking on behalf of the people at large. But he makes little attempt to hide the utter contempt that he felt toward the workers and peasants. Walkin starts with the Revolution of 1905. Why did the workers and peasants follow radical slogans? "It would be a mistake to conclude that the workers understood the significance of the slogans they heard."[20] Another question that immediately poses itself: How then does one explain the revolution if not as a *conscious* ideological move forward, as Marxists say? To that, Walkin would reply, "At the base of the Revolution of 1905 was the emergence of a primitive, elemental and anarchistic force."[21] This same force reemerged in 1917, according to this historian, because the administrative machinery broke down. Again, using Walkin's own words, one can see his innate class snobbery. "With the disappearance of administrative machinery in March 1917 full sway was given to the anarchistic and irresponsible tendencies of the primitive Russian workers."[22] What Soviet writers call the mobilization of workers under the Bolsheviks after March, Walkin refers to as a mob of violence and anarchy: "The still primitive masses, who degenerated into mobs seeking to gratify what they understood as their rights, without regard for their obligations to the law, the general interest or the rights of others."[23]

Of the two, Seton-Watson is the more important figure and the more dangerous. His language is not as vicious, and it is easier to be misled by his implied assumption that one need not seek out class alignments, because it is sufficient to speak vaguely of democracy.

Another bourgeois approach that can be quite effective is the subjectivist one, which does not start by examining reality as it exists but rather puts forward for the reader a set of evocative images that come from his own mind—words such as "dictatorship," "terror," and even "communist" are used to convey the required impressions. This carries history into the realm of narcotic drugs—such historians really taking one on a trip.

13

A good example of this type of writing comes from R. N. Carew Hunt, widely believed to be a British intelligence agent, who parades as a scholar and authority on the Soviet Union. His best-known work is a dictionary: *A Guide to Communist Jargon*.[24] Marxist writers have inevitably had to find new terms to describe society in the way it is seen by the members of oppressed classes. The language lacks the urbanity and refinement that the bourgeoisie developed as an expression of its own disassociation from sweat and cow dung. But of course, in their supercilious manner, bourgeois scholars like Hunt see nothing in Soviet and other Marxist writings except "jargon." The subjectivist approach of Carew Hunt and many other bourgeois scholars often reflects itself in their preoccupation with individuals rather than with broad social forces. An extreme example of this is found in the book on Stalin by the American historian Francis Randall. Everything that happened in the Soviet Union between 1925 and 1953 was personally attributable to Stalin, as far as Randall is concerned.[25] It should be noted in passing that Soviet and other Marxist writers are not always exempt from subjectivism, nor from traits such as concentration on personalities rather than social forces. But the vice is far more widespread among bourgeois writers because their ideological preparation does not equip them to deal with objective reality.

Bourgeois historians can be led into absurd positions, through their failure to perceive the deep-rooted contradictions in human society. An example of this absurdity is seen in the work of Bernard Pares, notably his *The Fall of the Russian Monarchy*.[26] He calls it a "study of the evidence," but the evidence of whom or what? His evidence comprises memoirs of the Russian ruling class. He admits that the Empress Alexandra's letters were his chief source. His object is an intimate knowledge of the internal workings of the government. This is not even good bourgeois history—it is feudal in its sole preoccupation with what kings and queens did.

When Tsar Nicholas agreed to have an audience with Prince Bergius Trubetskoy in 1905, Pares comments, "the emperor at last found himself in intimate contact with men who were really representative of the public."[27] That is to say, his idea of the "public" does not extend beyond the tiny circle of aristocrats and bureaucrats who participated in tsarist politics. Pares's class prejudices lead him to be exclusively concerned with an inconsequential section of the whole picture. He sees that area of court life as the most fundamental aspect of the whole picture, and he concludes that the revolutions came not at all from below but from above. In his view the revolution of February 1917 did not spring from the sort of fundamental contradictions about which Soviet historians write, but rather it occurred because the ruling class of the tsar and his advisers fell asleep and never woke up. This is an elitist notion that seeks to deny the working class any role in history. It is a notion fundamentally opposed to a socialist conception of the dignity of the working class.

To understand the hegemony of the bourgeois view of history, particularly of interpretations of the Russian Revolution, we need to interrogate the university institutions that are responsible for the vast majority of research and publications in the field. From a Marxist materialist standpoint, the university is an important element of the superstructure. If the production relations in the society are capitalist, then the superstructure of belief and action is also capitalist, and the university would obviously serve the interests of the capitalist or bourgeois class. Even from a non-Marxist standpoint, the above contention is invariably upheld directly or indirectly. It is well understood at all levels of English society that the upper strata of the ruling class receive their education at certain universities, and before that at the exclusive public schools. In the United States, there are perhaps more illusions that the universities are meant to serve the pursuit of truth, justice, aesthetics and the like; but studies devoted to the subject invariably come up with different conclusions. G. William Domhoff, in his book *Who Rules America?*, explicitly states that his starting point is not Marxist, but he is in no doubt with concern to the role of America's leading universities as tools of the big capitalists. Domhoff writes as follows: "Control of America's leading universities by members of the American business aristocracy is more direct than with any other institution which they control . . . These mechanisms give the upper class control of the broad framework, the long-run goals, and the general atmosphere of the university."[28]

The long-run control of the big bourgeoisie is not compatible with a limited degree of freedom in day-to-day affairs, which allows for some deviation within the universities. Therefore, it is not impossible for a materialist world view to come from a writer within a western and bourgeois institution. Besides, progressive non-Marxists' views can also challenge the standard bourgeois approaches. However, it is the rarity of such occurrences that must be stressed. There are several factors at work toward the elimination of any rebel or non-conformist tendencies. At one level, there is direct action to remove those who step out of line. Those who are familiar with the politics of university appointments, tenure, promotions, et cetera, know it to be a ruthless business.[29] One tendency is that where there is a powerful, pampered professor in a certain field, he surrounds himself with a chorus of sycophants, and the non-conformists are weeded out.

Above all, when any group of scholars works together closely in an institution, they tend to develop common approaches to problems. Indeed, this tendency links together universities in the national and international context, leading to the formation of broad schools of thought within particular disciplines. As far as the Russian Revolution is concerned, a very potent influence has been exercised in this sense by Russian émigrés who were given favored positions in academic institutions because of their familiarity with the language, their plausibility in terms of having lived most of their lives in Russia, and their compatible ideological outlook. These émigrés were usually "White Russians," hostile to the Communist government of the Soviet Union and grateful to their capitalist hosts in the United States and other countries. They did not hesitate in declaring their bourgeois orientation.

The strong bourgeois émigré interpretation made itself felt directly through the widely circulated works of such scholars as Michael Karpovich of Harvard, George Vernadsky of Yale, and Michael Florinsky of Columbia.[30] Besides, their influence was indirectly exercised through the generation of native American (white) scholars whom they trained on the Russian Revolution and other aspects of specialization of Soviet studies. The "acknowledgement" page of numerous prominent American historians of the Russian Revolution invariably reads like a "who's who" of Russian émigré circles as far as the academic world is concerned.

In England, the London School of Economics was one institution where Soviet studies had a special bourgeois flavor under the guidance of Leonard Schapiro, a staunch anti-communist of Central European background. Schapiro prefaces one of his works on the Soviet Union by stating, "I do not pretend to conceal my predilection for a society based on the established legal order."[31] Every society is based on an established legal order, so either the learned professor was saying absolutely nothing, or he had something else in mind. The fact is that such are the curious sophistries by which many bourgeois scholars admit to support of the established order of capitalist society.

From time to time, the bourgeois scholar does reveal his ideological prejudices in a frank manner outside of the body of his study. An entertaining example of this type is to be found in Adam Ulam's preface to one of his books on the Soviet Union, entitled *The Unfinished Revolution*. He writes, "It is perhaps appropriate in view of one of the main themes of the book, that this study of socialism should have been assisted by Guggenheim, Rockefeller, and Carnegie, the names being those of the foundations which have been very generous."[32] One would have to search very hard in the history of capitalism to find another trio of capitalist exploiters bigger than Guggenheim, Rockefeller and Carnegie! Their "philanthropic" foundations sponsor academic research and publications to promote the bourgeois ideology and the capitalist system. It would be unfair to say that everyone who receives money from such capitalist foundations necessarily shares the values of the capitalists who give the money, but in the case of Adam Ulam, he himself is affirming that his purpose and conclusions with regard to his study of socialist Russia do justice to his capitalist sponsors.

Adam Ulam is a foremost American scholar on the Russian Revolution based at Harvard, where he is a professor of government at the Institute of Russian Research. That fact is also prima facie evidence of his bourgeois commitment and orthodoxy, because not only is Harvard a bastion of the ideological superstructure in the United States, but that particular Russian center has been exposed as a very active instrument of the American state.[33] In other words, some institutions are more compromised than others within the bourgeois camp, and studies emanating from such institutions are more compromised than others within the bourgeois camp, and studies emanating from such institutions are unmistakably of a certain ideological flavor, as are studies emanating from a Soviet university under the aegis of the Soviet Academy of Sciences and/or the Communist Party of the Soviet Union. One such institution, which is most relevant to a study of views on the Russian Revolution, is the Hoover Institution for War and Peace at Stanford University.

The Hoover Institution is notorious for its connections with the CIA, the Pentagon and the State Department. The kinds of projects for which they make funds available are the publication of accounts by Russians hostile to the Communist regime, or other Americans writing diatribes against Communism. In 1955, the Hoover Institution published Harold H. Fisher's *The Communist Revolution*. Fisher took the stand that "the Soviet-led Communist movement seeks the same ends by the same means and threatens our liberties and those of other free peoples."[34] The reader would need to ask whether he or she is included in Fisher's collective "our," and whether he or she wants to be included, bearing in mind that the "free people" to whom he refers include the oppressed masses of Spain, Portugal, Greece and Latin America, plus (in 1955) all the colonized and exploited people of Africa and Asia and all the oppressed black people within the United States!

If one were to single out a bourgeois writer whose studies on the Russian Revolution are least redolent of the above assumption, that it is a revolution that threatened "free people," the most likely candidate would be E. H. Carr. Carr is a perceptive historian whose reflections on the writing and meaning of history are well known.[35] The Russian Revolution has been his major field in a long academic career, and his multi-volume history of the Russian Revolution is worthy of consideration as one of the few texts that have already come to be considered "classics" on this subject.[36] These volumes, and other studies by this English historian, display considerable sympathy for the Bolshevik Party that led the Russian Revolution and for the Russian people who reaped the fruits and sufferings of the revolution. It is illuminating to notice what an orthodox bourgeois reactionary says of Carr. The above-mentioned Schapiro, in the preface to his own book *The Origins of the Communist Autocracy*, mentioned that "Mr. E. H. Carr read the manuscript at an early stage in its existence, and made a number of comments on points of detail which I was glad to adopt. I regret that I was not able to adopt some other suggestions, because our interpretation of the facts diverged too fundamentally."[37]

Soviet Overview

One expects to find certain basic Marxist features within the Soviet analysis, such as emphasis on contradictions, technology, class and ideology. The basis of the Marxist world outlook is the notion of dialectical materialism. It is a notion that first of all recognizes that change and historical movement are dependent upon the contradictions within things and between things. Any form of logic other than dialectics assumes that when one has a given object the object remains constant and discrete in itself. The dialectical notion stresses that every phenomenon is constantly transforming itself, owing to its own internal contradictions and to contradictions between itself and other phenomena.

Thus, bourgeois logic expects to find a bourgeois class in existence at a particular point in time and to see that same bourgeois class in existence one hundred years later. Marx stressed that the bourgeois class was evolving because of its own internal contradictions, because of contradictions between itself and other classes and because of the basic contradictions between man and nature.

According to the classic formulation of dialectics, one can always discern a pair of opposites in operation—thesis and antithesis, giving rise to synthesis, which in turn is merely a thesis in relation to another opposite. Hence the law of the unity of opposites. How can one have a proletariat without a bourgeoisie? And so long as one has them both, one has a contradiction, just as there was previously a contradiction between the bourgeoisie and the aristocracy.

The vital role of technology comes about because technology is required to solve the oldest and most persistent of all contradictions—that between man and nature. For Marx, it is within nature and the material conditions of existence that one must find the motive forces in history. There were others who believed in dialectics, but who believed that all history flowed from ideas. This was the case with Marx's predecessor, Hegel. Marx, however, insisted on the primacy of matter over ideas, and having given priority to the material conditions of man's existence as the mainspring of history, he naturally gave similar high priority to man's tools or technology for achieving mastery of the material environment.

According to their way of earning a living, men in society fell into definite categories. In feudal times, those who earned their living through possession of land were the aristocratic class, while those who earned theirs by working on the nobles' lands were the serfs. Under capitalism, those who owned the factories (the principal means of production) were the bourgeoisie or capitalists, while those who sold their labor to exist were the workers or proletariat. Within society itself, this contradiction between classes was the most dynamic force, and it led to revolution at certain junctures in history when the class in power was overcome by its challenger.

Ideas came after matter. The ideas in men's heads were the reflection of their material environment, their state of technology, their class position and the ideas that they inherited historically, which too were ultimately traceable to material conditions. The sum total of ideas in men's heads can be called "ideology" of consciousness. Since men in society fell into classes, their ideology of consciousness had the stamp of a particular class on it. There was feudal ideology, bourgeois ideology and proletarian ideology, which is socialism.

When the Soviet historians look at the old regime in Russia, they first explained how the development of *technology* had produced and transformed classes. The bourgeoisie had been produced out of the peasantry and the aristocracy; the proletariat had been produced out of the peasantry. They explain how the presence of large factories affected the character of the proletariat and how the backwardness of agrarian technology affected the peasants.[38] They identify the principal class contradictions as being that between the bourgeoisie and the workers, and that between the aristocracy and the peasants. In addition, they note the contradictions between the semi-feudal and semi-capitalist state and the mass of the people.[39] They see the contradiction between Great Russia and the colonial parts of the Russian Empire.[40] They note the contradictions between Russian national interests and the interests of the Western capitalists.[41] *They explicitly commit themselves to the side of the workers and peasants.*

As far as ideology is concerned, one can gather directly or indirectly from Soviet presentations that the bourgeois ideology was only partially represented in the Russian state structure. Bourgeois elements wanted to go further—to remove feudal traces and remold the state structure to bring it in line with the bourgeois democracy of Western Europe. Besides, there was also the Marxist socialist ideology, which attacked not only feudalism, but capitalism as well, and this ideology was carried forward by the Bolsheviks.

The Soviet view combines the above elements by saying that the various contradictions were sharpening during the late nineteenth century and led *inevitably* to the outbreak of revolution in February and March 1917. The bourgeoisie thereupon tried to take over state power through the Provisional Government. However, *guided by Marxist theory and the Bolshevik Party*, the workers and peasants overthrew the bourgeoisie in October 1917. Subsequently, the Bolshevik party spearheaded the people's struggle to build a socialist society.

Soviet historians would draw attention to two further factors that aided the workers and peasants in their seizure of state power both in February and October. The first was the contradictions between the capitalist/imperialist powers in the form of the world war, and the second was the contradiction between Great Russia and the colonies, leading to nationality struggles.[42]

If it was not already a common understanding, then it should now be clear from this brief preview that sharp differences can appear among scholars professing the same fundamental world outlook. The debate within ideological camps or between them is sometimes about "facts" or the validity of sources. But all serious studies on the writing of history concur in stressing what the historian brings to his sources: the prejudices and biases that reflect an individual's distinctive social group and particular historical epoch in which she/he lives. To categorize a view as either Marxist or bourgeois—materialist or idealist—is to identify its most important bias. Furthermore, the differences between the materialist and idealist modes of perception emerge more strongly in some kinds of discussions than in others. A discussion of the Russian Revolution is certainly one instance where the ideological biases are highly relevant, and most striking. Besides, to approach the debate with an ideological schema is to focus on the most important issue of our time: the confrontation between capitalism and socialism, incorporating all the world-shaking problems of national liberation, racial emancipation, economic development and the liberation of man.

2

The Russian Regime and the Soviet Revolution

In assessing any historical event, one must have the clearest possible idea of the social context in which it took place. This is most essential when one is dealing with a revolution, which by definition is a major transformation of society. That is why all historians of revolutions pay such great attention to the old regime. What a historian claims to be the nature of the old regime is directly relevant to the conclusions he will draw, such that describing the sociopolitical structure is itself an act of historical interpretation. Therefore, the following sketch of Russian social structure before 1917 cannot be neutral, but it does attempt to concentrate on features that have been commented upon by a wide range of historians both bourgeois and Marxist.

The Feudal Order

There is some disagreement as to whether Russian society was ever "feudal," because of divergences from the pattern of feudalism established in places like Germany, France and England. However, the common understanding is that "feudalism" is a term broad enough to cover the Russian situation in the sixteenth, seventeenth, eighteenth and nineteenth centuries.[1]

Under classic feudalism, there were two classes: the aristocracy or the landowning class, and the serfs. A serf was not very different from a slave. He was the property of the landowner and could be bought and sold. Legally the only difference between a serf and a slave was that the serf could not be removed from the land on which he was born. He could be sold to another owner only if that owner bought the estate. Serfdom meant that the direct producers did not own the principal means of production—the land—and that was the essence of feudalism.[2] As late as 1861, serfdom still existed in Russia. That was the date at which the landowning class agreed to grant legal freedom to the serfs, whom one can thereafter refer to as peasants. Since serfdom was abolished only in 1861, it is understandable that in 1917 Russia could still be considered a semi-feudal country.

After the emancipation of the serfs, the Russian nobility continued to own most of the land. The biggest landowner was the emperor or tsar. In the early stages of feudalism, the king or emperor was on the same socioeconomic level as his largest noble vassals. This was described by the Latin phrase *primus inter pares*—first among equals. But the king represented the notion of centralization, while the nobles represented decentralization, so there was a conflict between them on that score. The conflict between king and nobles could resolve itself in three different ways: (a) The nobles could triumph and keep the state decentralized. This happened in Germany, and as a consequence Germany was not united until the late nineteenth century under Bismarck. (b) The nobles could decide to accept centralization and themselves take over power in the central government. This was what the English nobles did. They forced the king to sign a Magna Carta or Great Charter, which was an agreement to rule through consultations with them. (c) The king could triumph and impose centralization on the nobles, thereby depriving them of much of their political power. This was the alternative developed in France by the time of Louis XIV, and it was the alternative that was found in Russia. It meant that the tsar of Russia had sufficient personal power to be called an autocrat, although in the final analysis, he still ruled on behalf of the landowning class. Most of the bureaucrats were nobles, and they were kept close to the tsar at his courts as well as served as officers in his armies, as cabinet ministers, and as the upper echelons of the Orthodox Church. There was another sense in which Russia was semi-feudal by 1917: namely, the fact that classes characteristic of capitalism had made a major impact on Russia by the late nineteenth century, and Russia was involved in a web of money relations that were part of the capitalist mode of production. There had arisen an indigenous Russian bourgeoisie in the modern sense of the word—that is, there was a small manufacturing bourgeoisie. Marx noted that the bourgeoisie as a class did not appear overnight. It came about as a result of a long process of evolution with revolutionary ruptures or transformations, such as the English Civil War and the French Revolution. In the eighteenth century, the nascent bourgeoisie were still mainly merchants, while in the nineteenth century they became manufacturers and industrialists. The French Revolution, therefore, was a bourgeois revolution in two senses. In the first place, the predecessors of the modern bourgeoisie were prominent in making the revolution, the last vestiges of feudalism were removed, money relations were fully established, and the application of science and reason led to the development of industry and the rise of the modern bourgeoisie. The paradox is that at one level the bourgeoisie caused the revolution, while at another level the revolution gave birth to a new type of bourgeoisie.

The new type of bourgeoisie was well entrenched in Russia by the late nineteenth century, adding to the other members of society who would be described as "middle class." They manufactured a variety of goods ranging from steel to light consumer goods. The government itself was also an investor and a participant in industry.[3] Unlike the old regime in France, the old regime in Russia possessed an authentic urban proletariat. This follows logically from the fact that they had a manufacturing bourgeoisie. If a bourgeois owns a factory and he has capital to run that factory, he must hire labor to work there. Those workers are the proletariat. The two—the bourgeoisie and the worker—form a dialectical unity. The worker in the factory is quite different from the peasant and from the kind of people who were called the "crowd" in the French Revolution. The artisans of the French Revolution were survivors of the feudal epoch, while the workers of Russia were the products of the new capitalist or bourgeois order where the factory and its machines were fast becoming the dominant means of production. By its possession of a small bourgeoisie and a small but influential proletariat, Russia in the late nineteenth century was further removed from what could genuinely be termed feudalism.

There is yet another factor that forces us to recognize Russia as a blend of feudalism and capitalism. That factor is the relationship between Russia and the capitalist states of Western Europe. In many ways, Russia had a colonial relationship with countries like Britain, France and Germany. Russia sold them agricultural products such as wheat and raw materials such as timber, while purchasing manufactured goods in return. Even more significant was the fact that Western Europe invested heavily in the Russian economy and loaned large sums to the Russian government. Most of Russia's oil industry and its iron and steel industries were owned by foreigners. Its railways were built by loans extended by capitalists to the government, and this represented the mortgaging of the economy, given the high rates of interest.

Yet in turn, Russia was an empire in that it had a dominant metropolitan center, known as Great Russia, that had colonized and subjugated a large number of peoples and states. There were numerous languages and cultures within the Russian Empire, but the dominant metropolis imposed its own language, culture and religion as the official language, culture and religion. Great Russia sent out its colonizers and its administrators and subjugated others in an essentially colonial fashion. As more than one writer has pointed out, the only difference between the British Empire and the Russian Empire was that one was an overseas empire and the other was territorially adjacent.

To interpret the events of the Russian Revolution, one has to know the social background as well as certain facts about what occurred. However, "facts" have to be verified by other established "facts" and by a process of logic. One can begin by taking only the minimum established agreed facts. Below are some of the basics relevant to the revolution, presented in as neutral a manner possible.

(a) There was opposition of various sorts to the semifeudal autocratic Russian Empire. This reached a high point in 1905, when there was a revolution that failed. One consequence was a moderation of autocracy through the establishment of a duma or parliament. In the countryside, slightly more freedom was given to the provincial town and village councils, the *zemstvo*. These were in the hands of the nobility and better-off landowners.

(b) There were political parties, those on the left being illegal. The most important were the Cadets, the Socialist Revolutionaries, the Bolsheviks and Mensheviks.

(c) In February and March, there was social violence and the tsar was toppled. The Duma was instrumental in getting a Provisional Government established that had representatives of the Right and center. At the same time, Soviets or councils of workers and peasants sprung up throughout the country. The most important was in Petrograd.

(d) In October and November of the same year there was more social violence and the Provisional Government disappeared. This was the October Revolution. Power passed into the hands of the Bolshevik Party, supported by some Socialist Revolutionaries and some Mensheviks.

(e) After 1917, the Bolshevik government consolidated itself and directed the transformation of the economy up to and beyond the outbreak of World War II. For our purposes, the discussion will be taken up to 1939, and that transformation is a very vital aspect of the Soviet Revolution.

The February Revolution

In the winter of 1916–17, living conditions for the workers and peasants in Russia reached an unbearable point. There were strikes involving nearly a quarter of a million workers in Petrograd, and after a bread riot led by women, the people took to the streets.[4] There is a close similarity with the French Revolution in so far as there was an immediate connection between hunger and revolutionary action. The Russian people were hungry and so they stood grieving for bread for hours in the cold, their patience sapped. Yet hunger and suffering alone does not cause a revolution. The discontent within Russian society was so widespread that it affected even the armed forces that were the instruments used by the landlord class to oppress peasants and workers. In February, the Cossacks and other troops who were supposed to control the crowd were indecisive. Many units mutinied, and others were reluctant to fire on the crowd. The crowd released political prisoners and burnt the police files, and by the end of February, the tsar's rule in the capital was effectively ended. Meanwhile, violence had been triggered in other parts of the country. This offered the opportunity for all political parties to come above ground and many revolutionaries set out for home after having been in exile.

The tsar was in the south of Russia holidaying at a place called Mogilev, and he sent telegrams telling his commander in Petrograd to quell the "mutiny." He had to be informed by his own advisers that it was a "revolution." In fact, his advisers (nobles and bourgeois) decided to jettison the tsar. First, they tried to place his brother, the Grand Duke Michael, upon the throne, but Michael refused the dubious honor. Then the tsar's ministers, military leaders and top bureaucrats felt that he should abdicate. This he did, and in the interval, the Duma formed a committee that chose individuals to form a Provisional Government. This was to rule until the people elected a Constituent Assembly to decide on the future of Russia.[5] Obviously, the example of the French Revolution was in their minds.

Soviet writers refer to February as the bourgeois democratic stage of the revolution. Those who made the revolution comprised a cross section of the population. Workers and peasants did the fighting, while the bourgeoisie were the people who sought to take state power through the Provisional Government. The true organs of the will of workers and peasants were the soviets, which had first appeared in 1905. The Bolshevik Party was the most faithful guardian of the interests of the exploited classes.[6] Most bourgeois historians who have written on the February Revolution argue that the Provisional Government was a genuine instrument of national consensus, and that it was committed to revolutionary change. These bourgeois historians are here reflecting the opinion of the Provisional Government itself, which sought to speak on behalf of the nation as a whole. But what they have to say is very inconsistent. Alexander Kerensky was the first minister of justice in the Provisional Government and later prime minister. He called himself a socialist, which is itself a debatable point, but in any case, he agreed that all the other ministers in his cabinet were non-socialists![7] In other words, the cabinet had ten bourgeois ministers and one doubtful socialist, and yet they claimed to be the true spokesmen of the millions of Russian peasants and workers. *The Provisional Government was selected by the Duma*, and when they appeared before the people, there were shouts of "Who chose you?" To this question, the bourgeois minister Miliukov replied, "We were chosen by the Revolution."[8]

George Katkov's *Russia 1917: The February Revolution* is a useful example of the bourgeois historiographical approach. He never accepts the Marxist or Soviet description of the Provisional Government and uses the word "bourgeois" in inverted commas. Directly or indirectly, most bourgeois writers would make the point that the Provisional Government represented all parties except the "extremists"—namely, the Mensheviks and the Bolsheviks, and even the Mensheviks gave it support on vital issues. Yet, Katkov is in many ways self contradictory. His own evidence can be used against him. He admits, for instance, that "the Provisional Government did not on the whole substantially differ in its composition from the projected cabinets which would have come to power if a 'government of public confidence' had been granted by the tsar at an earlier date."[9] In other words, if the tsar had voluntarily agreed to *reforms* and to bourgeois constitutionalism, he would have peacefully achieved a government like the Provisional Government. By that argument Katkov admits that the Provisional Government represented reformist bourgeois interests and not the mass of oppressed people in Russia. Katkov also admits that the Provisional Government had no real national basis when he says, "It was never made clear by what right the small committee of constantly changing personalities who called themselves the Provisional Government issued laws binding on the country and its armed forces."[10]

Most bourgeois writers say that political parties flourished under the Provisional Government. Within the government, there were several parties such as the Octobrists, the Cadets, the Socialist Revolutionaries, the Trudists, et cetera, while the Bolshevik Party itself enjoyed legality. Later on, the Bolsheviks imposed a one-party tyranny—so they say. A very pertinent question that should be answered is to what extent does the existence of several parties indicate that government is democratic? There are two parties in the United States, both representing the interests of capitalists and whites. If they were to merge, it would make no difference whatsoever. In Tanzania, there is a single party representing the workers and peasants. The number of parties in existence is quite irrelevant—the issue is, to whom are they responsible? And whose class interests do they represent? All the parties in the Provisional Government were bourgeois parties, as can be seen from an examination of the personnel involved.[11] P. N. Miliukov was a middle-class professional historian and a member of the reformist Cadet Party. Prince G. E. Lvov was a member of the aristocracy with nothing but personal differences against the tsar. M. V.

Rodzyanko was a large landowner, prominent in the tsarists' dumas, and considered *reliable* enough from a tsarist viewpoint to be entrusted with choosing other members of the Provisional Government. A. L. Guchov served as first war minister and was an Octobrist, supporter of the notorious Minister Stolypin, who carried out bloody repression of peasants and workers after the revolution failed in 1905. V. V. Shulgin, another large landowner, edited a right-wing, anti-Semitic newspaper. And finally, let's consider its figurehead, Alexander Kerensky—a lawyer, freemason, and right opportunist of the first Socialist Revolutionary order. He eventually escaped through the US embassy and served his American supporters faithfully until his death in 1970.[12]

The *policies* of the Provisional Government were what, in the final analysis, would determine to what extent they represented a break with the past and could be called a genuine government of the people. This was the time of the First World War, and the principal public issue was the question of war. All writers agree that the war was vastly unpopular. But the Provisional Government insisted on carrying on this war. Soviet historians refer to that as the perpetuation of capitalist, imperialist policies.[13] Foreign Minister Miliukov agreed to carry on the war to serve Russia's imperialist territorial ambitions in Turkey. The only argument by bourgeois historians put forward to justify the conduct of the war is that it was *patriotic*, and that because the Bolsheviks refused to fight, they were *unpatriotic*.

The notion of patriotism must be understood in a class context—one can be patriotic in defense of a capitalist state or in defense of a workers' state. These are two different things, for when a worker is patriotic in a capitalist state he is just serving as his own oppressor. But bourgeois historians use the word as a cover for their own class interests. Seton-Watson, for instance, praised the right-wing Russian general Kornilov as a patriot. General Kornilov was a tsarist army officer who was so reactionary that he wanted to overthrow the Provisional

Government and bring back tsarism. Seton-Watson says of him, "General Kornilov was not of noble birth, a monarchist or a reactionary . . . He was a patriot."[14] The truth is that Kornilov was a reactionary long before he was a patriot, because he only defended the fatherland when it was ruled by reactionaries. People like him attacked their country when it fell into the hands of the Bolsheviks.

Part of the denunciation of the Bolsheviks is that they were in the pay of the Germans, because Lenin was brought back from exile in a special train arranged by the Germans. The charge that Lenin was therefore a German spy or an agent has been proved false, but the story is revived by Katkov, in great length, to make the point that Lenin was a conscious *ally* of the Germans.[15] He accuses Lenin of lying on this matter. Here is a typical instance of bourgeois subjectivism and mistaking the wood for the trees. Even assuming that Lenin was completely aware that the German capitalists financed and organized his return to Russia, how does that compromise Lenin as a revolutionary? It is a basic principle of revolution that one utilizes and exploits contradictions among the enemy. The overall enemy was capitalism; the specific enemy was the tsarist regime. Why should not a Russian revolutionary exploit the contradictions between the German capitalist and the Russian capitalist?

Katkov is fully aware of the tactical implications of Lenin's acceptance. He is aware that "on arrival in Petrograd, Lenin openly admitted that the German government had let him through for the sake of their own imperialist aims, and that he had taken tactical advantage of this."[16] Why, then, make the issue a point of major inquiry? It is merely to cast doubt on the integrity of the leader of the Russian Revolution. Of course, Lenin returned to Russia after the February Revolution, so the question is often asked, *who led the February Revolution?* The Soviets would give a large part of the credit to the Bolshevik Party, and this is vigorously denied by all bourgeois historians. They put forward the following arguments:

(a) Most prominent leaders were abroad or in Siberia. Lenin was in Austria, and Trotsky was in the United States. They both returned after February.

(b) Local party leaders who remained inside of Russia and in the capital (Petrograd) were of a lesser caliber and could not make revolution.

(c) Most local leaders admit that they were napping. A favorite statement is that by Maslovsky, a member of the Socialist Revolutionary Party, who said that the February Revolution caught all professional revolutionaries asleep "like the foolish virgins in the Bible."[17]

The bourgeois position on the February Revolution was advanced most effectively by the American historian William Chamberlin, and it is known as the theory of the spontaneous origin of the revolution.[18] Trotsky reviewed the arguments about spontaneity in his *History of the Russian Revolution*. What he has to say constitutes one of the most perceptive pieces of historical analysis that one could find. Trotsky quotes one contemporary who disagreed with the notion of spontaneity. This writer argued that the notion of spontaneity was unscientific—things just did not happen of themselves. He said that owing to "the fact that none of the revolutionary leaders with a name was able to hang his label on the movement, it becomes not impersonal, but merely nameless."[19] In other words, we do not know the names of the leaders, but they did exist, because it was a process in which individuals had to exercise initiative and leadership at various levels. It was these small decisions by such individuals that made the revolution.[20]

Trotsky argues that the Bolshevik Party should receive the credit for the fact that workers were able to act in the manner of that tramcar conductor.[21] The Bolsheviks, through their underground organization and their press, had been raising the level of consciousness of these workers and had thereby equipped them to exercise the initiative when the revolutionary opportunity arose. "To question, who led the February Revolution? We can then answer definitely enough: conscious and tempered workers educated for the most part by the party of Lenin."[22] That is Trotsky's conclusion on the February Revolution.

No bourgeois scholar has been able to counter the force of Trotsky's argument, which, for that epoch, is essentially the same as the argument of the present Soviet historians. Attempts to argue against this viewpoint have been very ineffective. One example is that of Oliver Radkey's *The Agrarian Foes of Bolshevism*. This is a piece of Hoover Institution propaganda, which is full of self-contradictions. "The February Revolution was in the fullest sense a popular phenomenon. It proceeded from the people itself, in a purely spontaneous and wholly unorganised fashion," writes Radkey.[23] Yet, he timidly accepts Trotsky's argument about the importance of the street leaders and tries to say that they were mainly trained by the Socialist Revolutionaries. Earlier, he had already made the point that the Socialist Revolutionaries had little or no contact with the masses![24]

Katkov, who has already been cited, comes out against the theory of spontaneity to explain the February Revolution. Instead of accepting that it was the Bolsheviks who must take credit, he goes back to his favorite theme of German agitators.[25] This is a beautiful example of subjectivism. The bourgeoisie insist that the only time people rise is when there are outside agitators. They are always looking not at the grievances of the people and the contradictions within society, but to the possibility of outside interference. This was the attitude of the colonialists. This is the attitude of the American government to black revolt; this is their attitude to students' rebellion. It is pure bourgeois subjectivism.

In spite of himself, Katkov gives evidence that shows the little ways that leadership matters in a revolutionary situation. He tells the story of one Bolshevik, Bonch-Bruevitch, to whom some Cossacks went and received advice not to fire on the crowd. Katkov tries to explain this by saying they were all of the same mystical sect, but the fact is that Bonch-Bruevitch was a prominent Bolshevik, and the Cossacks would not have gone to him if it was not felt that he could give a clear political directive.[26] Katkov also provides evidence of the activity of the Bolsheviks in the Putilov factory that brought 30,000 workers into the street.[27] Then too there was the activity of Trotsky's supporters inside the factories and on the streets. Their task was to simply transform economic demands into political demands, and that is how the Revolution of February 1917 became possible. It is at the level of the ordinary worker on the factory floor that one has to look for revolutionary leadership. The bourgeoisie cannot see that because of their contempt for the masses, and their disbelief in the creativity and capacity of ordinary workers.

The October Revolution

One noticeable difference between the February and October Revolutions is that the latter was planned and carried out by a single party—the Bolsheviks. No historian discusses the question of spontaneity in October. Everyone accepts that the Bolsheviks engineered the takeover of power from the Provisional Government, which by October was under the leadership of Kerensky.

Soviet historians present the October Revolution as a proletarian one compared to the bourgeois revolution of February. In their view, the Bolsheviks (led by Lenin) had taken command of the revolutionary situation, representing the interests of workers and peasants. They set up a dictatorship of the proletariat or a regime of workers' democracy.[28]

Bourgeois writers, with the notable exception of E. H. Carr, interpret the events of October as the work of a determined *minority*: the Bolsheviks. Implicitly and explicitly, bourgeois historians suggest that the Revolution of October was an imposition on the Russian masses. Radkey of the Hoover Institution says that October marked "the triumph of a minority" and showed "the ability of a small group hungry for power to subjugate and victimize the mass of their fellow beings."[29] Another historian of the same camp, George Vernadsky, claimed that "the Soviets established authority over a stunned and demoralized Russia."[30]

A second aspect of bourgeois interpretation is the charge that the Bolsheviks were *demagogues*: that they said things pleasing to the crowd or "mobs" as part of a ruthless Machiavellian plan to get power for themselves. Some bourgeois historians actually use the word coup d'état. A coup is not a revolution, because it is a mere exchange of one group of leaders for another. One bourgeois historian, Ivar Spector, goes as far as to consider the October Revolution as a "counter-revolution."[31] (that is, that the real revolution was in February and March).

To substantiate their positions, bourgeois historians go back to what they term the popular nature of the February Revolution. They go forward to the *Constituent Assembly*, which was voted into power in November 1917, less than three weeks after the Bolshevik "coup," to use Schapiro's words.[32] In the elections to the Constituent Assembly, the Bolsheviks polled just under a quarter of the 41 million votes recorded. In January of the following year, the assembly was dissolved after its first meeting. To bourgeois historians this is overwhelming evidence of the dictatorial, undemocratic nature of Bolshevik rule.

Among the historians prominent in this debate, there were a few who were participants in the events. One of these is Miliukov, and even better known is Kerensky. An individual such as Kerensky has also considerably influenced later views, through his active presence in the United States. Radkey refers to Kerensky as "this elder statesman who has done much to broaden and deepen the author's understanding not only of the events in 1917, but of other aspects of Russian society."[33]

There is really no argument that the Bolsheviks were a minority. Soviet historians describe the Bolsheviks as the "vanguard" of the proletariat—as the most conscious element of the working masses. There has probably never been a single party of active adherents whose membership constituted a majority of a nation, and it is not unusual within bourgeois democracy for a party to take office on a minority of the votes cast. The president of the United States often receives in votes a number that represents a small minority of the total citizens of the United States, and he is supposedly a "democratically elected" president.

As we have already seen with the February Revolution, the real issue concerns the interests that a party represents. The most vital question is whether the Bolsheviks represented the interests of the Russian masses. There are several ways in which this can be tested. Attention has to be paid to the new institutions called "soviets," and the Petrograd Soviet in particular. Within the Petrograd Soviet, the Bolsheviks started off with a minority after February, but their slogans were the ones adopted. When the Socialist Revolutionaries and the Mensheviks began to cooperate with the Provisional Government, the workers lost faith in them, and by September the Bolsheviks had a large majority inside the Petrograd Soviet.

Next, one should consider the *demonstrated support* for the Bolsheviks among the workers and soldiers. It was a well-known fact that the Bolshevik position was accepted in most army units, and especially among the Petrograd garrison, as the months progressed.[34] In contrast, Kerensky and his government were really in command of the armed forces, as Kerensky firmly admits. The Russian workers showed their support to the Bolsheviks in things such as operating the railways as directed by Bolsheviks. They did not do that for tsarism, and they were increasingly skeptical of doing it for anybody but the Bolsheviks.

The best example of this demonstrated support of workers and soldiers is the Kornilov affair of August. The Provisional Government, and its henchmen among other so-called left parties, were incapable of dealing with the threat posed by the right-wing Kornilov. Christopher Hill quotes Miliukov as saying, "For a short time the choice was free between Kornilov and Lenin. Driven by a sort of instinct the masses—for it was with the masses that the decision lay—pronounced for Lenin."[35] This observation from a conservative viewpoint is in effect saying that the Bolshevik minority was considered by the masses as their most faithful representative. The Bolsheviks linked with the masses through an uncompromising political program. Bolsheviks demanded peace, bread and land, when others were concerned with the imperialist war, with protecting capitalist speculators, and with delaying tactics vis-à-vis the land question.

The Bolsheviks encouraged the soviets as proletarian structures of government. For anyone brought up to accept voting in constituencies, and for several parties as the only form of democracy, it is often difficult to understand that there are alternatives—and superior alternatives. Lenin recognized that bourgeois parliamentary democracy was an advance over feudalism, but that it was also a system in which the worker was reduced to choosing his oppressors once every four or five years. Against this Lenin projected *proletarian democracy*, where the government would be in the hands of workers chosen by other workers at their place of work. The representatives would be paid wages just like other workers, they would remain at the level of workers, and they would be subject to recall at any time—not just in a given period.

Lenin expected the soviets to be just that sort of government, and in April, 1917, he indicated that the soviets, and not parliaments, were to be the future government of Russia as far as the Bolsheviks were concerned.[36] This gives the lie to the argument that the Bolsheviks dissolved the Constituent Assembly in November 1918 after they saw that it had a minority of Bolsheviks. As early as April the previous year, Lenin had already said that the Soviet and not the assembly was the highest authority.

Previous to the calling and dissolution of the Constituent Assembly, there had been two meetings of soviets drawn from all over Russia. It was in these gatherings that Bolsheviks argued their case most forcefully, and the second All-Russian Congress of Soviets had passed legislation supporting all the major Bolshevik positions.[37] The Constituent Assembly refused to accept the legislation of the soviets, and the Bolsheviks interpreted this as evidence that the revolution had moved beyond the positions of the Constituent Assembly. The speed of revolutionary events had left the Constituent Assembly behind even before it had got started.

A revolution by definition is a tremendous speeding-up of change, so that old forms of behavior and activity become out of date in a very short time. The French Revolution is a good example of the leftward shift which was reflected in the Constituent Assembly, the Legislative Assembly, and the Directorate. In Russia, things happen more quickly. It is as though the Legislative Assembly came before the Constituent Assembly, so that when the latter appeared it was an anti-climax.

A number of moderate bourgeois writers realized that the Constituent Assembly was not the pillar of democracy that the other bourgeois writers made it out to be. Melvin C. Wren said of the Constituent Assembly, "Its passing was little mourned. The people had been indifferent to its election ... and one could claim that it reflected the sentiment of the nation."[38] The same sort of view is expressed by the historian J. P. Nettl.[39] Both he and Wren indicate that it was unrealistic to discuss the Bolsheviks versus the other political parties as though the latter were truly representative of the masses of people. Indeed, historians of a conservative stamp admit that leaders in parties like the Socialist Revolutionaries and the Mensheviks were out of touch with the people they professed to represent. They were being left behind because of the development of revolutionary ideas and demands.

We find Stanley W. Page admitting that "the views of the Socialist Revolutionary and Menshevik leaders of the Soviets were much closer to members of the Provisional Government than they were to the desires of those they supposedly represented" on war, on the Constituent Assembly, on land and on national minorities.[40] He concludes his discussion on this topic by saying that though the majority of the Russians did not support the Bolshevik party, they did not oppose it. That is as far as he is prepared to go. However, it can be maintained that the majority did support the Bolsheviks in a great variety of ways, and that bourgeois historians indirectly admit this when they raise the charge of *demagoguery* against the Bolsheviks.

The very word "demagogues" indicates a high level of popularity. It indicates further that the popularity was due to mere use of words and dishonest techniques, but even before we deal with that, it must be understood that it is an admission that the crowds went behind the Bolsheviks. One contemporary observer, Rheta Door, wrote that "the mob liked their line of talk"—referring to the Bolsheviks.[41] This was a contemptuous reference to the masses of people, and because Rheta Door was in Russia at the time, she was actually denounced as a bourgeois by Russian workers. Rheta Door was particularly disturbed because there were so many ruffians on the trains. They paid for third-class tickets and went into the first-class compartment. She complained and was told to "get off and walk, you boorzhoil!"[42]

I have already made reference to the contemptuous attitude of the bourgeoisie toward what they call the mob, the rabble, the gullible masses. The charge of being demagogues is based on the sort of assumption made by Walkin that the workers and peasants did not understand the meaning of the slogans they supported. In fact, the earlier references to Seton-Watson were within a context where he accused the Bolsheviks of being demagogic manipulators. He admits by inference that the Bolsheviks were powerful within the soviets and that this was important. He says that their strategy was to take over the soviets, because (unlike the Provisional Government) the soviets did not have professional politicians; they were comprised of simple and guileless workers and peasants: "If by attractive demagogic slogans the Bolsheviks could capture the Soviets, and through them gain control of the masses, they would cut the ground from under the set of their rivals. Power could be theirs before any parliamentary system could be established."[43] In the same tone, Seton-Watson says that the Bolsheviks went to deceive the ordinary workers within the factories, and that Lenin went to the congress of peasant soviets and used his demagoguery against the peasants. According to Seton-Watson, the delegates "were mostly simple peasants, elected by their fellows, who could be and were won away by Lenin's arguments and stage managing."[44]

All of the above statements are extremely revealing. They admit, in spite of the author's intentions, that the Bolsheviks were the most popular group among workers and peasants, and the only explanation he offers for that popularity is that the Bolsheviks were clever devils and the mob was simple-minded and led astray. Indirectly Seton-Watson also admits that there was a clash between the soviet system of power and the parliamentary type, and that the first was a replacement of the second. The Soviet historians are saying the same thing with a different perspective. They are saying that they (like Lenin) prefer the soviet to the parliament, while Seton-Watson is saying that he prefers the British Parliament. At bottom, it is a clash of values and class interests. Similarly, Schapiro indicates boldly that he has a preference for the "rule of law" and British constitutional arrangements. He would have liked to see the Constituent Assembly function in Russia, and when it disappeared quietly without anyone even grumbling over it, he described this as due to the political immaturity of the Russian workers and peasants: "The political immaturity of Russia, as often in her history, favoured the most resolute, if most unscrupulous, political force of the time."[45]

The notion of Bolsheviks as a resolute band of conspirators is occasionally put forward in a very refined and sophisticated way. Without abusing the Bolsheviks unduly, this interpretation virtually praises them for being efficient. They were the best-organized party within Russia, the best political tacticians, and the most disciplined. Such a view praises the Bolsheviks for entirely the wrong reasons, and in the process, it really denounces them—because it says nothing of the superiority of their ideology, of the genuineness of their intentions, or of the wide mass support which they enjoyed. It reduces the question of the taking of power to purely mechanical dimensions, and one could equally well say that Hitler's fascist party came to power in Germany because it was efficient and disciplined.

One of the prime exponents of this theory of mechanical efficiency is Merle Fainsod, described in the Adams collection as "the brilliant American political scientist," who has provided a "judicial analysis" of the Russian Revolution.[46] His analysis is undoubtedly less crude than that of some other bourgeois writers, but precisely for that reason it is even more essential to give it close scrutiny. In essence it is no different from that of other bourgeois writers. Fainsod speaks of the "coup" of October 1917, and he attaches great importance to the Bolsheviks being a minority. He also regards the Constituent Assembly as the last free institution in Russia. Fainsod speaks of the Bolsheviks using the soviets to camouflage their intentions and to give them a pseudo-legality.

Who is Merle Fainsod? He, like Ulam, is from the Russian Research Center at Harvard, and has been there for a long time. The proposal to set that center up was written by a former Office of Strategic Services (OSS) operator and it was submitted through the Carnegie Foundation.[47] Its function is to serve the State Department, the armed forces and the CIA. Fainsod is an integral part of that machinery, accepting its values and its objectives. One should not be surprised that the Russian Revolution appears in a certain negative light when viewed by Fainsod from the Russian Research Center at Harvard, but then neither should one be taken in by statements purporting to establish the Olympian detachment and objectivity of such scholarship.

3

Marx, Marxism and the Russian Left

Marx's Prediction

There is an important trend running through the historiography on the Russian Revolution suggesting that, in a number of important ways, the revolution contradicted or refuted predictions made by Marx and Engels. Among the most common criticisms of this sort is the charge that, according to Marx, a revolution should never have broken out in Russia because the material conditions there, and the modes of production and the classes, were not developed to the extent that Marx himself laid down as prerequisites for social revolution. This view stresses that Russia was one of the most backward countries in Europe, barely out of the feudal stage in 1917. They note the small and weak bourgeois class in that country compared to Western Europe. They urge that the great preponderance of the Russian population were peasants and that Marx considered the peasant as reactionary. By all of Marx's yardsticks and his own conclusive statements, Russia should not have had its revolution prior to the proletarian revolution in the developed section of Europe. In Marxist terms, therefore, it is impossible to explain how the working class took power in 1917. If ever there was a revolution, it should have been a bourgeois revolution, because Marx said that there were certain stages of development—namely, feudalism to capitalism then to socialism via a Dictatorship of the Proletariat. In an essay titled "Karl Marx and the Study of History," H. R. Trevor-Roper refutes Marx's prophecy, in part by arguing that Russia established communism *before* becoming industrialized.[1] But was communism ever established? Klaus Mehnert's *Stalin Versus Marx* argues that "the Revolution had contradicted the Marxist forecast . . . by breaking out not in a number of advanced countries but in a single backward one, Russia."[2] David Mitrany, in his book *Marx Against the Peasant*, writes: "History knows no other instance of a vast social movement being so misread and misnamed as the agrarian revolution that has spread over half of the world since 1917. It has suited the Communists to advertize it as a Marxist revolution; but Marxist theory had nothing to contribute to it."[3] He refers to the Bolshevik revolution as "a Marxian and dogmatically anti-peasant revolution." Marxism "was a doctrine based upon the facts of industrial evolution and devised for the benefit of the industrial workers."[4] Finally, in his essay, "Lenin's 'Revolutionary Democratic Dictatorship of the Proletariat and the Peasantry,'" Kermit E. McKenzie complains that the Russian Revolution did not follow the various successive stages of society laid down by Marx. There should have been a bourgeois revolution, but instead Lenin and Trotsky brought in their alien doctrine of permanent or uninterrupted revolution, by which the proletariat took power. Lenin, in other words, bucked the "pattern of historical development which Marx perceived and elaborated, at least in relation to Western Europe."[5]

Taking McKenzie first, is it true that Marx's principal outline followed certain stages as suggested by McKenzie? The answer is yes. Feudal, capitalist and socialist orders correspond respectively to rule by nobility, bourgeoisie and proletariat. McKenzie said this did not happen in Russia. Is he right? The answer is yes. The February–March revolution was the revolution of the bourgeoisie. It was supported by the constitutionalists, the liberals and the moderate socialists—all either capitalists or groups sharing bourgeois ideology and aspirations such as bureaucrats, teachers and well-to-do peasants. However, Lenin and the Bolsheviks decided to overthrow the bourgeoisie immediately and lead the proletariat to power.

So, McKenzie is right in the points he raises, and yet his conclusion is totally irrelevant. Go back to his original statement and underline the phrase "at least in relation to Western Europe." There is no point in him making this qualification and then writing the rest of his article without taking it into account. Was Russia Western Europe? Obviously not. If we want to know whether the Russian Revolution upset Marxist prediction, we must ask what Marx said about Russia, and if he said nothing then we must apply Marxist method to an analysis of Russian conditions and consider what sort of conclusion a Marxist would arrive at (or Marx himself). The second operation is more difficult, but fortunately for Russia we do have some writings by Marx and Engels that we can consider.

Let's take the question up chronologically. The first statement by Engels on Russia was made in 1875 in a piece entitled "On Social Relations in Russia."[6] It is essentially a polemical reply to Narodnik leader Pyotr Tkachov, dealing firstly with the question of classes. Tkachov had argued that Russia could become socialist without a bourgeoisie. Engels's answer was that the bourgeoisie was as necessary a precondition of the socialist revolution as the proletariat itself. The Russian Revolution certainly did not disprove this. While both the bourgeoisie and proletariat were weak as compared to Western Europe, all observers agree that the development of capitalism was extremely rapid in late-nineteenth-century Russia, and this gave strength to the two classes that coexisted under capitalism—the bourgeoisie and the proletariat.

Russia, therefore, could not become socialist without some substantial development of the bourgeoisie and proletariat, but there was absolutely no reason why it could not have a revolution based on the peasants. Engels is worth quoting at length:

It is clear that the condition of the Russian peasants since the emancipation from serfdom, has become intolerable and cannot be maintained much longer, and that for this reason alone, if for no other, a revolution is in the offing in Russia . . . Her financial affairs are in extreme disorder. Taxes cannot be screwed any higher, the interest on old state loans is paid by means of new loans, and every new loan meets with greater difficulties; money can now be raised only on the pretext of building railways! The administration, corrupt from top to bottom . . . The entire agricultural production . . . completely dislocated by the redemption settlement of 1861 . . . The whole held together with great difficulty and only outwardly by an Oriental despotism the arbitrariness of which we in the West simply cannot imagine; a despotism that, from day to day, not only comes into more glaring contradiction with the views of the enlightened classes and, in particular, with those of the rapidly developing bourgeoisie of the capital, but, in the person of its present bearer, has lost its head, one day making concessions to liberalism and the next, frightened, cancelling them again and thus bringing itself more and more into disrepute. With all that, a growing recognition among the enlightened strata of the nation concentrated in the capital that this position is untenable, that a revolution is impending, and the illusion that it will be possible to guide this revolution along a smooth, constitutional channel. Here all the conditions of a revolution are combined, of a revolution that, started by the upper classes of the capital, perhaps even by the government itself, must be rapidly carried further, beyond the first constitutional phase, by the peasants; of a revolution that will be of the greatest importance for the whole of Europe, if only because it will destroy at one blow the last, so far intact, reserve of the entire European reaction. This revolution is surely approaching.[7]

So as early as 1875, Marx and Engels were predicting revolution in Russia. If anything, the charge might be leveled at them that they were premature, not that they did not see the coming event. Tsarism lasted longer than many people expected because the agricultural dislocation of which Engels spoke was partially remedied.

In 1877 Marx wrote a letter to the editor of the Russian publication *Otecestvenniye Zapisky*, in response to a critic who took *Das Kapital* to task for its inability to explain the historical trajectory of Russia. With respect to *Das Kapital*, Marx explained, "The chapter on primitive accumulation does not pretend to do more than trace the path by which, in Western Europe, the capitalist order of economy emerged from the womb of the feudal order of economy."[8] McKenzie was right in saying the theory was based on Western Europe, and he has no justification for applying it uncritically to Russia. This is what someone did in 1877, to which Marx replied,

> Now, in what way was my critic able to apply this historical sketch to Russia? Only this: if Russia is tending to become a capitalist nation, on the model of the countries of Western Europe—and in recent years it has gone to great pains to move in this direction—it will not succeed without having first transformed a large proportion of its peasants into proletarians; and after that, once it has been placed in the bosom of the capitalist system, it will be subjected to its pitiless laws, like other profane peoples. That is all! But this is too little for my critic. It is absolutely necessary for him to metamorphose my historical sketch of the genesis of capitalism in Western Europe into a historico-philosophical theory of general development, imposed by fate on all peoples, whatever the historical circumstances in which they are placed.[9]

Marx's position demonstrates, in other words, that his historical or dialectical materialism is a method that can be applied to different situations to give different answers. Marx's comments on Western Europe were based on a thoroughly comprehensive study of the evidence that he had before him in the nineteenth century. Hence to say anything about Russia would also require close study of what was going on in Russia. This is exactly what Marx did: "In order to reach an informed judgment of the economic development of contemporary Russia, I learned Russian and then spent several long years studying official publications and others with a bearing on this subject."[10] This kind of thoroughness was characteristic of Marx and later Lenin. In analyzing Western Europe, he was concerned primarily with the proletariat and the bourgeoisie, and gave very little attention to the peasant. But looking at Russia in the nineteenth century was almost like looking at Tanzania today—the vast majority of the people were peasant producers, so naturally Marx concerned himself with the Russian peasants.

Let's take another glance at Engels's "On Social Relations in Russia." There he took up the question of the Russian commune. This was the social organization in which the great majority of the peasants lived. It was a farming community responsible for dividing the land among its members, and it had control over the crops out of which it paid taxes and other levies to the tsarist state. It had certain, definite political and legal powers in relationship to its own membership. Many Russians hoped that this would be their salvation in the sense that it would provide a socialist or communist form without having to pass through capitalism. Both Marx and Engels seriously considered the possibility. Engels felt that if the commune could develop to the level of a modern, large-scale co-op then it would indeed provide an economically and socially viable form. But he noted that at that particular time, Russian communal forms simply served as the basis for tsarist despotism because they were not progressive social forms. Because of inadequate land, conditions of usury and high taxation, the commune was helping the landlord and the tsarist state to exploit the peasant. Under those circumstances, communal agricultural life was not a blessing, and many peasants were already running away from the commune. The commune could only be saved and regenerated if there was a proletarian revolution in Western Europe.[11]

Marx himself took up the question in a letter to Vera Zasulich in 1881. He repeated much of what Engels had said, stressing that the communes would gradually disappear unless there was a social revolution in Europe.[12] There was no revolution in Europe, and the communes did disappear, so there was no contradiction of Marx's prediction on this point. In their preface to the Russian edition of The Communist Manifesto (1882), Marx and Engels further developed their arguments: "If the Russian Revolution becomes the signal for a proletarian revolution in the West, so that both complement each other, the present Russian common ownership of land may serve as the starting point for a communist development."[13] This is a clear admission of the possibility of the Russian Revolution preceding the proletarian revolution. A decade later, in a letter to Russian Marxist Nicolai Danielson, Engels still held on to the view that conditions in Russia accelerated its economic development, perhaps more so than even an advanced capitalist country like the United States. He reminds Danielson that

> the U.S. are modern bourgeois from the very origin; that they were founded by *petits* bourgeois and peasants who ran away from European feudalism to establish a purely bourgeois society. Whereas in Russia we have a groundwork of a primitive communistic character, a pre-civilisation *Gentilgesellschaft*, crumbling to ruins, it is true, but still serving as the groundwork, the material upon which the capitalistic revolution (for it is a real social revolution) acts and operates.[14]

The crucial points of rebuttal of certain bourgeois criticisms are that Marx and Engels did not pay keen attention to the problems of the peasants in Russia. "Nowhere will one find signs that Marx had seriously studied the actual state of the peasants in any one land," writes Mitrany.[15] Mitrany then shifts his ground when he looks at Marx on Russia; he says that admissions on Russia amounted to an abandonment of the revolutionary analysis of *The Communist Manifesto*. This is a good example of bourgeois mental confusion and aberration. Mitrany accuses Marx of dogmatism, of neglecting the peasant on the one hand, while on the other hand, when he faces this example, he says this denies the validity of the theory as applied to industrial society.

Avrahm Yarmolinsky's *The Road to Revolution: A Century of Russian Radicalism* is in agreement with the Marxist position on the peasantry, although he is by no means a Marxist. His accusation is that the Russian Marxists departed from Marxism, which is another charge altogether.[16] Yarmolinsky attempts to show that the events of 1848 were different. The workers had to take a much more active role in their own interests. In their address to the Central Committee of the Communist League, Marx and Engels urged the communists to play a role independent of the bourgeois league in the 1848 revolutions, organizing themselves into municipal councils, and seeing to it that the workers were armed and organized. Their job was to "make the revolution permanent ... until the proletariat has conquered state power."[17] This is a new conception of awareness instead of passivity, of combined and yet independent action. Both Lenin and Trotsky were to develop this and apply it to the conditions of the Russian Revolution.

The question of Marxist prediction and its relation to the Russian Revolution does not end here. One will find that historians debate whether other aspects of Marx's schema were applicable to Russia. Marx had spoken of the dictatorship of the proletariat; did this ever come about during or subsequent to the Russian Revolution? Marx had said that with the establishment of socialism the state would gradually wither away; did the events in Russia justify or disprove this contention? These questions relate to the period after the revolution proper in 1917, so we'll shelve them for the moment while we find out more about the period before 1917.

Pre-revolutionary Russian Thinkers

Prominent bourgeois historians advanced a line of argument that it was not Marxism that was the dominant intellectual force behind the Bolsheviks in 1917 and after. Instead, they claimed that the Bolsheviks were merely extending an intellectual tradition handed down by pre-Marxist Russian revolutionaries.

Undoubtedly, Tsarist Russia had a rich tradition of revolutionary thought, particularly in the nineteenth century. These revolutionary ideas did not take the form of political or philosophical treatises, which would have been banned by the tsarist censor. Instead they assumed a literary form—novels and drama in particular—which, with some subtlety and luck, enabled them to evade the censorship. The principal revolutionary writers and thinkers who are credited with being the foundations of Bolshevism include such figures as Alexander Radishchev (1749–1802); Pavel Pestel (1793–1826); Nikolay Chernyshevsky (1828–89); Vissarion Belinsky (1811–48); Pyotr Nikitich Tkachev (1844–86); Sergey Nechaev (1847–82); and Andrei Zhelyabov (1851–81). The historical controversy centers on whether Lenin, Trotsky and Stalin had more in common with Radishchev, Belinsky and Tkachev than with Marx and Engels.

As a subsidiary issue, one also finds in the literature on this subject the assertion that the Bolshevik regime after 1917 showed peculiar resemblances to the tsarist state. In other words, both intellectually and politically, the Bolsheviks were supposed to be heirs of the Russian past. There is a large body of literature on this subject.[18] This is the first external criterion we can use to judge the importance of any aspect of historiography. Later, we could ask how much of it is really relevant to the Russian Revolution and whether the problem warrants so much ink. But for the moment, we can survey the literature.

Avrahm Yarmolinksy, one of the earliest writers on the theme, is an émigré who starts with the events of 1917 in his mind and sees those events as arising out of a revolutionary tradition. He sees socialist thought as one aspect of this tradition and populist propaganda as another (that is, propaganda among the people); and a third aspect is the doctrine of violent revolution put to the end of social reconstruction. His conclusions I find perfectly reasonable. He isn't throwing out one thing for another. He claims that certain ways of acting and thinking that were current in the nineteenth century persisted into the twentieth and influenced the Soviets, and that "it is doubtful if the doctrine of Leninism can be fully understood without taking account of the indigenous social revolutionary traditions as it developed in the second half of the nineteenth."[19] With E. Lampert's *Studies in Rebellion* (1957) and *Sons Against Fathers: Studies in Russian Radicalism and Revolution* (1965), and Franco Venturi's *Roots of Revolution* (1960), we come to the histories that are interested in the nineteenth century for its own sake. Sometimes this can lead to mostly sterile history, but it often illumines a lot, as contemporaries saw it, allowing us to draw out conclusions. Certainly, in the case of Nicolas Berdyaev's *The Origins of Russian Communism* (1937) and *The Russian Idea* (1946), one gets the impression that he starts with an idea and treats the nineteenth century as an attic through which he can rummage for interesting little bits that prove his point.

Who is Berdyaev? He tells us that he belonged to a generation of writers in Russia before the revolution who were part of the Marxist tradition but had broken with materialism and were pursuing idealism in literature, religion and metaphysics. There is in his writing some indication that he has an appreciation of dialectical method, especially in *The Russian Idea*, which is extremely perceptive in relation to nineteenth-century Russian literature. *The Origins of Russian Communism* is a more mystical affair, but it is more relevant to the historiography of the Russian Revolution and is frequently cited by bourgeois historians.

The opening lines of the introduction tell us exactly what the argument is about:

> Russian Communism is difficult to understand on account of its twofold nature. On the one hand, it is international and a world phenomenon; on the other hand, it is national and Russian. It is particularly important for Western minds to understand the national roots of Russian Communism and the fact that it was Russian history which determined its limits and shaped its character. *A knowledge of Marxism will not help in this.* [20]

He then lists some general characteristics that distinguish the Russian people and the Russian intelligentsia, and that also distinguish the communists:

(a) Russian people seek membership in some orthodox faith (Communism being one such faith).

(b) There is always a search for the kingdom of justice.

Then he turns to the Russian intelligentsia:

(c) Carried away by social ideas.

(d) Intolerant.

(e) Adopting Western ideas and making them dogma (whether Hegel or Marx).

(f) Messianic idea of the unique destiny of the Russian people—their capacity to liberate the rest of the world.[21]

Berdyaev considers Radishchev the first significant member of the intelligentsia. He doesn't spend much time on him, though he is covered in many other sources. His novel in the form of a dream, entitled *A Journey from St. Petersburg to Moscow* (1790), was a hostile comment on serfdom, which led to his being exiled. The implication is that Radishchev established the tradition of opposition to serfdom and an interest in the condition of the peasantry that was inherited much later by the Bolsheviks.[22] Then there is Pestel, a colonel who was involved in the famous uprising against the tsar in December 1825. The people who carried out this uprising (the Decembrists, as they came to be called) were themselves fairly conservative, but Berdyaev singles out Pestel as a socialist precursor. I've seen Pestel referred to as "a Russian Jacobin," and in Berdyaev's view, "he demonstrated a will to power and the violence which in the twentieth century appeared in the Communists."[23]

Vissarion Belinsky, touted as the founder of literary criticism in Russia, occupies a place of special importance in Berdyaev's schema: "Belinsky is the central figure in the history of Russian thought and self-consciousness in the nineteenth century. And he, more than any other, must be regarded as an intellectual ancestor of Russian communism."[24] Belinsky was a believer in the Russian people, in the tradition of Radishchev, and this belief, called "Narodinichestvo," remained a central feature in Russian revolutionary thought. In effect, the *narod*, or people, were identified with those who worked the land. But Berdyaev also notes that Belinsky, unlike other Narodniks, recognized the positive importance of industrial development and was ready to admit the importance of the bourgeoisie, though he could not bear them—much like the Marxists later on. Berdyaev makes the further point that the philosophical approach of Belinsky was the same as the Marxist-Leninists. With Belinsky, "there was the characteristic Russian search for an integral outlook, which will give an answer to all questions of life, unite the theoretical with the practical reason, and give a philosophical basis to the social need." The same idea of wholeness, Berdyaev writes, can be found in Marxism-Leninism.[25]

Nikolay Chernyshevsky was also a literary critic and writer, whose legendary novel, *What Is to Be Done?* (1863), was later re-echoed in Lenin's 1903 pamphlet of the same name. Marx and Plekhanov held Chernyshevsky in high regard. Berdyaev commends him in this context because he posed the problem of whether Russia could evade capitalist development. His answer was that Russia could shorten the capitalist period to nothing and go straight on to socialism. "The communists are trying to do just this," says Berdyaev. Secondly, Chernyshevsky sought the type of culture that triumphed in communism—the dominance of natural and social sciences, the rejection of religion and metaphysics, and the subservience of literature and art to social aims.[26]

Alexander Herzen, known in some circles as the "father of Russian socialism," had deep Narodnik sympathies but wrote mainly from the West. As an exile, he could write straight political denunciations of tsarism and call for revolution. He typifies the Narodnik view as well as the messianic idea. There is a special path of development for Russia (the commune); thus they would escape Western capitalism and solve their social problems better and more quickly than the West. Here again, communism had powerful elements of the Narodnik view.[27]

Berdyaev also sees Mikhail Bakunin, the leading anarchist who fought bitterly with Marx, as having a lot in common with the Bolsheviks—their militant atheism as well as a strong messianic streak. "To Bakunin," writes Berdyaev, "light will flare up from the East and enlighten the darkness of the West, the darkness of the bourgeois world. The Russian communists also will come to the same view in spite of their Western Marxism."[28]

Finally, Berdyaev draws direct lines between Sergey Nechaev and Pyotr Tkachev. The former was a revolutionary terrorist who founded a society called "the Axe of the People's Justice" and authored a manual of revolutionary asceticism, *The Revolutionary Catechism* (1869). His oft-quoted line, "To the revolutionary everything is moral which serves the revolution," was repeated by Lenin, Berdyaev asserts.[29] Tkachev was even more directly identified as a forerunner of Lenin. "Tkachev," writes Berdyaev, "is above all a socialist and his socialism is not of the democratic sort, in which respect, he is like Lenin and the communists." And like Lenin, he advocated "the seizure of power by a revolutionary minority."[30]

In addition to the revolutionary thinkers, Berdyaev insisted that Peter the Great (1682–1725) is also a kind of political descendant of Lenin. Peter the Great was a revolutionary from above, a Bolshevik in type (namely, in his contempt for religion). His reforms were carried out by violence and with no mercy on the religious feelings of the people. The Petrine and Bolshevik Revolutions display the same barbarity, violence, forcible application of certain principles from above downwards, the same rupture of organic development, et cetera. With these several ingredients, Berdyaev moves on to his great climax. Lenin, he says "united in himself traits of Chernyshevsky, Nechaev, Tkachev, Zhelyabov, with traits of the Grand Princes of Moscow, of Peter the Great and Russian rulers of the despotic type."[31]

Ideally, detailed knowledge of eighteenth- and nineteenth-century history and of the literature is useful to decide whether interpretations of given figures are satisfactory—but even without this knowledge, one can challenge the logic and the methodology of a historian and question what presuppositions induce him to come to certain conclusions. Berdyaev belongs to [the school of thought] that Marxism was not applicable to the Russian Revolution. He puts forward that Marx was a Menshevik—that is, if he were alive in Russia at that time he would have taken the position that Russia was not ripe for a proletarian revolution: "On the basis of an evolutionary determinist interpretation of Marxism it is impossible to justify a proletarian revolution in a peasant country."[32] He has the quotable statement that Lenin "brought about the revolution in Marx's name, but not in Marx's way."[33] Because he feels that Marxism is not relevant, he looks for alternatives. His basic assumption can be questioned on the grounds that it is a gross misunderstanding of Marxism to imagine that it could not be applied to Russia. Taking arbitrarily various bits from various people's writings and characteristics is ridiculous, and almost dishonest. No matter how dissimilar two people were there could be some trait in common, so it is not surprising that Berdyaev finds some of Lenin's characteristics in a large number of pre-Marxian revolutionary thinkers. In fact, one gets the feeling that Berdyaev first selected about a dozen things he considered characteristic of the Bolsheviks. He then looked at Russian history and said that Pestel has characteristic one—Tkachev has two, and so forth. Finally for number twelve, since he can't find a revolutionary, he throws in Peter the Great, and so he completes his compilation.

Berdyaev entirely glosses over points at which these individuals have held views and committed acts that were completely incompatible with the Marxist position:

- Nechaev—was committed to revolutionary asceticism, but he "despised the people and wanted to drag them forcibly to revolution."[34]
- Bakunin—As Berdyaev admits, Bakunin was anti-state and that's why he broke with Marx; his position was completely alien to Lenin's preoccupation with the state.
- Narodniks—on the whole did not come to grips with the question of the state, but were generally antagonistic toward capitalism.
- Zhelyabov—leader of the People's Will, was not in his general point of view a forerunner of Russian communism, but in his methods of organization and his action he was.
- Peter the Great—The difference that he admits between Peter and Bolsheviks is that the Bolsheviks by violence "liberated forces which were latent in the masses and summoned them to take their share in making history," while Peter had "widened the gulf between the people and the upper classes."[35]

This, after all, is the crucial difference. It would be a useful exercise to take the bits Berdyaev leaves out and stick them together just to demonstrate the complete arbitrariness of his methodology—half-truth with half-truth to make total lie. The next point of logic is that if you show parallels in the past, you then have to relate them to the present in some concrete way.

One must show the *connection* between Bolsheviks and these pre-Marxian thinkers, not just the parallels.

While I have indicated my total dissatisfaction with the manner in which the question of the pre-Marxist intellectuals was handled by Berdyaev, it does not mean that there is no validity whatsoever in such a position. If we reflect upon an African example, we realize that a phenomenon such as nationalism had its roots deep in the past, incorporating elements of opposition to the earliest imposition of colonial rule and going back beyond the first coming of the Europeans in some respects.

Take the example of religious protests. It now seems clear that social stress in African societies, more often than not, manifested itself in a religious form—the rise of prophets, the creation of new spirit cults, the growth of witchcraft eradication movements. When Africans reacted against the Europeans, the movements often took exactly the same form as they had always assumed—the Maji Maji revolt, to take a major instance, was a protest movement against colonial rule and policies, which took the form of reliance on a religious medicine, the water used on certain spirit cults.[36]

This is precisely what Marx and Engels had emphasized; the form of a socioeconomic conflict is usually decided by elements in the superstructure such as religion. The English Civil War is another example where this occurs. Consequently, the idea put forward by Yarmolinsky and exaggerated by Berdyaev—that certain modes of acting and thinking which were prevalent in nineteenth century Russia persisted into the twentieth century and affected the Soviets—is perfectly reasonable. Anything else would be difficult to conceive of. One could go further and expect that some specific individuals would have influenced the revolution just as much, if not more, than Marx and Engels. In Cuba, where they are now building socialism, Marx, Engels and Lenin have to share honors with José Martí and Antonio Maceo. These were the pre-Marxian Cuban revolutionary thinkers who made a giant contribution to the liberty of Cuba and to the revolutionary thought and action of Fidel Castro.

Similarly, in China, great respect is paid to pre-Marxist revolutionary, Sun Yat-sen, although Li Ta-chao (1918) introduced Marxism.

The Russian situation, therefore, is not unique. From a historical point of view, we have to get down to the task of showing the connection between early ideas and thinkers and the revolution of 1917. A number of Russian intellectuals and political formations wrestled with the question of how a socialist transformation might unfold in the empire well before the February Revolution. Georgii Plekhanov and the Mensheviks, for example, insisted that far from avoiding capitalism, Russia must go through every phase of capitalist development, with the corresponding political states. Then there were the legal Marxists, the followers of Peter Struve, who had a very curious position. They said that according to Marx a bourgeois state was necessary as a progressive phase following feudalism. Russia was feudal and hence a Marxist should look forward with enthusiasm to the bourgeois state. Struve and the legal Marxist were so enamored of the bourgeois state that they did not even follow the Mensheviks in thinking about a proletarian revolution in the distant future. They were perfectly satisfied with capitalist society. No wonder Struve joined the Cadet Party of Miliukov.[37]

Then there were the Economists who stressed economic demands but did not want to move towards political action. Here again the Bolshevik position was clarified in relation to two antagonistic viewpoints. On the one hand, the Bolsheviks were seeking to break with the Narodnik tradition that Russia was ripe for socialist revolution on the basis of the commune, and at the same time, they bitterly assailed Mensheviks, Legal Marxists and Economists with arguments first put forward in the extreme form by the Narodniks—namely that the peasant provides a way out, without Russia having to go through all the stages of capitalist development as had been experienced in the West. The significant point is that the theories grew not from parallels, which after all are things that have no contact, but by tensions between contradictory viewpoints—tensions that were creatively resolved in the philosophy of Marxism-Leninism. That, then, was the way the Narodnik ideas on the commune and capitalism gave rise to Bolshevik thought and practice.

The issue of terroristic methods followed much the same pattern. Marxist methods were a direct reaction to the bankruptcy of the old terrorist methods. With the assassination of Alexander II and his replacement with Alexander III, tsarist reaction grew fiercer, and it completely wrecked the last of the terrorist organizations—"The People's Will," organized by Vera Figner. The Bolsheviks posed disciplined propaganda as an alternative to the discredited methods of terror, which nevertheless remained a potential weapon, useful under certain circumstances. To quote Louis Fischer again, "Violence was in the Russian air and in the Russian tradition, but whereas violence to Tkachev and Nechaev was a principle and supreme political weapon, to Lenin it was a subordinate means."[38]

The next question we have to ask is what relationship the changing ideas had to the socioeconomic developments. One can see the extreme revolutionary tradition as itself a function of the operation of the law of combined and uneven development. On the one hand, there was the sociopolitical superstructure. On the other hand, there were the liberal ideas emanating from the capitalist west. Some Russians reacted by stressing that they could follow their own path and surpass the West (these were the Slavophiles). Others hoped to imitate the West. But all realized that no change was possible without coming into sharp conflict with the feudal state—hence the revolutionary tradition. It was initiated by the nobility themselves, followed by declassed individuals. The declassed persons were produced by the maturing of capitalist relations within the feudal society. Feudal nobility who went to the wall, failing to keep up mortgages, et cetera; lesser clergy who could no longer find pickings; lesser bourgeoisie and bureaucrats who found places in the universities and peasants who became landholders after emancipation. Herzen and Bakunin were of the nobility, but Belinsky was one of the new breed, who intensified their attack on the decadent tsarist regime.

However, the attacks against tsarism in the 1860s and 1870s were still being carried out in a society that was preponderantly agrarian, by which in comparison with Western Europe at the time could hardly have seemed to offer much opportunity for capitalist development. The agrarian character of the society and the particular mode of production, the commune, was thus the focus for all theorizing. The vast inchoate mass of the peasantry did not represent a coherent, unified and self-conscious class. Revolutionaries found it impossible to use this class to overthrow tsarism. When they went to the people, the people gave them to their Little Father, the tsar. Consequently, terror became a favored political ideology in a situation lacking a revolutionary class.

Ultimately, it was the intensification of capitalist development in Russia that made Narodnikism and terrorism anachronistic. With capitalist development, the commune was breaking up, the bourgeoisie were growing stronger and more numerous, and above all a very disciplined and self-conscious proletariat was arising. New theories could therefore be put forward. Russian Marxism was only called forth at a particular phase of its historical development, although Marxism was abroad in Europe for forty years.

I want to recall something Engels said when reviewing Marx's *Critique of Political Economy*: "Political Economy is the theoretical analysis of modern bourgeois society and therefore pre-supposed developed bourgeois conditions."[39] Marxism, in other words, does not have any special claim for itself; as a set of ideas, it is part of the superstructure and should be historically explained as a consequence of certain socioeconomic changes. Naturally, the rise of the new mode of thought is not sudden, nor is it unrelated to the prevailing modes, especially given the fact that the prevailing modes were themselves changing and being modified. This is another complication, but it has to be introduced to avoid the impression that things were static, which they very seldom are. Under the impact of changes in the modes of production (that is, the rise of capitalist relations and decline of feudal relations like serfdom), the Narodniks and the terrorists were themselves moving to a more progressive position. They had to consider the reality of capitalism as Chernyshevsky did; they had to start thinking of working men and reading and translating Marx, as Lenin's brother did; and some of them were rethinking their position on terrorism. So when people like Plekhanov and Vera Zasulich broke with the old movements and embraced Marxism, this was not so much a sharp and sudden break, but the culmination of an evolutionary process in the realm of ideas, reflecting the evolution of technical changes and the balance of the class forces within society.

What I have attempted to do is to show that Berdyaev's statement that knowledge of Marxism is entirely irrelevant to an understanding of the question of pre-revolutionary thinkers is wholly incorrect. On the contrary, Marxist analysis offers the best understanding of the development of revolutionary thought in Russia from the late eighteenth century right up to the revolution in 1917. A glance at the official Soviet histories at our disposal shows that they do not regard the pre-revolutionary thinkers as having made a contribution and that they applaud Chernyshevsky in particular for carrying the analysis as far as it could go in a Russia still tied by feudal relations. The limitation from our point of view is that we have a couple of general Soviet histories that could scarcely spare more than a few pages to any given topic. Measured against the mass of bourgeois publications, this work appears inadequate.

What we have been doing so far is taking literature as the basis of historical evidence, but these revolutionary writers were very seldom in the front rank of novelists. If the historian is to analyze cultural developments or to utilize evidence provided by writers, he would have to come to grips with

Pushkin, Tolstoy, Dostoyevsky, Turgenev and Maxim Gorky, to mention only a few of the literary lights of the pre-revolutionary period. Most historians do refer to them. Ivar Spector calls his book *An Introduction to Russian History and Culture* and writes that "no study of Russian history can be complete without a parallel study of Russian culture."[40] However, I've yet to come across a history of the Russian Revolution that does justice to the literary antecedents of the revolution, with the possible exception, curiously enough, of Berdyaev. We have to go further and place these major writers in the same revolutionary tradition that everyone admits existed in the nineteenth century. Either that or we admit that the greatest of the novelists ran counter to the stream that led to the Revolution of 1917. Superficially, this is so, because both Tolstoy and Dostoevsky were extremely religious and expressed hostility toward revolutionaries.

However, Berdyaev sees that it was the same theme of social revolution (which was a class affair) that aroused the creative conflict in the Russian writers. Some carried this conflict directly into the social sphere, while Tolstoy and Dostoevsky expressed it in religious terms, but in a manner no less hostile to the status quo. They both believed in the simple rightness of the common people; they both strove after truth and justice. Tolstoy went so far as to repudiate his own aristocracy, class privileges, wealth and fame. The conviction of the wrongness of the ruling class therefore found a very intense expression in the thought and actions of the greatest of the nineteenth-century writers. Berdyaev's Marxism is noticeable here—a method not easy to apply and easy to misapply—but because it aims at a total view of life, at identifying all the processes and tracing them back to the material conditions that determine our existence, it certainly provides more insight than the whole plethora of bourgeois historians, economists, literary critics and the like.

Bolsheviks versus Mensheviks

The October Revolution was made in the name of Marx. Karl Marx and Frederick Engels, writing mainly in the third quarter of the nineteenth century, produced *an integrated theory of society and history* that won numerous adherents before the nineteenth century was out. The comprehensiveness of their writings needs to be stressed. Because Marxism has attempted to grapple with the totality of human experience everywhere at all times, it is no easy matter to come to an agreement over precisely what constitutes the "correct" Marxist interpretation of this or that phenomenon. As we are all aware, within the camp of those who see themselves as Marxists, there have been frequent and sometime irreconcilable disagreements in the application of Marxism since the founder of the theory died.

By the end of the nineteenth century, multiple interpretations of Marxism developed in Russia. And while all self-proclaimed Marxists spoke the language of revolution, they split among themselves. The two principal groups were the Bolsheviks and the Mensheviks; and the political and ideological differences between the two were later reflected in a conflict between Soviet (Bolshevik) historians and Menshevik historians.

In the early part of this century, there was also a wider-reaching debate on Marxism involving all European Marxists, so that before and during the Russian revolution, the actions of the Russian Marxists were subjected to close scrutiny by Marxists in other parts of Europe. At the same time, Russian Marxists also had a great deal to say about Marxists in Western Europe. To some extent, the contemporary debate between Bolsheviks in Russia and other Marxists in Western Europe has its historiographical reflection in the differences between Soviet historians and those European historians who today accept a political philosophy known as "social democracy." However, for the present purposes, little will be said of this aspect of the historiography, largely because it blends into the broader confrontation between Soviet writers and bourgeois writers.

It is obvious that bourgeois writers, having a different view of the world from Marxists, would try at the intellectual level to belittle or disprove the validity of Marxist analysis. In one way or another, at one time or another, every bourgeois writer feels it his duty to put in a word against Marxism. The unanimity with which bourgeois writers of all descriptions combine in attacking Marxism is itself sure evidence that Marxism is not just one of many philosophical world views, but one that is qualitatively different from and hostile to the several varieties of bourgeois thought that are espoused in the modern world. G. A. Kursanov made this point in a publication entitled *Fundamentals of Dialectical Materialism* (1967): "The unity with which all bourgeois philosophers fight dialectical materialism is evidence of the fact that they recognise it as a philosophy opposed to all bourgeois and petty-bourgeois doctrines."[41]

However, it is not beyond bourgeois writers to side with one Marxist against another for purely opportunist reasons—that is to say, as a lever for the more complete denunciation of Marxism. Almost invariably, when attempting to adjudicate on a dispute among Marxists relative to the Russian revolution, bourgeois writers take the side of those Marxists hostile to the Soviet position. Their aim is not only to challenge Marxism at the intellectual level, but also to separate it from (a) the concrete revolutionary conditions of 1917; and (b) from state power such as is represented in the Soviet Union. (The same points apply to the Chinese Revolution.)

If a bourgeois historian could make the point that the Bolsheviks were incorrect in their interpretation of Marxism, then they (the bourgeois intellectuals) feel that they could convince others that Marxism was irrelevant not just to the Russian Revolution but to any other revolution. This is not a mere academic debate—it is a matter of life and death. So, the bourgeoisie are out to convince their own workers, as well as the peoples of the world at large, that Marxist revolution such as was made in Russia and China is irrelevant to the needs of mankind. It is against the above background that one must assess the legitimacy bourgeois historians and social scientists give to the views of the Mensheviks, Social Democrats and any other Marxist or quasi-Marxist who disagrees with the Soviet interpretation of the Revolution of 1917. The fact that most of the writing took place in the period of the Cold War is also significant.

The Menshevik-Bolshevik confrontation was one of the most important events in the political history of the tsarist state in the years prior to 1917. Russia had a single Marxist workers' party in 1904, founded by Plekhanov.[42] In 1904, the party split into two factions—Bolsheviks, headed by Lenin, who of course later became the government of Soviet Russia, and the Mensheviks, whose most prominent leaders were Julius Martov, F. Dan and M. I. Tseretli. A few of the Mensheviks were later loyal citizens of the Soviet Union, while others fled the country and lived as émigrés in the West. In 1917 and subsequently, the Mensheviks maintained that they had a better grasp of Marxism than did the Bolsheviks. They claimed that the Bolshevik seizure of power in 1917 was a violation of Marxist formula and did not conform to Marx's predictions about revolution in society.[43]

The split between the Mensheviks and Bolsheviks in 1904 had very little to do with the differing interpretation of Marxism—it was a dispute about tactics and organization. However, in the years after the break, it became clear that profound strategic and ideological differences were developing between the two factions. Two of these differences came out very sharply when the war broke out: namely, on (1) the approach to the international workers' movement, and (2) the related question of attitudes toward the Russian national bourgeoisie.

The Bolsheviks were uncompromisingly opposed to Russian workers and peasants participating in the First World War. They were equally opposed to German workers and peasants fighting for Germany, because they argued that workers were being used as cannon fodder by the bourgeoisie of Europe. Instead, they urged Russian workers and European workers in general to turn their guns against the bourgeoisie and carry out revolutions within their own countries. The Mensheviks, for the most part, acquiesced to the war, and especially after February became active supporters of the Provisional Government in the conduct of the war.

The Menshevik support for the Provisional Government after the February Revolution was not merely a tactical maneuver. It was rooted in the interpretation of Marxism that suggested that after feudalism there should be a bourgeois stage. The Mensheviks argued that Russia was in the feudal stage up to 1917. The February Revolution marked the beginning of the bourgeois stage. In their estimation, workers had no option but to support the Provisional Government, so that the bourgeois revolution would be successful in overthrowing and banishing feudalism forever.[44] At a later stage, new contradictions would mature within bourgeois Russia and would eventually give rise to a proletarian revolution.

The Bolsheviks by 1917 had come to the conclusion that conditions in Russia and internationally were such that it was possible to pass immediately to a proletarian revolution. Thus, they organized the seizure of power in October 1917, when the bourgeois Provisional Government had been in power for only seven months. The Mensheviks argued that the seizure of power by the Bolsheviks was a serious miscalculation and a most un-Marxist maneuver. Some of the Mensheviks wrote memoirs and historical accounts. One of these at our disposal was written by Raphael Abramovitch. His major thesis is that the Bolsheviks acted "against all the teachings of Marxism and history."[45] The time was not yet ripe for a proletarian revolution. The proletariat itself was too small and underdeveloped. How then could the Bolshevik Party be so arrogant and un-Marxist as to seize state power on behalf of a proletarian class that was not strong enough? He uses a very effective quotation form Engels, who once wrote, "A revolutionary party is irretrievably lost if it attempts to seize power in a society which is not yet mature enough for the domination of the class which is present."[46]

Soviet historians are very harsh on the Mensheviks and their historical view, which claims to be more authentically Marxist than the Soviet view. Soviets denounce the Mensheviks as "opportunists" and call them various rude names.[47] That is part of the technique of abuse that characterizes sectarian and factional debates among different adherents of Marxism. There are no real grounds for questioning the motives and revolutionary integrity of several of the Menshevik leaders and followers. What is more accurate is the Soviet charge that the Mensheviks put forward a dogmatic and mechanical interpretation of Marxism, without regard to the historical and objective conditions in Russia and Europe by the second decade of this century.

It was dogmatic because the Mensheviks took a historical sketch that Marx derived from Western Europe and tried to apply it uncritically to Russia. As we have already seen, Marx himself, in his own lifetime, had warned some of his critics as well as some of his own followers that this notion of historical development in Western Europe was not a model that was to be followed every other place on the globe.[48]

So the Menshevik view that Russia should have a long period of bourgeois rule is precisely the kind of dogma Marx could not have encouraged. That aspect of Marxism which lays claim to universal validity is its method—the scientific method of dialectical materialism. Like any other scientific method, it produces results on being applied to a given set of data or conditions. Thus a mature Marxist approach to Russia's problems up to 1917 was to see what were the specific local conditions within Russia, and what were the prospects of revolution based on those local conditions and the conjecture of international events. The Mensheviks can rightly be accused of having made a very superficial analysis of Russian society, and in place of real facts about Russia, they substituted preconceived notions they had taken from Marx's studies of the more developed areas of Western Europe.

From a theoretical standpoint, some of the weaknesses of

the Menshevik position can be understood by appreciating the points raised by Mao Zedong's "On Contradiction"—that is, in a discussion of dialectical materialism. Mao draws a distinction between what he calls the "universality of contradiction" and the "particularity of contradiction": (1) Contradiction exists in the process of development of all things at all times; but (2) there are qualitative differences between one contradic tion and another and *every form of society has its own particular contradictions.*[49] Even what superficially appears to be the same contradiction in different societies must be studied to decipher its distinctive features. For instance, bourgeois versus peasant in a highly developed capitalist society is not the same contradiction as bourgeois versus peasant in a semi-feudal society, or in a colonial society. To understand the specific content of the contradiction in the given society, one must look at the particular features of the two aspects of the contradiction— that is, look closely at the bourgeoisie and also at the peasants in the context of the given society. This is really an argument stressing the study of objective local conditions, and Mao condemns dogmatists for failing to study the particularity of contradictions in their local settings.[50]

The Class Struggles in Russia

Conflicting Marxist interpretations pose the question, "when is a society ripe for revolution?," and as a supplement to that, "when is a class ready to perform revolutionary functions?" In Russia, these questions need to be asked with specific reference to the bourgeoisie and the proletariat. According to Marx, the bourgeois class was revolutionary in the eighteenth century and in the early nineteenth century because changes in the mode of production *had given it the lead over all groups and individuals opposed to feudalism.* Some bureaucrats and professional men were opposed to feudalism because it offered them insufficient opportunity for the exercise of their own

71

grievances against survivals of feudal exploitation. Artisans were dissatisfied with the society. In expressing their grievances against the government and the state, all of these groups followed the lead of the bourgeoisie. The professional middle class acted as spokesmen for all elements of the bourgeoisie, providing an ideology for challenging the feudal structure in toto.

Marx, in an essay entitled "The Bourgeoisie and the Counter Revolution," said of the French Revolution, "In 1789, the bourgeoisie was allied with the people against the monarchy, the aristocracy, and the established church."[51] He went on to explain that the bourgeoisie formed the vanguard of the movement. The proletariat and other non-bourgeois elements either had no interests separate from that of the bourgeoisie, or they did not yet constitute independently developed classes. Under those circumstances, they fought in the interests of the bourgeoisie against the aristocracy and against feudalism. In *The Class Struggles in France*, Marx returned to the question. As Frederick Engels wrote in his 1895 introduction to the book's reissue,

> All revolutions up to the present day have resulted in the displacement of one definite class rule by another; but all ruling classes up till now have been only small minorities in relation to the ruled mass of people. One ruling minority was thus overthrown; another minority seized the helm of state in its stead and refashioned the state institutions to suit its own interests. This was on every occasion the minority group qualified and called to rule by the given degree of economic development, and just for that reason, and only for that reason, it happened that the ruled majority either participated in the revolution for the benefit of the former or else calmly acquiesced in it.[52]

One needs to consider whether the bourgeoisie in Russia in the early part of this century was capable of taking the revolutionary lead similar to that taken by sections of the emerging bourgeoisie in France in 1789. The Russian bourgeoisie was in some ways more advanced by virtue of being connected with modern manufacture, but it was tied up much more closely to feudalism than its English or French counterparts. The Russian bourgeoisie was directly aided by the Russian state because industrial development ever since the time of Peter the Great was sponsored by the state. Many of the bourgeois were from the feudal landlord class and had been using serf labor in factories. This was a different situation from either France or England, where many bourgeois were of independent peasant origin and hostile to state control. Besides, the Russian bourgeoisie relied on the tsarist state to keep workers in check.

Many of the Russian capitalists had advanced loans and mortgages to the Russian landed class. They had thereby become intertwined in exploiting the peasants in the countryside and were in no position to take a clear stand in ending the exploitation of the peasants. During the French Revolution, the fact that the bourgeoisie owned a great deal of land was a moderating factor in the revolutionary zeal of the bourgeoisie. However, when threatened by peasant uprisings, they passed legislation on the night of August 4, 1789 that sacrificed the rest of the feudal lands to the peasants on such a basis that the individualist capitalist peasants rose to the positions of strength. Although the French bourgeoisie and some peasants did clash at certain points of the revolution, it can be said that the French Revolution managed to provide a capitalist solution acceptable to the peasants; the Russian landholders also lacked the force that, in the final analysis, could crush peasant unrest as the French bourgeoisie did at Vendée.

The revolutionary bourgeoisie in France had won the support of the embryo working class, because the workers had no independent strength and no ideology of their own. The bourgeoisie was happy to use the muscle power of the "crowd," for they could control them. Subsequently, during the nineteenth century, the bourgeoisie came to realize that the growing proletariat was a threat to its power. The Russian bourgeoisie knew of the attempted workers' revolutions in Germany and France, and they knew of Marx. The Russian bourgeoisie feared its own proletariat with which it had been engaged in constant battles before 1917. This made the Russian bourgeoisie timid. They were afraid to abandon the protection of the tsarist state and landed class, lest the workers swallow them up. Under such circumstances, the Russian bourgeoisie was reformist rather than revolutionary. They joined the Cadet Party and were interested in peaceful change through the Duma. The Cadet Party was led by individuals like Miliukov who wished to institute reforms precisely so as to avoid revolution.[53] When the masses took power in February 1917, these reformists rushed in to try and control the situation; but they lacked the strength to defend the revolution. Were it not for the Bolsheviks and the workers, the Kornilov counterrevolution would have succeeded and tsarism reinstalled.

One of the potent factors in the weakness of the Russian bourgeoisie was the manner in which it was dominated by foreign capital. Half of the capital in Russian joint-stock companies in 1900 was from outside. France controlled 33 percent, Britain 23 percent, and Belgium 14 percent of foreign capital by 1916. No wonder, then, that the Russian bourgeoisie were not free to withdraw from the war that their capitalist bosses were fighting; and that war was clearly not in the interests of Russian workers and peasants. A study of the particularity of the Russian bourgeoisie suggests that the Mensheviks were dreaming when they imagined that such a class would effectively deal with the task of putting an end to feudalism in Russia.

Conversely, the Mensheviks underestimated the strength of the Russian working class, which they described as immature and weak. However, there are several important points to consider that would later emerge from the work of Soviet historians such as Trotsky and Western Marxists like Christopher Hill. First, the actual working and living conditions were atrocious. Russia was at an early state of industrialization—at the point where exploitation was brutal and the misery of workers great. In Western Europe, the phase of early miserable industrialization passes by without revolution. Workers in Western Europe bettered their conditions because of improved technology as well as profits brought in from outside Europe. The Russian working class in 1917 was smaller than its counterparts in Western Europe, but they were more committed to change because of the level of their sufferings.

Second, the Russian working class had a clear ideology. When Western European workers were at their most miserable stage in the eighteenth and early nineteenth centuries, they had no ideology or line of action that could represent their own particular class interests. They merely repeated the phrases of the bourgeoisie—liberty, equality and fraternity—and they were appendages of the bourgeoisie. When they started to adopt socialism as their own philosophy in the early eighteenth century, the ideology was not well defined and not an effective revolutionary tool. That was socialism in its utopian phase. In Russia, workers were exposed to scientific socialism, and Bolsheviks and Mensheviks alike had long been speaking of worker power. The Russian worker was much more self-confident at that stage of his development than the Western European worker. It is a very questionable statement to say that Russian industry was young and therefore that Russian workers were immature.

Third, the process of industrialization in Tsarist Russia did not follow the same path as in Western Europe. Because Russia was industrializing late, it did not move step-by-step from small factories to medium-sized and then large concerns. On the contrary, it moved directly to the building of large factories so as to catch up with the West. The consequence was that workers in Russia were to be found in large factories where the sense of class solidarity developed rapidly. It is significant that one of the areas of most successful Bolshevik activity was in the Putilov works in Petrograd. In January 1917, the whole contingent of Putilov workers were in the streets after a lockout—30,000 of them. Such a group of workers might be historically young relative to Western Europe, but they were in a condition where they matured rapidly. This is a feature commented on at great length by Soviet historians and by Trotsky.

Finally, the Russian working class was the only class in a position to take up national leadership. Given the structure of society, national leadership had to be exercised from urban and industrialized areas. The peasants rose against the status quo, but they had no control over the central organs of power. The workers, however, were strategically situated in the cities and had control of the transportation and communications as well as arms. This was the role played by the bourgeoisie in the French Revolution. It was a role that only workers could play in Russia in 1917. A detailed examination of the bourgeoisie and proletariat in Russia before and during 1917 shows that the bourgeoisie were not in a position to give the leadership to the revolution as was the case in 1789, nor were the workers so weak that they would be prepared to follow the bourgeoisie meekly.

Thus, Raphael Abramovitch's claim that the Bolsheviks prematurely seized state power before the full development of the proletariat, thereby ignoring Marx's fundamental premise, does not stand up to scrutiny. He does not recognize the weakness of the Russian bourgeoisie in comparison with the French revolutionary bourgeoisie, and yet he condemns the Bolsheviks for seizing power from the bourgeois Provisional Government. Events after February 1917 suggest that the consciousness of the workers and the Bolshevik party had passed the stage when they would passively allow the bourgeoisie to rule. They saw by the end of August that even the feudal state would not be defeated if it were not for the efforts of workers; and once the Bolsheviks had taken power they had to put an end to both feudalism and capitalism so as to institute socialism. It is interesting to note that Abramovitch felt that the Bolshevik government would fail to maintain itself in power. This is the logical conclusion from his premise that the society was not ripe for the takeover by the workers. When he cited Engels that "a revolutionary party is doomed if it attempts to seize power in a society that is not ripe enough for the class which it represents," Abramovitch felt that the Bolsheviks were doomed. The Bolshevik government survived and passes the stern test of reality. People like Abramovitch had not really analyzed the situation. They *hoped* the Bolshevik party would fail, because it dismissed the Mensheviks in the Constituent Assembly. Through that hope, they joined with the bourgeoisie in criticizing and actually working against the Soviet state. Such people, in spite of their Marxist position, lend themselves as tools to capitalism. Thus the bourgeois writers are quite willing to sponsor Abramovitch. The introduction to his book is by Sidney Hook, who says that "the Bolsheviks claim to be the only true heirs of Marx," but here we have another Marxist proving them wrong.

In the final analysis, Abramovitch's Marxism is very much in doubt. Understandably, as a Menshevik he disagrees with the Bolshevik interpretation and actions after February 1917, but even with respect to the February Revolution itself, he takes a most undialectical approach. He sees the war as the cause of the revolution: "If there was a single cause for the Russian Revolution of 1917, it was undoubtedly the first world war." It seems that in the atmosphere of the United States, Abramovitch abandons even the Marxist view of the coming of the February Revolution and accepts the view of his fellow tsarist and bourgeois émigrés.

The length of time spent on this writer is not due to his intrinsic importance, but rather as a means of discussing the position of the Menshevik Party, and as an introduction to bourgeois criticisms of the irrelevance of Marxism to the Russian Revolution. The sort of points raised by Abramovitch will be found as the standard stock-in-trade of most bourgeois writers, to the extent that they seldom bother to make any argument to that effect, but merely snide remarks on the assumption that the case has already been proved against the Bolsheviks. This technique of untested but assumed premises is a very important one used by bourgeois historians and social scientists in general; and in this specific context, it is very important that one fully appreciates the static, erroneous and dogmatic interpretation of Marxism, so as not to confuse the issue of what revolutionary theory is all about.

4

Trotsky as Historian of the Russian Revolution

Trotsky ... the historian can be fully appreciated only by those who have read from the beginning to end the *History of the Russian Revolution.*

—Irving Howe[1]

Born Lev Davidovich Bronstein on November 7, 1879 to a Jewish family of farmers in the Ukraine, Leon Trotsky would go on to rival Lenin in terms of his preeminence in the Russian Revolution. As a result of his political organizing among the workers, he was exiled to Siberia in 1898, only to escape to London and join other exiled radicals—notably Georgii Plekhanov, Julius Martov, and Vladimir Lenin—around the political journal *Iskra* (Spark) and the Russian Social-Democratic Labour Party (RSDLP). When the party and the editorial board split in 1903 between the Bolsheviks and the Mensheviks, Trotsky sided with the latter and momentarily parted ways with Lenin. During the 1905 Revolution, Trotsky was a key participant, as an editor, agitator, and ultimately chairman of the St. Petersburg Soviet—the center of the revolution. Forced again into exile following the defeat of the 1905 insurrection, Trotsky eventually joined up with the Bolsheviks and returned during the outbreak of World War I, just as the

Russian Social-Democratic Labour Party was undergoing a reorganization and realignment. Trotsky was appointed chairman of the Military Revolutionary Committee, which took power in October 1917. He was also peoples' commissar of war in the first Soviet government (that is, leader of the Red Army), where he distinguished himself as both a brilliant military strategist and revolutionary.

Trotsky's star began to fall after Lenin's death in 1924. In April 1925, he was removed from the post of war commissar and transferred to lesser administrative jobs. He was dismissed from the politburo in July 1927, expelled from the party in December, and exiled to Turkestan in January 1928. One year later he was exiled from the USSR, and he then moved to Turkey, France, Norway and Mexico, engaging in a constant battle of words with Stalin's regime. In August of 1940, he was assassinated in Mexico.[2]

We will have more to say about Trotsky's role in the Russian Revolution, but for now we will concentrate on his role as a historian of the revolution. A prolific writer possessed of boundless energy, Trotsky wrote several works, including a biography of Lenin and an autobiography. His first major historical analysis, "The Motive Forces of the Russian Revolution," which appeared as a chapter in *1905*, was produced soon after the split in the RSDLP. As one would expect, it is an analysis of classes—as suggested by the very headings and subheadings (proletariat; bourgeoisie; the modern city, where they both dwell; the nobility). He reveals a keen understanding of the fundamentals of class behavior. Compare his treatment of the feudal nobility to that of George Vernadsky, who wanted them to commit class suicide. Trotsky explains that it was class interest and not folly that caused the landlords to resist the reformist plans of a group like the Cadets.[3]

However, Trotsky's power as a Marxist historian lies not only in his grasp of fundamentals, but also the tremendous sophistication and refinement with which he uses historical materialism as a tool. No pedantic follower of Marx on Western Europe, he insists on the objective analysis of Russia, stressing the country's uniqueness and specificity. In the West, the bourgeoisie was largely indigenous, whereas in Russia it took the form of foreign capital. Lenin fully developed most aspects of bourgeois class formation, character, and the peculiarities of Russian capitalism that seem obvious now, but at that time Trotsky demonstrated originality and clarity of historical perception:

> When European capital nipped in the bud the development of Russian handicrafts, it also tore bourgeois democracy from the social soil that would make it grow. Can the Moscow or Petersburg of today really be equated with the Berlin or Vienna of 1848 or, a fortiori, with the Paris of 1789, where the railroad and the telegraph were not even dreams and where a factory with three hundred workers was considered a major industry? We don't even have a memory of that four-square burgess class, schooled for centuries in self-government and political action, and then allying itself with an as yet undifferentiated proletariat to take the feudal Bastille by assault.[4]

So what, Trotsky asks, does Russia have in place of a home-grown, politically mature bourgeoisie? "A new 'middle class' of professional intelligentsia" with no power or significance of its own. Looking for a "massive social class" upon which to lean, it finds support in the landlords.[5] Meanwhile, as bourgeois democracy proceeds in Russia as, in Trotsky's memorable words, "a head without a body," the class of most significance is the young proletariat, which in 1897 accounted for 10 million people, or a little more than one-fourth of the Russian population. Its critical importance was determined by its role in the modern economy. Thus 3.3 million workers in mining and manufacturing, industry, transport, construction and trade produced more than half of the national income.[6]

These ideas were put together and brilliantly developed in Trotsky's major work, *History of the Russian Revolution*, written at Brest-Litovsk in 1918 (before March). The three-volume edition was published in 1930–32 and edited by the American Trotskyist Max Shachtman. In the preface, Trotsky stresses that he is operating as a historian from documents rather than personal recollections. As to impartiality, he says, no one has yet explained of what this consists. With sympathies and antipathies open and undisguised, he set out to study the interconnection between facts and the movement of history. This monumental work is history at the highest level of analysis. Trotsky explains why Russia developed the way it did in the nineteenth century, why the 1905 Revolution took its particular course, why the war went the way it did and why the tsar behaved the way he did, and why there was dual power instead of just the bourgeois Provisional Government. He is sharply critical of the role of the party prior to Lenin's return, which differs pointedly from the Soviet view. His attitude toward other parties is sober, and references to himself are overmodest. His immediacy of style strikes a tone similar to John Reed's *Ten Days that Shook the World*, and yet Trotsky was using documents. In Irving Howe's pithy phrase, "The past and future were exchanging notes."

Trotsky begins with genuine Marxist interest in people, consciousness, and the agency of "men" to make their own history. While there are few fundamental disagreements between Trotsky and the official Soviet historians on the broad sweep of Russian history in the seventeenth, eighteenth, and nineteenth centuries, Trotsky has the capacity to use Marxist methodology skillfully and creatively, so that he actually enriches Marxist theory. Whereas the Soviet approach is a little heavy-handed in so far as they emphasize only the major conflict between the feudal and capitalist systems in the aggregate, reducing historical change to the flow of impersonal forces, Trotsky emphasizes people as agents of historical change. He writes firstly not about the modes of production but about consciousness among classes that make the revolution. "The dynamic of revolutionary events is directly determined by swift, intense, and passionate changes in the psychology of classes which have already formed themselves before the revolution."[7] Since the psychology or consciousness is determined by conditions, then it is in the historic conditions that formed Russia where we ought to begin to look for the roots of the February and March revolutions. By historic conditions he means the economy, classes, the state and the impact of other states. Further, since the enigma of the Russian Revolution is the fact that a backward country was first to place the proletariat in power, we must seek the solution in the *peculiarities* of the backward country.

What is peculiar about a backward country following the capitalist path? Although compelled to follow after the advanced countries, a backward country does not take things in the same order. In many respects, the backward country proceeds much faster, accepting the latest changes in the mode of production, as it has developed in the advanced countries. The privilege of historical backwardness compels the adoption of whatever is ready, skipping a whole series of intermediate stages. Trotsky presents a number of examples related to the United States and Europe, but we can see the truth of this observation by looking at East Africa. Take copper in Zambia and compare it with tin in Cornwall; take textile factories in Ubungo and compare them with Lancashire—take agricultural equipment or such a clear example as the motor car.

He puts it in this way: "Under the whip of external necessity their backward culture is compelled to make leaps."[8] On this basis, Trotsky puts forward a new concept that he calls the law of combined development, which he felt was applicable to Russia and other backward countries. By this he means "a drawing together of the different stages of the journey, a combining of separate steps, an amalgam of archaic with more contemporary forms."[9] This law reveals itself most clearly in the industrial field. Russia started late and adapted the latest achievements to its own backwardness. The economic evolution of Russia skipped over stages such as the craft guild, while technical stages that had taken decades elsewhere were simply leapt over. The paradox, however, is that when one sees the rapid industrial growth of Russia in the late nineteenth and twentieth centuries, one cannot say, as historian and economist Mikhail Pokrovsky asserted, that "we must abandon the legend of backwardness and slow growth."[10] The rapidity of growth was a function of historic backwardness. Combined development affected the nature of the classes. The proletariat in particular became more revolutionary because, on the one hand, they were subjected to conditions of backwardness in the form of tsarist oppression and, on the other hand, the rapid development of capitalism had involved them in a sharp break with the past.[11] As Christopher Hill points out, the annual deaths caused by industrial accidents in Russia were greater in number than the casualties of the Russo-Turkish War of 1877–78.[12]

From the law of combined and uneven development, Trotsky derived his famous idea of the *permanent revolution*. Marx in 1850 had said much the same thing about Germany in his "Address to the Central Committee of the Communist League." It was the task of the workers to arm themselves during the first stage of a democratic upsurge versus the old regime and to dictate conditions to the bourgeoisie. Alongside the official government, they were to establish their own revolutionary workers' governments, and to seize power from the bourgeoisie by any means they could. Meanwhile, the job of the Communist League (that is, the Communist Party) was "to make the revolution permanent until the proletariat has conquered state power."[13] Kermit McKenzie calls this a "minor theme," and George Lichtheim says it was anarchist influence on the immature Marx.[14] Both statements are nonsensical, but note the conditions in Germany—Trotsky was drawing on Marxist theory at its point of greatest relevance.

More than being a point of theory, the *permanent revolution* was a historical fact. Trotsky was not arguing whether it was good or not; he was saying that that was the situation in twentieth-century Russia. The Revolution of 1905 was "a prologue to the two revolutions of 1917."[15] Though lacking in complete confidence, the workers had taken arms *on their own initiative.* It was no party or theory, but rather the force of circumstances that guided them, the law of combined development pushing them to revolutionary heights. Nobody told the proletariat how to organize in 1905, but they did exactly what Marx wanted in 1850; namely, they set up their own independent proletarian organs of government in the form of the soviet. Trotsky pointed out that Struve wrote on January 7, 1905, "There are no revolutionary people in Russia as yet."[16] Two days later revolution broke out. The revolutionary masses are a fact—they fought with guns and they moved toward new political forms to counter the bourgeois state apparatus. Probably because Trotsky was the only major leader involved, he perceived that the soviet was going to be the basis of the new workers' state when it was formed. Lenin took some time to appreciate this.

Pursuing the theme of the development of consciousness of the classes, Trotsky presents key lessons of the 1905 Revolution: (a) Impressed by the force of the workers and peasants, the bourgeoisie had become more conservative and suspicious. (b) The proletariat was preparing to take the leading role. The Revolution of 1905 had thrown up the soviet, which was the ideal revolutionary form and which grew rapidly in 1917. However, there was a need for a revolutionary organization capable of mobilizing the popular masses and consolidating the momentum evident in a wave of political strikes. By Trotsky's account, some 1,843,000 workers engaged in political strikes, with another 1,020,000 participating in "economic" strikes.[17] After 1905, as the bourgeoisie became more timid and workers more determined, the revolution was bound to be permanent. The role of the political party was to understand this, and thus provide direction to the process. But in the period of reaction after 1907, most progressive elements suffered terrible blows.

Despite the tremendous growth of political strikes between 1912 and 1914, there was no revolutionary organization to take initiative.

In May 1917, Trotsky returned to Russia from exile in New York, ten weeks after the events of February. He devoted all of his energies to the revolution and, not long after his arrival, joined forces with Lenin and the Bolsheviks. His memoirs describe in great detail the events from the October Revolution to the negotiations at Brest-Litovsk to withdraw Russia from World War I. He always stressed the mood and consciousness of the masses and the need for the party to take up a correct analysis. For Trotsky, history is guided by action, but his is undoubtedly a history of the highest level.

Even within the military one could see the law of combined and uneven development operating. In the case of the First World War, Russia acquired some of the most modern weapons, but the problem was that cultural backwardness modified the effect of technical advances. There was no correspondence between the cultural level of the peasant soldier and modern military technique. The war was embraced by the Russian bourgeoisie, in part because they made huge profits: "patriotic virtue was rewarded generously."[18] It also made the bourgeoisie more and more afraid of social revolution. Following in the wake of the political strike wave between 1912 and 1914, the war put a temporary halt to the revolutionary movement. Trotsky asks the question, "Would the mass offensive of 1912–14 have led directly to the overthrow of tsarism if the war had not broken out?"[19] He is quite cautious on this question of inevitability, arguing that it is impossible to know for certain. "The process would inexorably have led to a revolution," he writes, "but through what stages would the revolution in those circumstances have had to go? Would it not have experienced another defeat? How much time would have been needed by the workers in order to arouse the peasantry and win the army?"[20] He nevertheless observed that the war later speeded up the revolution.

Yet, the peasantry remained in a strained relationship to the proletariat. It was pointless to expect a transformation in the mode of production while the peasant saw his backwardness in terms of too little land. No economic regime disappears before exhausting all of its possibilities. The peasantry by its own force could not have achieved the agrarian-democratic revolution. Trotsky cites the example of Pugachev's Rebellion of the late eighteenth century, which failed to become a revolution for lack of a "Third Estate." Without an urban industrial democracy, the peasant war could not become a revolution.[21] For the first time in world history, the peasant was destined to find a leader in the person of the worker. This was the unique feature of the Russian Revolution. Yet this itself further exemplifies the laws of uneven and combined development. In order to realize the Soviet state, it was necessary to draw together two factors— a peasant war characteristic of the dawn of capitalist development, and a proletarian revolution, which comes after capitalism has matured.[22]

Being a more complete work than the official Soviet publications, Trotsky's *History of the Russian Revolution* pays attention to the ruling class, devoting a chapter to the interrelations between the monarch, the upper nobility, the bureaucracy and the bourgeoisie. He sees the position of the monarchy as "a disgusting mixture of fright, superstition and malicious alienation from the country."[23] Because a revolution breaks out when the antagonisms of the old society are at their keenest, even the classes who benefited under the old society turn against the ruler. The question of the personality of the monarch is dealt with within the general dialectical framework. Trotsky was only prepared to concede that "this or that policy of the monarchy, this or that personality of the monarch, might have hastened or postponed the revolution, and placed a certain imprint on its external course."[24] Accumulating social contradictions were bound to break through to the surface.

The February Revolution was begun from below, overcoming the resistance of its own revolutionary organizations. The leaders were watching the movement from above. They hesitated, they lagged—they did not lead. Indeed, "We must lay it down as a general rule for those days that the higher the leader, the further they lagged behind."[25] In other words, *the revolutionary masses were a fact*. Yet he attacks the theory of a spontaneous and impersonal revolution as a liberal fiction. The revolution caught the government and the revolutionaries unaware only with regard to the exact moment. Both sides had been preparing for it for years. The fact that one cannot discover the identity of the leaders makes the revolution nameless, but not impersonal. The outbreak must be seen in the context of the generally propagandized condition of the workers, hence the "conscious and tempered workers educated for the most part by the party of Lenin."[26]

This leads to the theory of the paradox of the February Revolution. While the soviets were the only genuinely revolutionary body and the basis of the revolution, the "Executive Committee of Soviet Workers' Deputies" had no real organic link to the soviets. Unlike the 1905 Revolution in which the Executive Committee was elected by the soviet, this one was a self-constituted initiative of socialist intellectuals created in advance of the soviets and independent of the factory committees. It was made up of men who had hastened to place themselves in that position even before the fighting was over. For Trotsky, this was a critical matter that "until now [had] been left completely in the shade."[27] The Executive was conservative and it required months of reshuffling before they became organs of struggle and new insurrection. Through their representatives, the masses were drawn into the mechanics of the two-power regime. They now had to pass through this struggle in order to learn by experience that the Executive Committee could give them neither peace nor land. After the February Revolution, two things happened simultaneously. The central organs of power were taken over by the bourgeoisie, liberal landlords and the liberal intelligentsia; and the workers, peasants and soldiers turned to their own independent local councils—the soviets of 1905. The role of the Bolsheviks was first to capture soviet power and then begin the assault on total state power, but they were corresponding to, rather than dragging, the masses. From the July days until the seizure of state power in October, the masses were on the move. The task before the Bolsheviks was to determine how to take power and how to effect the alliance of the proletariat and the peasantry.

One final note: throughout the text, Trotsky hardly mentions himself, and yet his account is strongly protagonist. It was written and published in 1925, during the early years of his struggle with Stalin. He treats his rivals as veritable morons.[28] He insists that he has no intention of stirring up old quarrels, but he hints that "old Bolsheviks" are still dumb, and this launched an important chain of history as personal character assassination. Trotsky bit off more than he could chew. He searched, but Stalin made up his documents.

5

On the "Inevitability" of the Russian Revolution

Having dealt with the events of the year 1917, one has necessarily to turn to the Russian past to seek the roots and causation of the said events. Within the historiography of the Russian Revolution, the question of causation is often posed in the form of the question "was the Revolution inevitable?"

Soviet writers and some other Marxists say that it was— perhaps partly because they were the victors, and the notion inevitably gives them greater dignity; but more fundamentally because Marxists believe in certain laws of historical movement, based on dialectical materialism. They hold that antagonistic class contradictions must give rise to revolution; that the feudalist had to give way to the bourgeoisie in Europe; and that the workers will ultimately take over from the bourgeoisie.

Marx pointed out that man makes his history himself, but his consciousness in so doing is historically determined by factors such as technology, class, and previous ideas. It is precisely the limitations imposed by external factors on human consciousness that cause people within classes to behave in a certain circumscribed way. Landed classes will always seek to defend their own landed interests and, in the process, will continue to exploit the peasant and to restrict other classes like the bourgeoisie. The latter fought feudalism, but they cannot be expected to rise beyond bourgeois democracy and give full rights to the workers, because while seeking equality the workers would then threaten bourgeois profits, which are the source of all bourgeois activity. So the bourgeoisie continue to oppress workers, and that makes a worker revolution unavoidable at some stage. The consciousness that is relevant is essentially the consciousness of a given class rather than a single individual, and it is in analysis of class contradictions that Soviet and other Marxist writers feel convinced that the Russian Revolution was inevitable. The principal class contradiction was that between landlord and peasant. To understand the role of the peasants and the land question in the Russian Revolution of 1917, one has to go back to the period of fully fledged feudalism, before 1861. By the middle of the nineteenth century, the conflict between the serfs and the landowners had become extremely sharp. The serfs wanted freedom and land. They were engaged in a constant battle with the landlord (including the tsar). There were numerous sporadic rebellions, some of them quite large. According to one researcher, there were 556 serious rebellions of peasants under Nicholas I, between 1825 and 1855.[1] To put down peasant rebellions was very costly to the state. the regime of serfdom was holding back agricultural innovation, and it was holding back the development of industry, which needed free labor—that is, labor that is free to move from one factory to another.

After the Crimean War of 1854–5, the Russian government decided that their inability to crush Turkey was due to their backwardness, just as the efficiency of the small British forces was due to the industrial development of Britain. Therefore, when Alexander II came to the throne in 1855, this new tsar began to consider carefully the idea of emancipating or freeing the serfs. The tsar was the greatest serf master in Russia, so he began to work out proposals for his own serfs.[2] But he had to *persuade* the other nobles—the dukes and grand dukes, who were fellow member of the ruling class—that it was useless to continue with serfdom. This persuasion proved to be a difficult task.

Meanwhile, the serfs were still protesting and were growing more and more militant. As early as 1856, the tsar had warned the nobles that it was "better to abolish serfdom from above than to wait till it begins to abolish itself from below."[3] Eventually, in 1861 an act was passed for the emancipation of the serfs.

Soviet historians and many Western bourgeois historians agree that the act did not at all eliminate the antagonism between landlord and peasant. The inadequacies of the Emancipation Act were as follows:

(1) Peasants were given very small areas of land. Altogether the land that they were permitted to purchase was smaller than their allotments under serfdom.

(2) The landlords used the opportunity to part with most of the unproductive land.

(3) The purchase price was high, and was paid in installments known as "redemption payments," which hung like millstones around the necks of the peasants. It was not until the Revolution of 1905 that the redemption payments were abolished.

(4) The communal village, or *mir*, which served the landlords under serfdom became the new legal basis of rural society without the capacity to deal with problems. Peasants were tied to the commune, leading to overcrowding.

(5) Treatment of peasants was still semi-feudal—for instance, flogging as a punishment for offenses.

Given all of the above weaknesses of the Emancipation Act, Soviet historians contend that the contradiction between landlord and peasant grew more and more acute as the nineteenth century wore on. One very important factor was that the population doubled between 1850 and 1900. The Revolution of 1905 was largely an outbreak of peasant frustration. The lands of the mirs were overcrowded. Land was unscientifically farmed in strips with poor tools, so it could not give an adequate livelihood. The tsarist government was in no position to solve the dilemma of the land, and Soviet writers see revolution as the unavoidable consequence.[4]

A number of bourgeois writers believe that the land question could have been solved and revolution avoided. Prominent among these writers are the Russian émigrés: people connected in some way with the tsarist ruling class, who fled Russia in 1917 or shortly afterwards. Their ideas are sympathetic to the old regime of which they are a part, and they are concerned to defend themselves from the charge that they made revolution inevitable.

On the land question, the émigrés have a lot to say. Up to a certain point, they agree with Soviet and other historians that the way in which emancipation was handled merely carried over the problems of serfdom in a new form; for instance, Karpovich and Florinsky give very Marxist-sounding accounts of the peasant question.[5]

However, a few of the émigrés are inclined to engage in historical *hypothesis* about alternative ways of dealing with emancipation. Such hypotheses are sometimes necessary to try and arrive at valid historical conclusions, but they have to be based on objective reality. In this instance, there is a great deal of subjectivism.

Vernadsky and Spector concur in propounding the following hypothesis: Emancipation could have ruled out the possibility of revolution in 1917 if the serfs were freed without land, and then some of them should have been assisted on an individual basis to acquire land and become a solid peasant capitalist class. Or alternatively, the nobility should have been compensated and the serfs given the land free. This would have removed the question of heavy redemption payments.[6] This first suggestion is entirely unrealistic. The serfs already had land allotments under serfdom; since they were attached to the soil for generations, they considered it theirs. Part of the produce of the soil was theirs, and many areas remained common land that was used by the serfs rather than the landlords. The overwhelming desire of all peasants was to gain title to the land and obtain a bit more. They were not seeking freedom in the abstract. Even the reactionary tsar knew that. He had to offer all peasants the possibility of obtaining land if he was to avoid the revolution from below. George Vernadsky and Ivar Spector are blind to the fact that the surest way to have incensed the serfs in 1861 was to have told them that they were legally free, but that only some of them would be privileged to gain land. Instead of studying the Revolution of 1917, we would probably be studying that of 1861.

The second suggestion about compensating the landlords is equally unrealistic. What was "compensation"? If it meant token compensation, the landlords would have none of that, for it would be tantamount to giving away their land. If it meant the state paid the landlords, then this was also an indirect way of the feudal tsar and his government paying for their own liquidation as a class. Neither the tsar nor any other landlord was prepared to voluntarily deprive himself of his socioeconomic base. The tsar in fact did the very best he could under the circumstances, in the light of his own class position. He said to the nobles, "To avoid revolution, you must free the serfs and sell them some land." The nobles asked, "Where will the peasants get money to pay for the land?" In turn the tsar suggested that he would raise a loan and pay the nobles cash for certain pieces of land. The tsar offered them high prices for poor lands, thus giving them a subsidy or "golden handshake." The peasants were then asked to repay the loan in installments, hence the redemption payments. This is what the British did for the white settlers when Kenya became independent. The British ruling class was taking care of its own interest and those of the settlers, just as the tsar was taking care of the interests of the nobles. He could not do otherwise.

A much more substantial argument concerning the land question is the one that concentrates on the period after 1905. This argument suggests that the land question was being solved in the period after the Revolution of 1905, and that it was only the war which put an end to a period of improvement. The Revolution of 1917 was not inevitable; it was the unfortunate accident of the First World War that brought it. Historians in this category include Florinsky and Karpovich. They point out that after having been frightened by the Revolution of 1905, the tsar engaged in certain reforms, and that he had competent ministers who oversaw the new policy—men like Stolypin and Witte. Stolypin was ruthless. He crushed the peasants after the 1905 Revolution failed. But he was also foresighted enough to realize that some reforms would have to be put into effect if future revolutions were to be avoided. On Stolypin's advice, the redemption payments were discontinued; the movement out of the commune was made easier, benefiting both agriculture and industry; and consolidation of scattered strips became possible. Above all, the regime encouraged the formation of a class of capitalist farmers or kulaks. The tsarist state encouraged private property rights instead of family rights, by placing property entirely in the hands of the head of household. The government set up a land bank and lent money to those peasants who were already better off so that they could purchase land. In addition, settlements or homesteads were established in Siberia where some peasants were given liberal land grants.[7]

The purpose of Stolypin's policy was to create a strong peasant capitalist class, who could identify their interests with landlords and the bourgeoisie and thereby provide a strong social base for the defense of the status quo against revolution. While this was going on, Stolypin used bloody repression to keep the situation in hand. He was one of the most hated ministers and was assassinated in 1911. Lenin once paid tribute to Stolypin, calling his policies "progressive" for accelerating capitalist development and the bourgeoisie.[8] But Lenin had no illusions about his intentions: to crush the revolutionary movement. He realized that had Stolypin's policy succeeded, it would have made revolution *more difficult*. Of course he still maintained that the Revolution was inevitable, but Karpovich argues that "in view of this process it would be hardly correct to assert that the Revolution was absolutely inevitable."[9]

There are a number of weaknesses in the émigre perspective on the land question after 1905, based on a tendency to exaggerate and romanticize the limited improvements in that period. In the first place, the amount of consolidation of land and the creation of capitalist farmers was negligible in proportion to the vast majority who still farmed in the old communal way, with scattered strips, poor tools, and very little land. The vast proportion of the peasants were forced to share out among themselves an entirely inadequate portion of the cultivable land. In 1913, out of a total of 906 million acres, 41 percent was in the hands of estates owned by the crown, the church and nobility. The rest was in the hands of 20 million peasants. Secondly, the attempt to open up new lands was not very successful. By 1911, 60 percent of the settlers who went to Siberia with high hopes had returned to their original home areas.[10] The policy of new colonization is always a slow one, and it would have taken a very long time for Stolypin's bets to pay off. Thirdly, the government policies were creating new and dangerously antagonistic contradictions, between the kulaks and the poor peasants. Both the Russian and the Chinese Revolutions showed that conflict between rich and poor peasants could be just as bitter as conflict between peasant and landlord. And finally, not all improvements in agriculture should be considered as benefitting the peasants as such. Minister Witte encouraged the production of more grain by modern methods, but he exported the surplus to the West to pay capitalists for goods, loans, and interest on those loans.[11]

Apart from the land question, there were a number of other contradictions that Soviet writers discerned as being significant in the old regime, and that they felt led inevitably to revolution. One of these was the conflict between the backward, reactionary tsar and the citizens at large. This meant that the feudal state was opposed by all oppressed people as well as by the enlightened few of the bourgeois and landed classes. Since the latter knew of progressive developments within Western Europe, they were very conscious of the inadequacies of Russia. Indeed, long before the revolution, it was clear that the intelligentsia had come to the conclusion that the Russian regime should be gotten rid of by *any means necessary*, and violence against the state was a very common phenomenon.

Most individuals who could be termed "progressive" had accepted that violence was the only way of dealing with tsarism. The widespread commitment to revolutionary violence was due to the massive presence of reactionary violence. The tsar had closed most avenues toward peaceful change and instead was banking on his police and army to keep the regime going, no matter how unpopular it was. Russia was one of the first genuine police states in history. Censorship was widespread, the armed police were very visible, and secret police and agents provocateurs were widely used. The tsarist state had agents provocateurs in the Duma, the Zemstvo, the labor unions and all the left-wing parties like the Bolsheviks and the Socialist Revolutionaries. Two such notorious police agents were Malinovsky, one of the revolutionary police agents in the Bolshevik organization, and Father Gapon in the labor movement. Through Gapon, thousands of workers met their death in 1905.[12]

A police state of the tsarist type inevitably calls forth revolution—this is the view not only of the Soviets but of other historians too. However, most émigré historians argue that Russia was moving out of feudal darkness and backwardness before the First World War. Writers like Karpovich, Vernadsky and Florinsky claim that education was increasing in Russia, that municipal government had become more enlightened and that the Duma was proof that autocracy was no longer as rigid as it used to be. They also stress that industrialization and economic modernization were taking place.[13]

The question of political liberalization is particularly open to criticism. It can be countered by observing that after 1905 the tsar made concessions from a position of weakness, but he withdrew those concessions as the years advanced. The second Duma was dissolved because it attempted to take up a progressive stance; and the third and fourth Dumas had a much more restricted franchise. The émigrés reply in turn that other historians have gone too far in dismissing the dumas as having no democratic potential.[14] Thus, the debate goes back and forth.

One of the groups that suffered most under the tsarist regime was the working class. Soviet historians understandably have a great deal to say about the workers. They describe the intolerable conditions of the workers and point out that the frequency of strikes and industrial unrest was proof of the intense confrontation between the workers and their employers (including the state). The émigrés, on the other hand, would mention that trade unions had eventually been permitted in Russia, after having been illegal for a long time, and that it was once more the unfortunate intervention of the war which interrupted a situation that was improving.

Since these historians attach so much importance to the war, it is necessary to take a close look at the role of the war in relation to the revolution. Among the consequences of the First World War on Russian society were the following:

(1) Shortage of labor in agriculture and industry owing to the mobilization. Much of this labor was skilled, and it involved a withdrawal of horsepower from the farms. In addition, there was a "militarization of demand," so that food, textiles, leather and steel production went to serve the army first, and there ensued a great shortage of food and manufactured goods for the *civilian* population.

(2) Loss of territory and productive resources, especially since European Russia was the most highly developed economic region of Russia and the most hard-hit by war because of its Western location.

(3) Breakdown in foreign trade, internal transportation and fuel distribution.

(4) Alienation of the 15 million armed workers and peasants through defeat and mismanagement. The soldiers responded to pacifist propaganda and there were large-scale desertions.

In light of the above, Florinsky asserts that "the true and basic causes of the revolution were military defeats, staggering losses, demoralization of the army, plight of the refugees, economic hardships, lack of understanding of the objects of the war, and general longing for peace at any price."[15] The Bolsheviks at the time of the war themselves admitted the importance of the event. They called it the "mighty accelerator" of the revolution. That, of course, is different from Florinsky's position, for he sees the war as the basic cause. Soviet historians simply say that the war speeded up a revolution that was already in the making. In fact, to be precise, the war first held back the revolutionary movement by eliminating some of the most conscious, and then speeded it up by creating new and bigger contradictions between the working people and the ruling class. Soviet historians consider that a set of long-term causes were operating throughout the latter part of the nineteenth century and in the twentieth century, and these made the revolution inevitable. The war is seen as a short-term cause that created the correct climate by February 1917 in which the long-term contradictions came to a head. To use the language of chemistry, the war was operating as a *catalyst*—soviet historians say that it *precipitated* the Revolution of 1917.[16]

Because the émigrés feel that things were improving in Tsarist Russia, they discount the significance and the so-called "inevitability" of the long-term contradictions. To them the two operative factors in 1917 were the war and the tsarist government, rather than tsarist society as a whole. The émigrés have to admit that, improving or not, something was wrong with tsarist society or else it would not have collapsed during the war. Certainly, all societies do not collapse in war, and as Florinsky himself admits, a war is the great test of the fabric of a society. The émigrés usually proceed to argue that what was wrong with tsarist society was the poor quality of the leadership. They manage to discount the Soviet discussion on class contradictions by focusing not on the body of the society, but on the ruling circle of the tsar, his family and his advisers.

What then was the caliber of leadership of the Russian state by the time of World War I? The tsar, Nicholas II, is regarded as a ruler without much willpower. He was heavily influenced by his wife, a member of the British royal family. The empress in turn fell under the influence of a so-called "holy man," Rasputin, who was a Siberian peasant whose scandalous life earned him that name, which meant "dissolute." He was an able confidence trickster and became an adventurer among the women of the nobility, eventually reaching the tsar's court. His influence over the tsarina or empress stemmed mainly from his ability to stop the haemorrhaging of her son who suffered from haemophilia. By controlling the empress, he controlled the tsar, and the government came to be run depending on Rasputin's dreams and prayers. His scandalous personal life brought the court into disrepute, but even more important was the fact that while his word was law, it led to irrational interference in the government of the country and the conduct of the war. It would not be an exaggeration to say that in its last years, the tsar's government was being conducted on the basis of fraud and witchcraft.

Apart from Rasputin, there were a large number of other strange figures at the Russian court, and most of the ministers from 1914 to 1917 were of very poor quality. Partly because of Rasputin's intervention, but largely because of the underlying uncertainty of the times, the tsar found it necessary to change ministers with great frequency, depriving his administration of any stability. In the last year of the old regime, there were four different prime ministers, four different ministers of the interior, three different war ministers, and three different foreign ministers. A glance at some of the persons who held ministries and/or advised Nicholas would suggest that it was a circus rather than a government.

One of the most powerful men at the court was Konstantin Pobedonostsev, the layman appointed by the tsar to control the Orthodox Church in the office of procurator of the Holy Synod. He was a confirmed reactionary who would have made

Edmund Burke appear to be a radical. He was not simply against workers and peasants, but against all the freedoms of bourgeois democracy that had been fought for in the French Revolution!

What is this freedom by which so many minds are agitated, which inspires so many insensate actions, so many wild speeches, which leads the people so often to misfortune? ... Among the falsest of political principles is the principle of the sovereignty of the people ... Thence proceeds the theory of parliamentarianism, which has deluded and infatuated certain foolish Russians.

So said Pobedonostsev.[17] At least he was loyal to the tsar and he was relatively sane, which cannot be said for some others. Baron Boris Stürmer, one of the ministers, was very suspiciously connected with the Germans, while another powerful minister, Protopopov was subject to fits of lunacy, apparently the consequence of advanced syphilis.[18]

Given the influence of Rasputin and the odd collection of ministers, it may seem that a writer like Karpovich has a very strong point when he says, "The war made the revolution highly probable, but human folly made it inevitable."[19] In other words, Karpovich is saying that when tested by war, Russian society showed weakness at the government level. The human folly of the tsar and his ministers made a difficult situation impossible and led to revolution. Such an argument dismisses the long-term causes working during the "old regime" and gives us an apparently satisfactory reason for the revolution by concentrating on the period of the eve of the revolution.

A question that these émigrés do not ask is, why was it possible for a government of a huge country to fall into the hands of such utter reactionaries, charlatans and fools? Soviet historians, and Trotsky in particular, suggest that the stupidity of the government was itself the reflection of the irreconcilable contradictions in the society, which had upset the formerly secure feudal base. The rise of new classes was fast making the aristocracy irrelevant. To keep themselves in power, they made the state machinery more blind, more repressive and more out of touch with all enlightened opinion. It was only in an autocratic regime lacking in vitality that such a collection of idiots could govern. The "human folly" was thus a product or symptom of a very sick society indeed.

Some Western historians, without using a Marxian analysis, arrive at a conclusion very similar to that of the Soviet historians. Apart from E. H. Carr, this is true of B. H. Sumner, a British historian who is no friend of the Bolsheviks, but who, using his own terminology, in effect acknowledges that the feudal base of tsarist society had been eroded, and that this was the reason for the absurd behavior of the court: "It has already been said that tsarism had operated through the landowning class, the army and the police, the bureaucracy and the Church. By the time of the war the last was but a hollow prop, the first was as such a spent force."[20] In other words, the revolution in February 1917 was made possible because of the long-term forces that had been operating within feudalism to deprive the landowning church and nobility of their socioeconomic strength. This takes us full circle, back to the Marxist and Soviet argument that changes in the mode of production determined that there should be the birth of a new society, and that revolution was the midwife that brought the new society into being.

6

On Democracy: Lenin, Kautsky and Luxemburg

Karl Kautsky was a frontline European Marxist. He was a German who had known both Marx and Engels since his youth, and after their deaths he became their principal literary executor (in charge of all correspondence and manuscripts). Kautsky was one of the foremost Marxist theoreticians of the turn of the century. Lenin said of him, "Kautsky knows Marx almost by heart."[1] Obviously, therefore, Kautsky was taken seriously when he attacked the Bolsheviks in a work entitled *Dictatorship of the Proletariat* (1919). That was a contemporary analysis of the situation, the historiographical importance of which is that its criticisms of the Soviet state (like those of Raphael Abramovitch) have served as a model for bourgeois detractors. From Germany, Kautsky had extended his support to the Russian Mensheviks, so he begins by repeating the Menshevik position that Russia was not ripe for a socialist revolution.[2] More important, however, is Kautsky's rush to brand the Bolsheviks as dictatorial in the worst sense of the term. He explains Marx's use of the term "dictatorship of the proletariat" as being the equivalent of "proletarian democracy"—just as Marx used "dictatorship of the bourgeoisie" and "bourgeois democracy" interchangeably.[3] This interpretation is sound as a point of departure. But how does Kautsky apply it to Russia in 1917?

According to Kautsky, when Marx used the term "dictatorship of the proletariat" he did not intend that it should be taken literally. It should really mean the democracy that exists in a state where the bourgeoisie has been subordinated to the proletariat, who in theory would be in the majority. This would allow the term "proletarian democracy" to have real meaning, because it would represent the will and interests of the majority. But in Russia the working class was a small minority and thus could not provide the conditions for the dictatorship of the proletariat, used in this sense. The result is a dictatorship of the proletariat over the peasantry—that is, minority government, which was not a Marxist ideal. Kautsky therefore joined the school, comprising mainly bourgeois writers, who assert that the revolution contradicted Marxism in important ways, writing, "The Bolshevists are Marxists, and have inspired the proletarian sections coming under their influence with great enthusiasm for Marxism. Their dictatorship, however, is in contradiction to the Marxist teaching that no people can overcome the obstacles offered by the successive phases of their development by jump, or by legal enactment."[4] Furthermore, the Bolshevik party arrogantly claimed the right to represent the working class, but instead their members became the real dictators in the country. The proof of their dictatorial intentions was seen when the Bolsheviks dismissed the popularly elected Constituent Assembly and, in the absence of democracy, the Civil War broke out.[5]

Lenin's reply, published as a lengthy pamphlet titled *The Proletarian Revolution and the Renegade Kautsky*, is absolutely scathing. In his polemical tone, oscillating between the crude and the ironic ("How Kautsky transformed Marx into an ordinary Liberal" is a beautiful chapter heading), Lenin both attempts to set the historical record straight and advance a Marxist understanding of "dictatorship." By dictatorship, he meant the rule of one class over another. Such a dictatorship could take on a brutal form if there existed a military clique and a bureaucracy. Lenin takes issue with Kautsky's comparisons with Britain and the United States, insisting on attention to specific historical conditions. He writes,

> The revolutionary dictatorship of the proletariat is *violence* against the bourgeoisie; and the necessity of such violence is *particularly* called for, as Marx and Engels have repeatedly explained in detail (especially in *The Civil War in France* and in the preface to it), by the existence of *militarism and a bureaucracy.* But it is precisely these institutions that were *non-existent in Britain and America in the seventies, when Marx made his observations (they do* exist in Britain and in America now)![6]

In Russia, given the desperate struggle of the exploiters, it was necessary to disenfranchise the ruling classes.

There are also other works written by Lenin, both before and after Kautsky's attack, that are relevant to the problem of *The Dictatorship of the Proletariat in Russia.*[7] Altogether, Lenin's responses fall into three categories:

  (a) Lenin distinguishes between bourgeois and proletarian democracy.

  (b) Lenin considers the role of the peasantry.

  (c) Lenin deals with the problem of counterrevolution.

The first issue has already been discussed in the context of the October Revolution because the favorite argument of many bourgeois historians is to establish the dictatorial nature of the October seizure of power by pointing to the dismissal of the Constituent Assembly in January 1918. Lenin drew the distinction between bourgeois democracy as represented by the Provisional Government and the Constituent Assembly, and worker democracy as represented in the various soviets.[8] The Bolsheviks backed the soviets instead of the Constituent Assembly, based on their awareness that the soviets best represented the consciousness developed by the end of 1917. As already indicated, the superiority and genuine representativeness of the soviets and the fact that the Constituent Assembly was not the real organ of popular will were demonstrated by the absolute lack of public reaction to its dismissal—as admitted by bourgeois historians.[9]

Lenin went to great pains to elaborate the point that worker democracy needed different structures to express itself. The workers could not simply take over a bourgeois parliament and consider that the revolution was achieved; in fact, the whole apparatus serving the bourgeois state had to be destroyed and replaced by institutions which sprang from the working masses. This was one of the major points raised by Lenin in *The State and Revolution*.[10] The second point relating to the peasants was of crucial importance, because the peasants were the overwhelming majority of the Russian population—over 90 percent. Marx did not consider the peasantry as a revolutionary force. In fact, he tended to leave them out of his analyses of nineteenth-century Europe because he regarded the peasant as a social being in the process of disappearing: Peasants were becoming capitalists through their slow accumulation of capital, and the improvement of techniques since the Middle Ages. It was in peasant households that modern manufacture had developed. While a small number of peasants rose to become bourgeois, a far larger number eventually became members of the proletariat. The great majority of peasants in Western Europe were deprived of the opportunity of earning a living on the land and hence had to hire themselves out as laborers. At that point, they became workers or a proletariat in the modern sense.[11]

Changes in the mode of production were therefore creating a bourgeoisie out of peasants and proletarians out of peasants. Marx saw both the bourgeoisie and the proletariat as the classes to whom the future belonged. First, the bourgeoisie would take power from the feudal aristocrats, and then the proletariat would take over from the bourgeoisie and institute the dictatorship of the proletariat. In that scheme of things, Western European peasantry had no role. Marx's analysis corresponded to reality in a society like that of England, where the peasant had virtually been eliminated by enclosures and other means. However, Kautsky approached Russian society without any notion that his analysis should contemplate the contradictions between the peasants and the bourgeoisie that existed after February 1917. The editor of the 1964 edition of his book, J. H. Kautsky, who is very sympathetic, makes the point that "not once does Kautsky suggest that the Western pattern might not fit Russia; all his comparisons, even those regarding the peasantry, are with Western countries."[12]

The way that Kautsky ignored the peasantry was dogmatic indifference at its worst. It is not that Kautsky made an argument against the peasants—it just never entered his mind that the peasant was capable of actively participating in the revolutionary process and in the dictatorship of the proletariat. Lenin had carefully considered the role of the peasantry in his studies on the development of capitalism in nineteenth-century Russia. Several other writings and speeches addressed themselves to the role of the peasant in the revolution and in socialist reconstruction.[13]

On the basis of his assessment of the Russian peasantry, Lenin felt that the dictatorship of the proletariat in Russia would in fact be represented by an alliance of workers and peasants. What this meant was that there were contradictions between workers and peasants, but they were not antagonistic ones because their basic interests were the same and they were both considered the working people of Russia. The first concrete evidence of that alliance was that peasants should get their age-old ambitions fulfilled in the form of land. The second phase of the alliance was during the Civil War: The peasants sacrificed to feed the Red Army and the workers so as to ensure the victory of the revolution over its internal and external enemies. The third phase was the New Economic Policy (NEP), which was proclaimed in 1922 and continued after Lenin's death up to 1927. The NEP was a relaxation of the policy of War Communism, adopted during the Civil War, because that policy was asking the peasantry to bear all the burdens of the nation, and Lenin decided that their burdens should be lightened, even if it meant allowing certain capitalist tendencies until the workers in the towns were strong enough to supply the needs of the peasantry in a socialist manner. The fourth phase was one that Lenin did not live to see fully realized—it was the transformation of the peasants into workers within a collectivized and socialized agriculture. However, there were beginnings from 1921 right after the Civil War, and the principle Lenin followed was one that did not involve coercion of the peasant.[14] In line with his idea of an alliance of workers and peasants, the workers and the party were to set out to persuade the peasantry peacefully to adopt socialist forms of agriculture.

From the time that Lenin returned to Russia after the February Revolution, he cultivated both the soviets of workers and the soviets of peasants, and he paid particular attention to winning over the progressive members of the Socialist Revolutionary Party because they represented the poor and middle peasants, while the right-wing members of the same party spoke for the rich peasants and other landowners.[15] On the vital issue of the peasantry, Lenin showed his ability to translate Marxist theory into actual policy relevant to the conditions of Russia. This Kautsky did not attempt to do, and it is not surprising that this stand of Kautsky's is taken by bourgeois critics to be the essence of Marxism. It is always in the interests of bourgeois scholars to take Marxism as expressed in a rigid and dogmatic manner, because such dogma is then easily shown to be false when it is tested against experience.

Lenin also attacked Kautsky for failing to realize that a counterrevolutionary situation came into existence the moment that a revolution was made, and that one of the tasks of the revolution was to crush the counterrevolution at all costs. Kautsky seems to be saying that the undemocratic behavior of the Bolsheviks brought about the internal dissension known as the Civil War, which lasted from 1918 to 1921.[16] But the Civil War was nothing else but the counterrevolution. The armies fighting the Bolsheviks were tsarist supporters, armed and supplied by Britain, France, the United States and Japan. Such a reaction on the part of the tsarists and capitalists had nothing to do with the Constituent Assembly; it was a consequence of the fact that the revolution had expropriated their property and set up a system hostile to capitalism.[17]

As Lenin saw it, the dismissal of the Constituent Assembly and the fact that the bourgeoisie were disenfranchised in revolutionary Russia were necessary steps to ensure the dictatorship of the proletariat. If workers were to set up their own system of democracy, they had first to exclude the bourgeoisie, until such time as those bourgeois were transformed into workers. Furthermore, they had to deal harshly with all those elements who were plotting to bring about counterrevolution in one way or another. Immediately after the revolution, the dictatorship of the proletariat had to be a real dictatorship against the bourgeoisie. Within the context of the discussion as to what was "Marxist" and what was not, Lenin used as his authority statements made by Marx in his discussion of *The Civil War in France* (1871 Commune uprising) and remarks by Engels on the subject of "authority."[18] There Engels pointed out that the first act of the revolution must be to strengthen the state apparatus so as to deal with the enemy. To people who were arguing to the contrary, Engels said,

> Have these gentlemen ever seen a revolution? A Revolution is certainly the most authoritarian thing there is; it is the act whereby one part of the population imposes its will upon the other part by means of rifles, bayonets and cannon—authoritarian means; and if the victorious party does not want to have fought in vain, it must maintain this rule by means of the terror which its arms inspire in the reactionaries.[19]

Engels is taking "Revolution" to mean "armed revolution," and one could debate its relevance to a "non-violent revolution," but the accuracy of the statement can hardly be challenged with respect to revolutions such as the French, the Russian and the Chinese.

Kautsky's failure to perceive such an obvious truth—that the first task of the revolution is to guard against counterrevolutionary violence—needs to be explained. He simply was not a revolutionary, in spite of his profound involvement in Marxist thought. Kautsky was a theoretician, while Lenin was a revolutionary intellectual. Marx once wrote that bourgeois philosophers had set out to understand the world, but the real task was to change the world.[20] Individuals like Kautsky in Western Europe had ceased to entertain the revolutionary aspect of Marxism, and to all intents and purposes they had become bourgeois philosophers contemplating the world. Kautsky was representative of a school of thought known today as social democracy.

In the nineteenth century, the term social democracy included all Marxists. Up to 1904, the Russian Marxist party was also known as the Russian Social-Democratic Labour Party, and all Marxist parties were part of the Second International—a collective front of all European revolutionary worker parties.[21] However, the improvement in the standard of living of many Western European workers, based on colonial exploitation, caused their representatives to cease talking about revolution, and instead they began to follow the path of class collaboration with the bourgeoisie by the end of the last century. The foremost figure in this trend towards accommodating Marxism within the capitalist world was Eduard Bernstein, who is very often referred to in revolutionary Marxist circles as a "revisionist"—one who revised Marxist writings and took out the revolutionary content in the process.[22] It is interesting to note that Jean Jaurès, the well-known historian of the French Revolution, was also a revisionist social democrat who accepted a ministry in the cabinet of the French bourgeois government.[23] Not surprisingly, people like Jaurès took an opportunist line during the First World War and asked the workers to fight on behalf of capitalism and imperialism. Kautsky was not one of the founders of revisionism, but he gradually slipped into that position; the apparent rigidity of his Marxism in interpreting the Russian Revolution is a reflection of the debilitating effect of imperialism on the consciousness of Western European workers.

The old Social Democrats and the Second International suffered a steady decline in revolutionary zeal, until they ceased to be anything except bourgeois parties contesting bourgeois elections. The British Labour Party and the German Social Democrats are examples of parties whose ideological roots at one time lay in the working class, but who now alternate with other bourgeois parties in governing their countries according to capitalist principles, including the pursuit of colonial and imperialist objectives and support to fascist regimes such as those in Portugal, Greece and South Africa.

Consequently, if one asks what is today the historical view that social democracy has of the Russian Revolution, the answer would be that their view is identical with that of the bourgeoisie. Subsequent events have made clear that Kautsky's disagreements with the Bolsheviks in 1917 were not due to any personal errors on his part in interpreting Marxism; his inability to apply Marxism to a revolutionary situation was due to lack of commitment to revolution, which he shared as part of a new strata in Western European society: the imperialist worker elite and their intellectual spokesmen.

Rosa Luxemburg

It is not that every Marxist who disagreed with the Bolsheviks thereby ceased to be a Marxist, or became representative of a revisionist strain in Marxism. There is the example of Rosa Luxemburg, a revolutionary Marxist with genuine differences of position, opposed to those of the Bolsheviks. Born in Russian Poland, Luxemburg moved to Germany and became a genuine internationalist and revolutionary. An assistant to Kautsky in his better days, she made her contribution to the labor theory of value, capital accumulation, and imperialism in her book *The Accumulation of Capital.*

Her analysis of the Russian Revolution in English bears the title *The Russian Revolution and Leninism or Marxism?* She begins with an attack on Kautsky, who had suggested that the war would help bring about the fall of tsarism because German soldiers would free the oppressed peoples of Russia: "The freeing of Russia had its roots deep in the soil of its own land and was fully matured internally."[24] The war interrupted the revolution and then accelerated it. One way or another, it was acting on forces that were most obvious since 1905. In 1917,

> the sweeping march of events leaped in days and hours over distances that formerly, in France, took decades to traverse. In this, it became clear that Russia was realizing the result of a century of European development, and above all, that the revolution of 1917 was a direct continuation of that of 1905–7, and not a gift of the German "liberator." The movement of March 1917 linked itself directly onto the point where, ten years earlier, its work had broken off. The democratic republic was the complete, internally ripened product of the very onset of the revolution.[25]

On the question of the Constituent Assembly, Luxemburg supported an interpretation very close to that of Kautsky. Like the Bolsheviks, as the above quote indicates, she saw that the Revolution of February was the result of contradictions within Russian society that had matured by that time. She also agreed that the October Revolution was a logical necessity that was precipitated because the demand for peace and land set off the bourgeois elements. She continued to see eye to eye with Soviet and Trotskyist positions until October. As she put it, "The party of Lenin was the only one in Russia which grasped the true interest of the revolution in that first period."[26]

But she leveled a sharp and unremitting attack on what she thought were significant errors of the revolution. She attacked the Bolsheviks for dismissing the Constituent Assembly, which not only coincided with bourgeois interests, but enabled critics on the left to present her position as a challenge to the "authoritarian non-Marxist" Lenin.[27] Without attempting to impugn her Marxism, it is worth pointing out that it was Rosa Luxemburg who took a very authoritarian stand on major issues in Russia, which Lenin and the Bolsheviks had handled in a very democratic manner. She held the Bolsheviks responsible for the collapse and breakdown of Russia by encouraging nationalities, dismissing Lenin's "right of self-determination of nations" as "nothing but hollow petty-bourgeois phraseology and humbug."[28] And on the question of the land, for example, Luxemburg criticized the Bolshevik policy of redistribution to the peasantry on the grounds that it would simply reinforce private ownership and bar the way to development of socialist forms.[29] On strictly theoretical grounds, she was correct, but it was precisely in the interest of promoting a democratic alliance of workers and peasants that the Bolsheviks agreed to suspend collectivization of the land. In a similar way, Mao Zedong had to fulfill the wishes of the peasantry in China for individual land, and at a subsequent date deal with the problem of reeducating them to collectivize agriculture.

Luxemburg devoted much of her criticism to the question of democracy. She begins by acknowledging that the revolution was the first experience in proletarian dictatorship in world history, and to that extent an experiment. It occurred under the most difficult of conditions, and hence errors were to be expected. (The Soviet view, in contrast, is trite.) Indeed, her fear was that under the given circumstances of isolation in a backward economy, attempts at democracy and socialism were likely to be distorted. Luxemburg was, in effect, claiming that the Bolsheviks started off on the wrong foot. She insisted on the enfranchisement of all classes and saw the Constituent Assembly as essential.[30] However, criticisms about lack of democracy in the period 1918–19 are grossly overdone. What was the situation? Rival parties had been banned, the suffrage had been outlawed, and agencies of propaganda such as the press were controlled by the Bolsheviks. There was no regimentation affecting the majority of the people. Russia in those years was far removed from the totalitarian state. Such measures as were adopted to meet counter-revolution were entirely within the lines suggested by Engels. (Lenin was aware that it was an experiment.)

So Rosa Luxemburg was against democracy for the peasants, and she was against independence and autonomy for nationalities.[31] She was in favor of democracy for the bourgeoisie, refusing to agree with the Bolsheviks that they should be disenfranchised. This refusal to see that in a revolution one had to realize that a class opponent was a mortal enemy led to Luxemburg's own death. Her party in Germany was caught up in a revolutionary situation in 1919, and she was slow to act. Instead, the bourgeois reactionaries captured her and murdered her in cold blood.[32] That was the price that she paid for failing to recognize that a revolution is not a tea party. Her own subsequent experience tragically and cruelly exposes the limitations of her analysis of the Russian situation in 1918.

In a curious way, Luxemburg's criticisms had more relevance to the future than to the time she wrote. It was the long-term consequences of the dialectical relations between Lenin and the Central Committee, between the Central Committee and the members, between the bureaucracy and the people. Take the question of democratic representative institutions and the people. The living movement of the masses is a pressure on these institutions and gives them vitality. Only from the masses could one get the correction of shortcomings in social institutions. Furthermore, because the revolution and the dictatorship is an experiment, things must be done by trial and error, not by decree. People must not be obstructed in their improvisation and creativity. When the mass of people is alienated, bureaucracy grows, dictatorship emerges and there is "a brutalisation of public life."[33] This sort of prediction will be very important for assessing the period of Stalin's rule, and for relating it to the political ideas and institutions set up by Lenin.

7

Building the Socialist State

One of the most crucial tasks facing the Soviet regime was how to make the agrarian sector socialist. In 1917, the land was granted to peasants on the basis of individual ownership along capitalist lines. That had to be changed if the country was to become socialist. A dramatic attempt to transform the situation took place in 1929 and 1930, when the Soviet state embarked on a massive and enforced collectivization of agriculture. Within the peasantry itself, class stratification had been developing since the nineteenth century, and this was stimulated by the reforms after 1905. The same process continued after 1917, leading to the rise of a considerable number of rich peasants. This was the group that was most opposed to collectivization since they were already substantial capitalist farmers. Consequently, the Soviets decided to base their collectivization on the support of the poor and middle peasants, and Stalin announced a policy for the liquidation of the kulaks as a class.

Different types of collective farms were set up with the participation of the poor peasants, and a law was passed whereby a collective farm could take over the property of the kulaks in the district without their consent. The collectivization drive took place in the winter of 1929 and spring of 1930, and it was met with the determined opposition of the kulaks.

Violence spread throughout the countryside, and Stalin himself issued another order that brought forcible collectivization to a halt. In a famous speech, Stalin said that the collectivization campaign was marked by excesses, and that the people carrying it out had become dizzy from success, so that they lost their sense of proportion and engaged in activities which were not intended by the party and the government. In any event, numerous peasants lost their lives, and many others were deported to Siberia.

The tragic events of the forced collectivization of 1929–30 served as one of the main weapons in the arsenal of the bourgeoisie during the Cold War. Western historians never cease citing this as irrefutable evidence of the evils of Communism. Upon closer inspection, their claims are vulnerable to critique. First, there is a tendency to exaggerate the numbers involved. Jasny, for example, suggests that "perhaps two million peasants died," without attempting to provide any basis for his estimate. Second, bourgeois historians treat the kulaks as though they were innocent victims of some devilish plot, comparable to Hitler's attacks on Jews. Jasny goes so far as to deny that there were anything like kulaks, attributing the word to Soviet propaganda.[1]

The kulaks were a clearly recognizable sector within the peasant class. They owned a great deal of land compared to others who had little or none. They employed and exploited landless rural labor ruthlessly, renting farm equipment and animals to them at high prices and paying them very little. Kulaks were often the village moneylenders and charged high rates of interest. In that way, they came to take over the land and property of their debtors who could not pay.

A serious study of the peasantry will reveal that they cannot all be lumped together in the same category, and that the poor peasants suffer from real exploitation at the hands of the rich. This was the case in China too, as is very well brought out in William H. Hinton's outstanding book *Fanshen: A Documentary of Revolution in a Chinese Village*.[2] Because the poor peasant was so ruthlessly exploited by the rich peasant, he was very vindictive and ruthless when he got an opportunity to settle the score with his exploiters—and this opportunity came in Russia in 1929. It is quite clear that even the Bolshevik party did not realize what would happen when they directed the poor peasants to "liquidate the kulaks as a class."[3] Many poor peasants thought that this was a chance to liquidate the kulaks as human beings!

Most bourgeois historians dismiss Stalin's statement that the excesses of collectivization were not the policy of the Bolshevik party. Yet, if we examine the evidence of some of the most hostile bourgeois writers, we see that the violence was really something far beyond the party edict that stemmed from the bitterness that poor peasants felt towards kulaks. One example is that of Merle Fainsod. Secret documents containing accounts of collectivization in one of Russia's western provinces fell into the hands of US intelligence. Being a professor at the Russian Research Center at Harvard, Fainsod naturally had access to this material, on which he based a book, *Smolensk under Soviet Rule*. A small excerpt is found in Robert V. Daniels's edited collection *The Stalin Revolution: Fulfillment or Betrayal of Communism?*[4] There is little scope for quarrel with Fainsod's facts. He gives what appears to be a very accurate picture of the campaign against the kulaks, showing the seizures of property, the deportations, suicides among kulaks, and violence against their persons. He indirectly vindicates Stalin's claim that some people were dizzy from success in being able to turn the tables on the kulaks, writing that "despite apparently precise directives and instructions, many ... village authorities went their own way, interpreting the kulak category broadly to embrace middle and even poor peasants who were opposed to collectivization, and rarely bothering to supply supporting data to justify their decisions. In the first flush of the dekulakization campaign, excesses were commonplace."[5]

Fainsod goes on to give many minute examples of the violence to which kulaks were subjected. Kulaks were deprived of their clothing, shoes and warm underwear (sometimes stripped directly from their bodies), bonnets were taken from children's heads, food was taken straight from their pots, and their alcohol was consumed. The slogan of the dekulakization brigades of workers and poor peasants was "drink, eat, it's all ours." In one case a worker tore a warm blouse off a woman's back and put it on himself with the words, "You wore it long enough, now I will wear it."[6] Of course, Fainsod blames all the above things on Communism, but they could be much more accurately blamed on capitalist exploitation and oppression which had bred such hatred in the minds of those who suffered from it. The violence was part of the old and not of the new social system.

It is not possible for the bourgeoisie to understand the significance of the very facts that they present, because they do not know what exploitation and oppression means to the people who are the victims. The bourgeois writers present the kulak exploiters as poor sufferers who merit all our sympathy, while the peasants who beat them up are nothing but hooligans who were given the opportunity by Communists. We who have suffered from the same exploitation and oppression ought to be able to take a more understanding view of why the poor peasants wreaked personal vengeance on the kulaks and other well-to-do peasants. We can take a more compassionate view without necessarily saying that Stalin's policy was right or that the Bolshevik government should be free from blame. In the first place, it is the government that must shoulder all responsibility for acts committed by large numbers of its citizens, especially when those acts stemmed directly from laws passed by the government. In the second place, as socialists desirous of transforming a rural society into a socialist society, we have to take a stand against the use of force in this context. That is a matter of principle. It is all the more necessary that a socialist should reject the forced collectivization in the Russian case, because bourgeois writers state either explicitly or implicitly that such force is an integral part of socialist transformation.

The Marxist position is especially susceptible to this attack, because the notion of revolutionary violence is caricatured to mean violence at all times and places against opponents or those who disagree. In fact, revolutionary violence is the *social* violence that is necessary for the changeover of power from the hands of the bourgeoisie into the hands of the workers and the peasants. Once they have the power, a workers' government has to carry out the revolution by transforming society, and that is not done through violence.

Bourgeois historians may exaggerate the amount of violence associated with the collectivization of agriculture in Russia, and they might fail to understand the true significance of that violence as a reflection of capitalist exploitation. But a socialist can agree with them that the violence was undesirable.[7] Indeed, Soviet historians have for many years now been prepared to look at these events in a new light. Under Stalin, Soviet writers defended everything that he did. In subsequent years, a number of his policies came in for sharp criticism, including the way that he handled collectivization.[8] It is worth noting, however, that the Soviet criticisms concentrate on Stalin. They say his "dizzy with success" speech was an attempt to shift the blame on to local party officials, when he was responsible. The fact is that the whole party has to be held responsible.

The Soviet view is more enlightening when it points out how much Stalin departed from Lenin's position on the peasantry. Lenin had warned against undue haste, stressed the education of the peasants, and decided that collectivization should proceed in stages—from simple cooperation through common ownership of land and equipment and, finally, to communal production and consumption. Indeed, at the theoretical level and prior to 1929, the Bolshevik Party treated the peasant with great respect. Even the kulaks had been allowed to flourish, although Lenin believed that their activities should eventually be curtailed. But he quoted Engels to the effect that "perhaps it will not everywhere be necessary to suppress even the big peasant by force."[9] In any event, Lenin was determined that the middle peasant should be won over purely by persuasion, and one of the more unfortunate aspects of Stalin's policy was that the middle peasant was often treated in the same way as the kulaks.

Lenin translated theory into practice with the introduction of the *New Economic Policy*. Bourgeois writers invariably try to draw the implication that Stalin had to use force against the peasant since collectivization goes against the very nature of the peasantry. The assumption that underlies the work of most bourgeois writers on this subject is that Soviet collectivization was accomplished only because of force. Maurice Dobb, in his study of the Soviet economy, has effectively demonstrated that this assumption is false.[10] Coercion works only when coercion is consistently applied. As soon as it is removed, people cease to do what they were formerly forced to do. When Stalin relaxed the coercive measures, the result was that the great majority of peasant households that had been collectivized immediately decollectivized themselves. Different strategies had to be found to reenlist them in the collectives, relying on persuasion and economic incentives. That was the manner in which a more lasting and stable collectivization took place. So, the experience within the Soviet Union itself demonstrates that violence is inapplicable as a means of successful agrarian transformation. It is a complete reversal of the facts to say that the policy of dekulakization proved that collectivization can only be carried out by force. Besides, in the final analysis, all subsequent historical examples have conclusively demonstrated that bourgeois assumptions about the nature of the peasant are false. Because the peasant has historically been attached to private property, the bourgeoisie have claimed that he is by nature a capitalist and opposed to socialism. One bourgeois writer on the Russian Revolution, Leonard Schapiro, claimed that "what the peasant wanted was land, not socialism"—as though these two things were mutually exclusive.[11] The experience in China, Korea, Vietnam, Eastern Europe and Cuba has shown that the peasant can have the use of the land in a collective socialist form and be perfectly satisfied. The likelihood is that the African continent will in time produce other examples of the successful peaceful collectivization of agriculture and the institution of socialism in the agrarian sector.[12]

Another point on which bourgeois writers often lay stress is that the conditions of the rural masses in Russia were very depressed, and they present that as a consequence of Soviet policies. As will be shown later, it is true that Soviet policies favored industrialization. But it is certainly false to say that living conditions deteriorated under Soviet rule. The condition of the ordinary peasant under tsarist rule was miserable beyond words. Famine was endemic in the countryside, and all other interests were satisfied at the expense of the peasant. Infant mortality was extremely high, illiteracy was rampant and the life expectancy was low. All of these things were slowly but steadily remedied by the Soviet regime. To the extent that backwardness prevailed, it was precisely because so much backwardness had been inherited from the semi-feudal, semi-capitalist regime from which the regime took over.[13]

Underlying bourgeois historical writings on this issue is the assumption that the capitalist system is infinitely superior. Indeed, at most points of the evaluation, there is the implied comparison, especially since the whole object of the Cold War propaganda was to set up the capitalist system as a superior one. It is therefore very relevant to inquire how capitalism treated peasants. The answer is quite revealing. In Eastern Europe, the peasant was bounded off his land. Indescribable misery was caused by the enclosure movement and other devices that concentrated the land in the hands of big landlords. Outside of Europe, wherever Europeans established capitalist farming, they did so by expropriating the land of the indigenous peoples and often they virtually committed genocide. The latter applies with most force to the United States, while examples of crude treatment of the indigenous landowners are also to be found in South Africa, Australia, New Zealand, Kenya and Algeria.[14]

If bourgeois writers want to make a comparison between capitalism and the Soviet establishment of socialism, then they must include all points relevant to the comparison—that is, they must explain the historical genesis of capitalism. Doing so with reference to the peasantry and the establishment of capitalist agriculture would certainly make most of their criticisms of the Soviets sound extremely hollow.

Aspects of Soviet Industrial Transformation: Part I—The Soviet View

Marxist historians generally show a preference for *periodization*—namely, the setting up of time divisions that represent distinctive developments. According to the most recent Soviet writers, the process of economic transformation after the Civil War can be divided into three significant periods:[15]

(1) 1921–25, the period of rehabilitation
(2) 1926–32, the laying of the foundations of Socialist economy
(3) 1932–37/38, the completion of socialist economic reconstruction and victory of socialism

The first category speaks for itself. It was the period in which the Soviets had to rehabilitate an economy that had suffered four years of European war and two years of civil war. Russia was backward in 1913 on the eve of the First World War, but during that first period, the Soviet government was happy just to achieve the modest goal of returning to its 1913 output. By 1925, pre-war levels or near pre-war levels had been reached in agriculture and industry.

By 1926, an intense debate was underway over the manner by which the Soviet Union could escape from backwardness so as to equal and surpass its capitalist enemies. Soviet leaders decided to concentrate on industry as the only means of avoiding becoming an appendage of the capitalist world economy. In particular, they focused on *heavy* industry, namely the production of iron, coal, steel, engineering works, electrical power, petroleum and chemicals. These sectors were to be promoted at the expense of light industry and consumer goods, resulting in a tremendously high rate of investment. The first Five-Year plan (1928–33) called for the investment of between a quarter and a third of the national income in the economy as a whole. This was 2.5 times the rate of investment in pre-revolution Russia and twice that of pre-war Britain.[16]

The capital for investment came from internal sources. There were no foreign loans, and sacrifices had to be made to float internal loans. Above all, the existing industry and agriculture had to provide capital for investment. The amount of surplus grain and other agricultural produce had to be increased and either sold abroad or transferred to the urban areas to support the industrialization effort. But, the kulaks had control of 20 percent of the marketable surplus of grain, and they would much rather hoard their stocks or cut back production than release it cheaply to the state so that the state could accumulate capital. This was one reason why the kulaks had to be crushed and agriculture collectivized. The collectivization of agriculture was an integral part of the strategy of industrialization.[17]

All aspects of the economy were single-mindedly guided in the same direction because there was *central planning*. Thus, the financial institutions and foreign trade all served the same function of supporting industrialization and further developing the means of production. The Soviet Union exported farm products and other primary goods in exchange for machines, lathes, and plant and industrial materials.

Hundreds of enterprises were built between 1926 and 1933, and many old ones were rebuilt or renovated. In 1926, the gross output of heavy industry increased by 43.2 percent as compared with the previous year; in 1927 it went up 14 percent, and in 1928 by almost 25 percent.[18] The capitalist economies did not attain such high rates even in boom years, let alone in the late 1920s, when capitalism was on the brink of the crisis of 1929–33. There was a steep rise in the national income during this period. Podkolzin gives the following data: "If we take the 1913 national income at 100 per cent, we shall see that during the period under review it was as follows: 1926—103 per cent, 1927—110 per cent, 1928—119 per cent, 1929—138 per cent, 1930–167 per cent, 1931—195 per cent, 1932—217 per cent." National income was better distributed through the reduction of private ownership in industry from 10.5 percent to 0.5 percent, and at the same time unemployment was eliminated.

Achievements were possible because of a rise in labor productivity and drop in production costs and, in turn, living standards of the workers improved through increased wages, reduced unemployment, expansion of housing, and improvement in food access and quality. The net result of all the changes was the "transformation of the USSR from an agrarian country into an industrial power." This was envisaged in the first Five-Year Plan. Podkolzin quotes a German economist, Kraemer, who wrote at the time, "It would be grand if the five-year plan could be fulfilled in 50 years, but it is utopia." The working people of the Soviet Union gave the skeptics a lesson.[19]

Industry's share in the gross output increased from 48 percent in 1927–8 to 70 percent in 1932. At the end of the first five-year development plan, the USSR was second only to the United States in the level of world engineering output. Indeed, during the Great Depression, while the Soviet economy was advancing strongly, capitalism was suffering from crisis, which led to catastrophic falls in production. In the United States, industrial output decreased by 44 percent from the 1928 level, in Germany 45 percent, France 25 percent and Britain 20 percent. Not only were there quantitative changes, but also qualitative ones. In this regard, the improved location of industries proved to be of considerable importance. Before the revolution, Russia's industry was concentrated in the European part of the country. The first Five-Year Plan provided for large capital investments in the eastern areas.[20]

The evidence presented here by Soviet writers suggests the continued transformation of the economy along modern industrial lines. The first Five-Year Plan had been completed ahead of schedule (in four years) and so too was the second. Among its characteristics:

(1) More investments in armaments, owing to the threat of war.

(2) More attention to consumer goods, though heavy industry continued to take precedence.

(3) More investment in the Eastern regions (50 percent of new capital).

(4) More highly trained personnel accompanied by the "technical re-equipment" of the economy, particularly heavy industry.

(5) Some advances made in the rural economy, notably resolving some of the difficulties of collectivization and introducing large numbers of tractors.[21]

This list of achievements notwithstanding, it is difficult to see any real justification for drawing a distinction between the first and second five-year development plans. They both aimed at the same problems, and in the course of 8.5 years (1928–37) laid the foundations of a socialist economy. However, to say that socialism was actually achieved by 1937 or 1938 is very arbitrary. The same processes continued until World War II broke out in 1941, and the building of socialism resumed after the war. Thus, during the earlier period, the Soviets could only establish the foundations.

Marxists other than Soviet historians and economists have also taken an interest in the Soviet economy and in the arguments arising from Soviet transformation. One early example of a Marxist study made available in the West is Eugene Varga's *Two Systems: Socialist Economy and Capitalist Economy*. A Hungarian-born Marxist who emigrated to the Soviet Union in 1920, Varga completed his study of the Soviet economy in 1937 and had it translated and published in English in 1939. As the title indicates, the book compares Soviet development with capitalist development and uses statistical data to make his points. Here are some examples:

127

(1) In the Soviet Union, expansion of the means of production increased tenfold in the period spanning 1927 to 1936, while it remained the same level in the capitalist countries.

(2) Electrical energy from 1925 to 1935 increased eightfold in Russia and only twofold in Britain and Germany.

(3) For education, he gives increases in Russia relative to tsarist times. The number of elementary and secondary school children by 1937 had increased threefold since tsarist times; the number of university students had increased fourfold, and of those attending technical schools fivefold.[22]

Varga goes much further in emphasizing that the data conclusively proves the superiority of the socialist mode of production over the capitalist one. In line with Marxist theory, he proposes several principles that account for that superiority—the fundamental principle being that socialist production is rationally planned to supply people's wants. This contrast between the two systems has a number of consequences. First, socialism fully utilizes material and human productive resources, whereas capitalism does not. Capitalism cannot fully utilize its fixed capital or technological capacity because of depressions, limitations of the market, and various subterfuges in production. (During depressions, many factories go out of operation; factories cut back production when the market price is unfavorable; and inventions are shelved because they threaten established companies.) Capitalism cannot use all of its human resources because of "parasites" who exploit labor, and the "chronic mass army of the unemployed" who are superfluous and function to keep wages low and workers disciplined.[23] Second, socialism succeeded in eliminating what Varga calls "the tremendous faux frais of capitalist economy"—notably, periodic crises, competition, and advertising. Finally, the socialist planned economy promises a more rapid increase in the rate of accumulation and increase of production.[24]

Aspects of Soviet Industrial Transformation: Part II

The writing of history is not merely the work of historians. At the level of scholarship, a whole variety of social and even natural scientists are engaged in the writing of history. It is particularly noticeable within modern history that it is difficult and sometimes pointless to distinguish between historians, political scientists, sociologists and economists. This should already be evident since the writers under consideration in our study have been from several branches of the social sciences.

In dealing with Soviet industrialization and economic transformation, a number of arguments crop up that relate to economic theory. On the one hand, the validity of those theories are not dependent on an analysis of Soviet Russia. On the other hand, since the ultimate purpose of all theory is to apprehend and explain experience, then economic theory can be tested against the reality of the Soviet experience. That operation is itself part of the historical writings on the period.

One theory that has almost died as a result of the Russian Revolution is that socialist economics cannot work. Before the 1930s, bourgeois economists viewed a socialist economy as utopian because they could not conceive of a society different from the one based on the capitalist market. In 1938, Benjamin Lippincott made the following statements:

In the folklore of capitalism is the belief that a socialist economy is impracticable. Like many other beliefs in capitalist culture, this is widely held not only by the man in the street, but also by the economist. Of all the objections that have been raised against socialism, none have been more telling than this: that socialism cannot be worked out in practice. Men of goodwill might agree that a socialist state of the democratic type is superior to a capitalist state on social and moral grounds, but they have given little consideration to such a state, for they have assumed that it is impracticable.[25]

The concrete experience of Soviet economic transformation has shaken that aspect of bourgeois thinking, although it took time for the message to get home since most bourgeois scholars stubbornly resisted the new idea. According to one American economist, Harry G. Shaffer, it was not until after the Soviets launched their Sputnik in October 1957 that the Western world gave recognition to the practicality of Soviet Socialist achievement. In the introduction to his edited volume entitled *The Soviet Economy: A Collection of Western and Soviet Views*, Shaffer wrote,

> The widely-held view that a centrally planned, socialist economy could not function at all (and later the somewhat modified view that it could perhaps function, but at best very inadequately) deterred many social scientists from devoting their time and effort to the study of the USSR ... When the first sputnik began to orbit a sleepy globe, people all over the world awakened to the realization that an economic and military power had arisen in the East which presented a formidable challenge to the supremacy of the economic and political institutions of Western capitalist or semi-capitalist democracies.[26]

In effect, this bourgeois economist is making the very important admission that, as a consequence of the Russian Revolution, even the bourgeoisie has to take the socialist economic theory as something worthy of study, if only from the perspective that one studies a strong opponent.

Accepting that socialist theory is not pure fiction and utopianism also means accepting certain negative criticisms of the capitalist economy. This of course is unpalatable to the bourgeois economists, but socialist economists such as Oskar Lange and Maurice Dobb have been able to use the Soviet transformation as a model to renew Marx's own criticisms of the shortcomings of capitalism—such as fluctuations, severe depressions, unemployment and gross underutilization of human and technological potential. These attacks, coupled with the rise of the Soviet Union, China and North Korea, have put capitalist economic theory on the defensive. As Lippincott expressed it, the burden of proof has now been shifted to the capitalist economy to show why—in view of the demonstrable superiority of socialism—it must not be replaced by a socialist economy. Not surprisingly, on the question of the Soviet economy many bourgeois writers take up a very defensive position. On the collectivization issue, Western historiography has an aggressive ring and is quick to condemn Stalin's behavior. But on the economic issue, they are constantly on the defensive, trying to explain away why the socialist economy has shown capacities for growth unknown to capitalism, even though capitalists have exploited the whole world. Earlier, I maintained that the bourgeois writers had grudgingly accepted the facts concerning Soviet economic transformation. This is because they are caught in a dilemma where denial of the reality of socialism is no longer possible, and yet acceptance of that reality undermines the very basis of their own social system.

There are a few instances in which bourgeois writers give full credit to the Soviet achievements. One example is the British historian of Russia E. H. Carr, whose work on the 1917 revolution is also of high caliber. Carr's views can be cited at some length as a very reasonable introduction to the Soviet economy. In his book *1917: Before and After*, Carr writes,

Starting from a semi-literate population of starving peasants, [the Soviets] raised the USSR to the position of the second industrial country in the world and the leader in some of the most advanced technological developments, ... perhaps the most significant of all the achievements of the Russian revolution. Nor can the achievement be measured purely in material terms. In the time span of half a century, a population of almost 60 per cent urban has replaced a population more than 80 per cent peasant; a high standard of general education has replaced near illiteracy; social services have been built up . . . It would be wrong to minimize or condone the sufferings and the horrors inflicted on large sections of the Russian people in the process of transformation. But it would be idle to deny that the sum of human well-being and human opportunity in Russia today is immeasurably greater than it was fifty years ago.[27]

Most bourgeois writers make a number of qualifications before they accept the facts of the Soviet economic achievement. Alec Nove, for example, writes, "*Nonetheless*, no one can seriously doubt that the rapidity of industrial development and its peculiar challenge to the West are directly connected with the ideological beliefs of the Soviet leaders and their ability to impose the priority of growth on their subjects."[28] Likewise, American economist Harry Schwartz writes, "*Yet even after one allows for the propaganda exaggeration* . . . the magnitude of the Soviet production feat still commands attention as one of the fundamental events in modern history."[29] English geographer John C. Dewdney offers yet another set of qualifications meant to question the socialist system while acknowledging Soviet achievements. In his book *A Geography of the Soviet Union*, Dewdney writes,

> The Soviet Union has now been in existence for more than forty-five years and during that period the country has been transformed from one depending primarily on agriculture to the world's second greatest industrial power. The Soviet Union's achievements in the sphere of economic development have been very great and we should be unwise to delude ourselves by denying or minimizing this fact. At the same time, we should not make the opposite error of exaggerating the Soviet achievement and assuming that the rapid progress which has been made since the Revolution is due solely or even mainly to the superiority of the Communist system over alternative economic and political systems.[30]

At the time that the book was published, Dewdney was a professor of geography at Fourah Bay College, Sierra Leone; but his "we" means not "we, the Africans" but "we, the European bourgeoisie."

Dewdney gets into serious difficulties with his logic when he attempts to explain Soviet advances. The quotation above continues as follows:

> There is much truth in the assertion that economic development in the USSR over the past forty-five years has to a large degree been a process of "catching up" with the more advanced industrial powers and that the vast changes which have taken place are indicative of the backwards state of the country before the Revolution rather than a testimonial to the efficiency of Soviet planning as such.[31]

He sets out to explain why Russia advanced from being backward to a place of industrial prominence. The reason? Russia was very backward! How this fellow must have confused our brothers in Sierra Leone!

Bourgeois writers make a long list of qualifications of the Soviet industrial achievement, whether to reduce its impact or to show that socialism is not really superior to capitalism. The most important of those qualifications are listed below:

(1) Soviet statistics are queried.

(2) Soviet planning is criticized. Industrial growth is said to have been achieved at the expense of living standards.

(3) Forced labor was used on a large scale.

(4) Economic decisions were made on political grounds and hence irrational.

(5) There was unintelligent overwork to achieve fast rates.

(6) Developments were lopsided. Industrialization would have occurred regardless of whether there was a revolution.

We will take each of these critiques and qualifications in order.

Statistics

Some bourgeois writers claim that the government of the USSR deliberately falsified their economic statistics as economic propaganda to make people believe great progress occurred. Naum Jasny is in this camp. He argues that the Soviets falsified statistics in order to inflate growth rates and conceal declining levels of personal consumption.[32] However, most bourgeois writers no longer share Jasny's view. They argue that the manner in which Soviet statisticians compiled their figures was sometimes misleading. Schwartz, for example, points to methodological errors. First, in calculating the value of industrial production, Soviet statisticians did not take inflation into account, resulting in an exaggerated picture of industrial production in the 1930s. Moreover, the Soviet government retained the system of accounting even after the deficiency was discovered. Second, by shifting their accounting of crop output from net to gross basis, the Soviets deliberately or inadvertently hid losses incurred in harvesting and transporting. There is considerable literature on this subject, and on delving into it one finds that the bourgeois scholars have realized that Soviet statistics are not fabrications, and that any quarrel with them is on technical grounds. Thus, Alec Nove, in *The Soviet Economy*, asked "are the [Soviet] figures true or are they invented?" His answer was that "very few persons now believe that they were invented. The evidence against such a view is very strong. Despite captured documents, despite the presence in the West of various Soviet officials who had defected, no evidence exists that the central Soviet statisticians invent figures to order, to produce propaganda effect."[33] He then goes on to make several statements critical of the way Soviet statisticians compile their figures, but in the end this turns out to be a debate between professional statisticians on the best way to compile indices to reflect reality. And in this debate, Soviet statisticians also have a great deal to say on the shortcomings of bourgeois statistics.[34] The important thing to note is that the earlier Western view that the Soviets were simply falsifying their figures has now been largely overturned by their own research—some of which has been carried out by the US State Department.

Planning

Naum Jasny is also very hostile to the idea that the Soviet Union successfully demonstrated the role of central planning on economic development. He said in one of his last books that he had previously been fooled into accepting the Five-Year Plans as valid for periodization. Therefore, he replaces the five-year (or four-year) divisions with new time periods of his own, to which he gives attractive names, such as "Stalin has everything his way"! It is true that Jasny explains that while writing his book *Soviet Industrialization*, he was already over seventy-seven years of age and had only his pencil as an assistant, but that is no excuse for such crass subjectivism.[35] Jasny is representative of a school that is losing out, even with the bourgeois camp. Economists of different ideological persuasions have all come to accept or at least to pay lip service to the notion of central planning after its demonstrated capabilities in Soviet Russia. All "Third World" countries now have their Five-Year Plans, and the bourgeoisie is anxious to intervene and ensure that those plans are capitalist wherever possible. They cannot fight the idea of planning.

Alec Nove, while writing on Communist economic planning for the benefit of the American bourgeoisie, admitted that the Communist experience pointed to certain advantages of planning—such as avoiding recessions, coordinating investment decisions, and minimizing the waste of resources on advertising and consumer goods like cars and soft drinks. There is a fairly minor criticism made by Harry Schwartz of the Soviet plans, when he says that they were seldom accurate—some parts being overfulfilled and others underfulfilled. He compares overfulfillment to a train arriving and leaving ahead of schedule.[36] However, in most cases, a socialist society starts by setting modest and realistic goals in its plan, and then these can be overfulfilled by popular effort. This is entirely to the credit of the socialist revolution.

In Korea, there is a slogan called "Chollima speed," which is taken from Korean legend and means "to move at great speed." Korean workers usually fulfill the tasks set in their plans at Chollima speed. Time and time again, they were able to show overfulfillment of plans, and reported to Premier Kim Il Sung that they were working at Chollima speed. It was this Chollima speed with which the Koreans seized the US spy ship, the *Pueblo*, capturing the crew and all the sophisticated equipment that the imperialists were using to violate the sovereignty of the Korean people.[37] Once more, the superiority of socialism was on display.

On the Supposed Fall in Living Standards

In a short note on the question of comparing the Soviet and US economies, Harry Shaffer accused the Soviet Union of sacrificing food production for increased industrial capacity. Jasny, likewise, leveled similar vitriolic attacks, arguing that Soviet industrialization was accomplished by holding down consumption levels lower than anyone could believe possible. Industrialization was accomplished without its normal concomitant—the improvement of the living standards of the population.

Soviet historians deny that industrialization was accomplished at the expense of living standards. They point to wage increases, the elimination of unemployment, and the provision of social services. A prominent Western Marxist, Maurice Dobb, spent a great deal of time analyzing this problem, and he comes out in support of his Soviet colleagues. Dobb contends that while the first and second Five-Year Plans emphasized producer goods, they did allow for an increase in producer goods over tsarist-era levels, which had been restored by great effort after eight years of continual war. The goals of these plans were partially achieved, at least with respect to consumer goods. He points out that some targets for increased consumer goods were not reached because of external factors, such as adverse price movements and Western hostility. The latter caused a greater proportion of Soviet national effort to go into heavy industry for defense. The "kulak sabotage," or the destruction of grain and livestock in opposition to collectivization in 1932, also presumably resulted in the loss of a lot of agricultural stock. Dobb concludes that Russia succeeded in solving the problem of poverty in the years of transformation. It was not developing an economy based on the plentiful supply of consumer goods, as in capitalist countries, but providing the basic necessities the Russian masses previously lacked: food, shelter, clothing, schools, recreation, and so forth.[38]

A very curious factor in Jasny's analysis of the living standards of Soviet people is his singular concern with the purchasing power of wages vis-à-vis consumer goods. At no point does he take into account the major changes that had been made in the provision of social services, which previously were beyond the reach of the Russian working class.[39] When contrasted with this very sloppy kind of thinking, Dobb's presentation is very convincing.

Eugene Varga also makes a good case when comparing Soviet and Western living standards up to 1937. He compares Russia in the 1930s with its neighboring Eastern European countries, which were then still in semi-feudal conditions. In countries like Romania and Bulgaria, there were widespread reports of famine and people starving to death during the 1930s. (That, of course, was before those same countries took to the path of socialism). Varga also presents ample evidence of atrocious living conditions within capitalist countries and suggests that the condition of workers under capitalism must be judged not only by what went on in the metropoles, but by the conditions in places like Bombay, where Indian workers were also being exploited in the interest of world capitalism. For instance, he points out that during the Great Depression of 1929–32, capitalism in the Western countries succeeded in easing its position at the expense of colonies and economically weak countries. This last point is particularly vital and relevant to those of us in the parts of the world subjected to colonialism.[40]

When Schaffer said that Soviet industrialization sacrificed food production while capitalist industrialization was accompanied by increased food production, he was forgetting that Africa, Asia and Latin America were integral parts of the process by which Western Europe and North America became industrialized. Consequently, one must ask whether the industrialization was accompanied by increased food production in the total context. This question has to be answered in the negative. In fact, capitalist industrialization sacrificed food production within the exploited colonial areas so that raw materials could be sent to feed capitalist industries. The early period of industrialization in Europe was heavily dependent upon slavery in the Caribbean. While Britain was accumulating capital for industrialization through the profits of slave-grown sugar, the islands of the West Indies were made to concentrate almost exclusively on growing sugar rather than other staple foods. They became dependent upon the importation of food, and when the import was disrupted by war or any other eventuality, the people suffered famine.

Africa and Latin America are also very familiar with the food shortages and famine resulting from concentrating on crops like cotton, coffee and groundnuts. Gambia, a major rice producer before colonialism, had to import rice to relieve famine after the British colonialists had everybody growing groundnuts and cotton for export.

Similarly, within an international context, Jasny's assertion that improvement in the living standard of the population is the normal concomitant of capitalist industrialization is entirely false. Clearly, he knows nothing about the dark days of capitalism in Europe in the eighteenth and nineteenth centuries. He knows nothing, or does not care to know, about the living standards of black people in the United States both during and after slavery. He is entirely ignorant of the fact that the British promoted their cotton industry at India's expense. He was never told that Western industrialists in the late nineteenth century advanced on the shoulders of China to such an extent that they were deliberately trying to make the Chinese into a nation of dope addicts. And Jasny could scarcely have intended his comments about improved living standards to apply to the brutalization of peasants in Congo and South Africa—to name but two of the areas of vicious colonial exploitation in Africa.

All of the examples above are directly relevant to any attempt to make a comparative appraisal of socialist development within the Soviet Union and capitalist development elsewhere. In the years of socialist transformation, the Soviet people made tremendous sacrifices. This indeed has now been accepted by underdeveloped nations as one of the things they have to face up to in their own development. It was sacrifice based on self-reliance, while capitalist production has forced colonial peoples and workers in general to make sacrifices to develop the European bourgeoisie.[41]

Forced Labor

The charge concerning forced labor is quite an interesting one. It sets out to show that the Soviet system achieved so much, not because it was innately superior to capitalism, but because the Soviets used forced labor while capitalism relies on "free labor." The first thing to notice is that "free labor" means that the worker is theoretically free to refuse to work at all, or he can sell his labor to any employer. But in practice his choice is severely limited because otherwise he has no means of subsistence. (The criminal class is a small exception.) Socialist society demands that everyone should work as a right and a duty. This demand covers former bourgeois and any enemies of the state who are apprehended and imprisoned. It is mainly from this latter category that labor in the Soviet Union gained the reputation of having been "forced." In other words, it was alleged that the Soviet state had imprisoned huge numbers and put them to work in intolerable slave-like conditions.[42]

Schwartz has a lengthy section on the question of forced labor in the Soviet Union, especially in the period of transformation under discussion. He argues that there is an important element of coercion in all labor relations, and he cites, among other things, the fact that graduates of the Labour Reserve Schools, and of all universities and technical institutes, had to work for several years wherever the Soviet government assigned them.[43] On the basis of the same observation, one must conclude that there is an important element of coercion in Tanzanian labor relations.[44] Obviously, Schwartz could not appreciate that individuals educated by the workers and peasants had to place themselves at the disposal of the said classes after they had been educated. They could not even make the excuse that their own families had educated them, even though that in itself is a shallow excuse, for in a capitalist society it is the workers who permit the children of the bourgeoisie to be educated. Schwartz then proceeds to say that apart from the general coercion of all workers of all categories, there was the special coercion of prison labor. He mentions that in the early 1930s some foreigners were allowed to inspect the Soviet labor camps for prisoners and came back with reports that the picture had been exaggerated and distorted abroad. However, Schwartz feels that their evidence should be disregarded because the Soviets had time to alter conditions in any given area before the foreign inspection arrived. He concludes on the basis of reports from Soviet émigrés that "forced labor is a significant factor in the USSR's economy."[45]

There are two basic criticisms that can be made of the above view. First, it is strange that the capitalists who had encouraged slavery and forced labor for the last 500 years, both inside and outside their countries, should be so alarmed by prisoners being forced to work. Up to today, the jails of the southern states of the United States and of South Africa are full of prisoners who are there essentially because they belong to a given race. They are forced to work under the most brutal conditions and are dispatched like slaves to private firms to exploit their labor. Second, it can be argued that forced labor could not have industrialized Russia, since it is only effective in jobs of low skill. It can be used to get raw material for industry and to accumulate capital for industrialization, but in Tsarist Russia serf labor was not well suited to industrial development.[46]

Therefore, in Soviet Russia prison labor had a limited relevance to agriculture and related activities like timber cutting. This point is well brought out by the bourgeois economist Alec Nove, who feels that in so far as forced labor was used (as a by-product of political arrests) it was actually a disadvantage to the economy. He writes, "It is absurd to assert that the material achievements of the Soviet regime were directly attributable to terror and forced labor. Thus, it is no coincidence that the economic sector in which coercion played the greatest role—collective agriculture—remained the most backward."[47]

Jasny enters the debate on forced labor on a note of false sentimentality by complaining that the Soviet government forced women to work by law, even if this meant that a married woman would have to leave her family.[48] Jasny obviously feels that the woman's place is in the home—a view that is not accepted, even by women in the bourgeois societies. Today, this is a matter of considerable concern throughout the capitalist world, and women are mobilizing to advance their own interests. In fact, that sort of agitation started in the bourgeois world in the early part of this century, and the basic demands by militant women have been the right to work and the right to equal pay for such work—rights guaranteed by the socialist revolution.

Politically Inspired Irrationality

Some bourgeois writers put forward the view that the Soviet government makes certain decisions about the economy on purely political grounds that are economically unsound. Nove gives two examples of this. He says that Stalin put a lot of factories in the wrong place—removed from the source of their raw materials and hence having high operating costs. Secondly, Stalin started schemes such as "the plan to transform nature," which was an attempt to grow forest belts in previously unforested areas. In Nove's estimation, that sort of policy had more political motivation than economic sense. In fact, Nove dismisses it as the triumph of "politically inspired irrationality over economic common sense."[49]

In some ways, this is a minor criticism. Even if it were true, the Soviet economy nevertheless expanded. However, it is the expression of a very confused notion of economic development that is often exported to the underdeveloped countries. It must be dismissed as such, in our own interest of having a clear view of what the Soviet economy achieved. Nove was referring to factories that the Soviets built because they decided that industrial development should be evenly spread throughout the country. In some cases, a factory would use local products of an inferior quality rather than be dependent upon better supplies from another area that was already developed. In the short run, such projects might be "uneconomical" in the limited sense that their operating costs are higher than that of similar factories elsewhere. But in the long run, the project is part of an overall plan to raise the level of well-being in the district. Capitalist development has never

encouraged siting of factories with the motivation of benefiting the people of any given area. Factories are sited to make
maximum profits for the owner. Within capitalist countries,
there are usually serious discrepancies between the rate of
industrial development in different sections. At the moment,
Italy still provides an example of grossly uneven development
within a single country. While the North industrializes, the
South remains in rural backwardness. The result is that
Northern Italy continues to exploit the people of the South
and dominates them politically.[50]

In underdeveloped countries, bourgeois advisers have
long been deterring industrialization on the grounds that
according to "the law of comparative advantage," the underdeveloped country should specialize in agricultural produce
to which it is supposedly best suited, while developed countries should specialize in manufactured goods. According to
this argument, it is "uneconomical" for Tanzania to have a
textile mill because it could import cloth more cheaply from
Holland or Japan. Even assuming that the mill was more
expensive to operate than a similar factory in Europe, it still
remains true that for economic emancipation, the path of
industrialization will have to be started at some time—the
sooner the better.

Unintelligent Overwork

The charge is that Soviet progress during the first two Five-Year
plans was achieved through rapid but unintelligent work,
thereby jeopardizing future development. One example Nove
cites is that the Soviets extracted coal from the richest and most
accessible seams, in lieu of a long-term plan of balanced extrac-
tion.[51] He also alleges that machinery was brutalized and that
in the end this increased cost. It is quite possible that this criticism is largely or wholly true, for short-term production can
endanger long-term production. This has always been the case

143

with private capitalists who are concerned only with their own immediate profits, and not with the state of the environment they will hand down to later generations. For instance, timber dealers are often extremely indiscriminate in felling of trees that can take forty, fifty or one hundred years to grow. It is only in a few cases that bourgeois governments are wise enough and strong enough to enter the picture and regulate short-term production so that it will harmonize with the maximum protection of resources. Socialist development is in a much better position to carry out this regulation because the economy is planned.

To the extent that the Soviets did engage in short-term overwork in resources and machinery, this was because planning was then in its infancy. Today, planning techniques go up to twenty-five years, with five-year intervals, one-year programs, and monthly schedules.

Lopsided Development

The argument that the Soviet economy was lopsided bears a resemblance to the argument that it lowered living standards. It, too, presumes that the emphasis on heavy industry was so great that everything else suffered. Nove writes that "the economy has been stretched to the greatest possible extent in order to maximize industrial growth; this has led to a whole number of disproportions, which are becoming intolerable."[52] The only substance that lies behind this criticism is that the Soviet government did not produce consumer goods on the scale associated with capitalist metropolitan economies (especially the United States). Jasny notes that in 1955 only 1.5 motorcars existed in the Soviet Union for every 100 in the United States.[53] Quite apart from the fact that the American consumption level rests upon exploitation in Latin America, Asia, Africa and even Europe, it is very misleading to imagine that indices of consumer goods are any reflection of a country's development, especially since some of the "Third World" countries have extremely high rates of consumption.

Development comes through raising the level of productivity in such a way as to generate future growth and become self-sustaining. In a colonial economy, the manufacture of consumer goods is a slightly better alternative to the import of the same goods, but consumer goods industries remain dependent upon developed economies for their physical plant. They do not generate growth in other sectors of the economy, and they do not lead to the creation of a large technically skilled working class. At the present moment, the Soviet Union can concentrate on the extension of the production of consumer goods because it has the means to make the plant required. In other words, the Soviets have produced the means of production, and because they concentrated on that first, they triumphed. The very lopsidedness Westerners find problematic was a factor in their success.

It does not necessarily follow, however, that the Soviet model is the only path to socialist economic development. This was one of the wrong inferences drawn by some socialist scholars and Marxist revolutionaries. Subsequent experience in China has shown that, in contrast with the Soviet Union, emphasizing agriculture made more sense. In Korea, it was found that a balanced move forward in agriculture and light and heavy industries was possible, and desirable. Each revolutionary situation has to have solutions that fit the objective local conditions. In the case of the Soviet Union, it is difficult to conceptualize any alternative strategy that would have brought development with the rapidity necessary to make the first socialist revolution a reality in the teeth of the bourgeois opposition.

Transformation Would Have Occurred Anyhow

This point has been receiving increased attention from a number of bourgeois economists. It is the last place of refuge for the capitalists for hiding from the fact that the socialist mode of production is demonstrating its superiority over capitalism. By stating that the revolution would have occurred without the political revolution, they are trying to suggest that capitalist development can still continue in the present century, and that it has the capacity to transform a backward agrarian country into a modern industrial power.

The argument has a number of interrelated parts. Proponents pay attention to the industrialization process under tsarism, insisting that development was proceeding and Russia was on the path to greatness, were it not for the wars and the revolution. Here, of course, there is a marked similarity to the émigré position. By exaggerating the tsarist contribution and by minimizing the Soviet achievement, proponents conclude that there was a fairly constant line of development from the nineteenth century to the 1930s. The claim that the revolution brought about no real change is a classic technique of conservative historians. When de Tocqueville looked at the French Revolution and the ancien régime, he claimed that the two were intimately linked in that the revolutionaries were merely carrying through policies like administrative centralization, which had been followed by the French monarchs. Similarly, in looking at the French Revolution, Cobban says he sees no substantial change in the economic situation after 1789 or even in the nineteenth century. He himself has a very conservative interpretation, and it is not surprising that de Tocqueville was his model.[54]

Certain economic theories are peddled with a view to showing that every country independently comes to industrialization through stages. There is a slow evolution everywhere and then a "takeoff point." Once a country reaches the takeoff point, the economy then leap forward. W. W. Rostow is the eminent bourgeois theoretician of this point.[55] Accordingly, the bourgeois historians and economists contend that tsarism had reached the takeoff point, so that the transformation would have taken place without revolution, and the Russian people would have been better off since they would not have had to suffer under communism. The clearest example of the confusion inherent in this viewpoint is the work of Alex Nove. He writes, "We should not go so far as to attribute the industrialization of Russia wholly to the Communists, since the process would have gone on (albeit probably at a reduced pace and in different directions) without them."[56]

A little reflection will show that these very qualifications make the major premise meaningless. The notion of the rate of change is very important. Change is constantly occurring whether we like it or not, but economic development from backwardness to industrialization presupposes a rapidity of government-directed change at such a pace that other changes, both internally and externally, do not negate the efforts of transformation. For example, population growth and the depletion of certain natural resources are changes that are going on within the country, while technological changes going on outside the economy have a major impact on whether or not the economy develops. It is entirely possible for a country to increase its productivity and yet for its share of world trade to decrease, placing it in a worse position relative to the more developed economies. The Soviet Union had to compare its rate of growth with that of the capitalist countries. If their rate of growth was not rapid enough to catch up or surpassed them, then the socialist experiment would have been jeopardized. Even if their industrialization proceeded along capitalist lines, as Nove would have preferred, a slow rate of growth would still have jeopardized national sovereignty. Where would Russia have been in its capacity for self-defense by the time of Hitler's invasion?

Then the question of "direction" is perhaps more crucial. There is a world of difference between the direction of capitalism and the direction of socialism, especially when that capitalist growth was within the framework of imperialism. Before 1917, industry in Tsarist Russia was not merely capitalist; it belonged to foreign imperialists. Some figures have already been given concerning the level of British, French, German and Belgian investment in Russia before the First World War. It is worth noting that the proportion of foreign capital into textiles was 28 percent, in woodworking 37 percent, in metalworking 42 percent, in chemical industry 50 percent, and in the mining industry 91 percent.[57] The Soviet regime not only quantitatively increased industrial production, but it was all placed in the hands of the Russian people and not of foreign exploiters. One wonders whether in the industrial development envisaged by Nove there would have been a transfer from foreign capitalists to Russian capitalists. Nove gives the game away when he writes, "Nonetheless, no one can seriously doubt that the rapidity of industrial development, and its peculiar challenge to the West, are directly connected with the ideological belief of the Soviet leaders and their ability to impose the priorities of growth on this subject."[58] One can only assume that the alternative growth would have been slow and would have posed no challenge to Western capitalist interests in Russia or elsewhere.

The above historiography is directed as much to the "Third World" as to the citizens of capitalist countries. The message that they are trying to get across is that underdeveloped countries today need not take the socialist path, since they can develop just as well through capitalism. Nove makes the amazing statement that "the industrialization of China was held back by (and I agree) war, and would inevitably have followed the establishment of order under almost any conceivable government"![59] He is telling us that a government that did not take the land from the feudalists and that did not chase the foreign white devils out of China would have managed to make China the great power that it is today! Why then is there such a vast difference between India's and China's advances when they both had such similar histories before gaining political independence?

Today's most powerful industrial capitalist countries, such as the United States, Britain and Japan, developed in the eighteenth and nineteenth centuries through exploiting their own people and the resources of other lands. That option is no longer open to any young developing country. Today, the welfare of capitalism in America, Britain, Japan and so forth is incompatible with the development of colonized areas *even along capitalist lines*, because that development would mean the end of the parasitic relationship that is the essence of imperialism.[60]

To fully comprehend the problem, one has to realize the fundamental revolution in thought that Lenin brought about when analyzing the nature of imperialism. It was a revolution even within Marxist circles, and most of the criticisms made against Marxist thought as it is applied in the modern world can be forestalled by reference to what Lenin wrote on imperialism and on capitalism in this imperialist epoch. This can be illustrated with reference to the historical debate over the question of whether the outbreak of the revolution in backward Russia contradicted Marxist predictions.

It is held by most bourgeois writers that the very necessity with which the Bolsheviks were driven to transform the economy and society was proof that Marxist historical theory was incorrect, since Marx presupposed that socialist revolution would occur only in advanced industrial countries. One example is Klaus Mehnert's *Stalin vs Marx*.[61] The title itself reveals his conviction that the period of transformation in the Soviet Union basically conflicted with Marxism. At the root of his conceit lay the argument that the revolution had contradicted Marx's forecasts by breaking out not in a number of advanced countries, but in a single backward one. Hugh Trevor-Roper, a well-known conservative English historian, makes the same kind of criticism in an essay entitled "Karl Marx in the Study of History."[62]

The first level of analysis is to determine what Marx said or meant. At no point did Marx or Engels say that a revolution would not break out in a backward country, or that it would break out in a backward country only after it had occurred in the industrialized countries. As we have seen in chapter 2, in his 1875 essay "Social Relations in Russia," Engels painted a picture of tsarist society in which the contradictions were so sharp that he felt a revolution might break out at any time.

And in 1882, in their preface to the second Russian edition of the *Communist Manifesto,* Marx and Engels suggested that it was quite feasible and possible that Russia might have a revolution *before* the West. That was also in the context of discussing the Russian peasantry. Individuals like Mehnert, who make claims to the effect that nowhere does Marx or Engels discuss the peasantry and nowhere do they concede that revolution might take place in a backward country first, are guilty of a common bourgeois practice—the criticism of Marxism without ever having read Marxist texts.

The second level of analysis is to discuss not what Marx said, but what implications can be drawn by applying Marxist categories to the reality of the present century, for Marxism is not a finished and complete product contained in a given number of texts written by Marx and Engels. Marxism is a method and a world view. Neither Marx nor Engels believed their interpretations were unassailable given the limited amount of scientific and accurate data available to them, as well as their own human limitations. Furthermore, new situations arising after their time required new analyses. This is where Lenin made his major contribution, both in clarifying the position in Russia as well as enlightening us on imperialism.

There is no substitute for a careful reading of *Imperialism, the Highest Stage of Capitalism.* From his analysis of the nature of imperialism, Lenin concluded that by the time of the First World War, workers in the advanced countries had been lulled by the profits of exploitation carried on abroad, and that capitalism's principal contradiction was that between the bourgeoisie and the workers of countries like Russia—areas of investment for Western capital. The infusion of foreign capital is what made it possible for a "backward" country like Russia to move ahead to revolution before Britain and France. And the accuracy of Lenin's analysis has subsequently been borne out by the revolutionary process in Asia, Africa and Latin America.

8

The Transformation
of Empire

We are at the stage where we are talking about revolution as a process of *transformation*. When looking at Soviet industry in the last chapter, I noted that economic development was accompanied by regional unevenness and exploitation under capitalism, while in the Soviet Union there was a serious attempt to see that development was balanced over the whole area of the country. The question of balanced growth leads to another remarkable aspect of the social transformation of pre-revolutionary Russia: what can be termed the *transition from Russian imperialism to Soviet Federalism*. This is a transition that covers numerous fields, ranging from political structure and administration through industry and agriculture to education and culture. Before discussing the USSR and the national question in some depth, I will first briefly explore the character of tsarist-era colonialism under the following three headings: Russian Imperialism, Economic Exploitation, and Cultural Domination.

Russian Imperialism

By "Russian imperialism," I do not mean Russia's attempts to expand and to invest capital in countries such as Turkey,

Afghanistan and Manchuria. Certainly, this was a feature of the Tsarist Empire that ended with the revolution, but for our purposes we need to look more broadly at the structure of the Tsarist Russian state, which was built on the principal of colonial and imperialist domination. Here in Africa, given our own colonial experience, we automatically tend to think of colonialism and empire as related to overseas expansion, with Britain and France as the main culprits. However, we must also consider colonial domination as an overland annexation process, with one state colonizing its neighbors. This is precisely what prevailed throughout Central and Eastern Europe and in the Near East, from the Middle Ages right up to the nineteenth and twentieth centuries. The three great empires were those of Turkey, Austria and Russia.

There was a group of people known as Russians, who ruled over Finns, Poles, Latvians, Lithuanians, Georgians, Ukrainians, Armenians, Mongolians, and Turks, to name just a few.[1] The Russians monopolized political power and sent their governors and settlers into the countries of these other peoples. As in all colonial states, there was a legal distinction between the citizen (Russian) and the colonial subject.[2] The constitution of Tsarist Russia explicitly based discriminatory measures on the racial or national origin or religion of those affected. It was in some ways like the distinctions made under Portuguese and Belgian colonialism, and under South African and Rhodesian apartheid. In other words, Russian colonial rule hardly differed from that of the Western European powers. The British sent warships; the Russians sent the Cossacks. When its colonial subjects revolted, as Georgian workers and peasants had during the 1905 Revolution, the tsar, as we've seen, agreed to a few minor reforms but ultimately crushed the uprising and reverted to the old system of colonialism.

Economic Exploitation

A primary catalyst for Russian expansion was economic exploitation, for that is what colonialism is all about. The tsarist regime exploited the land and labor of the people, and as I hinted above, it sent Russian colonists who directly expropriated the land of the people in the colonies. By the late nineteenth century, Russia could be called imperialist, not only in the Old Roman sense by which a collection of colonies becomes an empire, but in the Leninist sense in which the investment of capital is the key element in the imperialist relation. Great Russians were investing capital in other areas of the country and taking the profits from those regions for their own accumulation. For example, landlords and capitalists invested in grain production in European Russia and Siberia; capitalists invested in cotton production and oil in Central Asia; and Russian and Western European capitalists invested in railroads and ports in the Far East, notably the Trans-Siberian Railway.[3]

Cultural Domination

Every colonial relationship in history has involved cultural domination, namely the imposition of language, religion and way of life on the subjugated peoples. In the Russian Empire, there were numerous other religions apart from the Russian Orthodox church. None of these were respected. The Catholics in Polish Russia were persecuted. The Jews were hounded wherever they were found, especially in the Ukraine. The Muslims were treated as enemies of Christian civilization. And those elements of the population who believed in their own family gods and traditional religion were the most despised of all, in the same way that European missionaries came to Africa and denounced African religion as devil worship and black magic.

Some of the peoples of the Russian Empire were socially and economically weak. Their material level of existence was low, they lived in small communities, and they lacked organization and weapons to defend their existence. Such was the case with the nomadic groups in Soviet Asia and with the hunters and fishermen of the Arctic. When faced with a more technologically advanced culture, such groups were victims of genocidal policies. This is what happened to the Indians in America, the Aborigines in Australia, and the Bushmen in South Africa. The same type of process was underway in the Russian Empire based on the cultural and economic imperialism of the Great Russians. Great Russians exploited the Yakuts to get furs but made no attempt to give them part of the civilization about which they boasted (just as in Africa). They did not build schools or health centers or facilities for the advancement of the colonized peoples. If someone saw a school somewhere in Soviet Central Asia, one could be quite sure that it was for the children of the Russian settlers who were taught in Russian, which was unintelligible to the local people. Incidentally, this cultural superiority readily gave way to *racism*. Inherent superiority is a good excuse for suppression.[4]

The USSR

At the constitutional level, there were a number of experiments leading up to the Constitution of 1936, which, with small modifications, constitute the basis of the present state. All the constitutions leading up to 1936 explicitly establish and confirm the principle of equality of all citizens of the USSR, irrespective of race and nationality. Constitutions and laws do not necessarily reflect actual social relations, so in and of themselves they cannot guarantee absolute equality and the elimination of discrimination in the Soviet Union. Yet, it is interesting to note that the American bourgeoisie is reluctant to grant even the legislation that will establish the principle of racial equality.[5]

As a federal republic, the basic constituents are the individual republics. However, at a lower level, a great variety of political and administrative structures are set up precisely for the purpose of guaranteeing the free political, economic and cultural development of each nationality. Administrative autonomy ensured a degree of self-rule and self-reliance. In other words, local government was important. However, none of these forms were fixed. They kept shifting them, experimenting, and trying to find forms to fit the process of transformation. Not surprisingly, these frequent constitutional and legal modifications did not settle down until 1936.

Behind all of this was the principle expressed in Lenin's *The State and Revolution*: that the old state machine, which was built for particular purposes, had to be destroyed and replaced by a new one.[6] Third World examples of new state forms include the People's Court in Zanzibar, the judiciary in Ghana and Zambia, the one-party state here in Tanzania, and the new revolutionary structures arising in Vietnam and Mozambique. In the USSR, the new state forms promoted balanced economic development, not just in industry but in agriculture. Economic changes obliged the state to help people adapt to the new arrangements, as some moved from peasant to proletariat, while others shifted from nomadism to sedentary agriculture. The new constitution tried to be attentive to cultural difference. All languages were encouraged. More than forty groups only had oral languages; thus creating written languages for all nationalities and ethnic groups was among the state's immediate tasks. These languages were enshrined in schools, in courts of law, and in literature.

Nationalities were granted control over particular soviets, oblasts[7] or occasionally republics. This was often done by identifying various subjugated groups and their relationship to one another. In many instances, extending self-governance to nationalities had the effect of ending sub-imperialism (for instance, Tatars exploiting Bashkirs). The transformation of education was the most important aspect of Soviet reforms. With its emphasis on scientific analysis, education provided skills for self-administration (localization) and permitted all groups to participate in the national life.

The National Question

The nationality question represents an area of historiography that mirrors many of the chief ideological differences discussed in earlier chapters. While both Marxist and bourgeois historians have tackled the question, the study of nationalities is predominantly a sphere of bourgeois scholarship. It follows, therefore, that bourgeois treatment of the subject is hostile to the Bolsheviks in 1917 and to the subsequent formation of the Soviet state. The Cold War, after all, was an intense period of class struggle. The importance of the subject is evident in the quantity of work produced by bourgeois scholars. Taken as a whole, these writers raise three sets of points. First, they make a case for the wide variety of peoples in Tsarist Russia, pointing to the huge number of linguistic, ethnic and cultural groups, to the several religions, and to the various political and administrative structures. Second, they emphasize the significance of tsarist policies toward nationalities and how they were related to the outbreak of both the February and October Revolutions in 1917, and to civil war. And finally, these writers critically examine the nature of Soviet policy towards the nationalities and minorities throughout the former empire.

The first point is very crucial, given the striking heterogeneity of the Russian state: from Petrograd to Astrakhan (Caspian Sea and Muslim culture)—tribes worship bears and trees in the Siberian forests and tundra. The USSR inherited an empire populated by all varieties of Europeans and Asians (Caucasus, the locus classicus of the European type; Eskimos, Mongols, Tungus, and Fakuts; Persians, Afghanis, Chinese, and Japanese), living under a range of political systems, from European feudalism and Oriental despotism, to small clans and bands. The physical landscape was equally diverse, ranging from forest to steppe to desert, perpetually snow covered; it was subject to intensive agriculture, nomadic pastoralism, hunter-gatherers, or simply "a thousand and one ways of starving to death."[8]

The effect of the combination of these factors depended on historical circumstances. The Western or European section of Russia was first peopled by Finns and Slavs, and later expanded with the influx of Scandinavians by the ninth century. The Tatar wave followed, which was pushed back from the sixteenth century by the Great Russians under the tsar. This process of Russian/Slavic expansion was taking place right up to the end of the empire in various ways, in the form of conquest as well as through relatively peaceful colonization. Expansion was comparable in some respects with American westward settlement, but in most cases it was distinctly *colonial*: direct rule, indirect rule, settlers (Cossacks), one-crop economies and exploitation of major natural resources (primarily minerals and timber) by extractive industries. Hence the state under tsarism took on a distinctly colonial character. The core settlers were Europeans, Orthodox Christians, who extended their control over other Europeans, including Finns and Poles (the latter being Catholic), and ultimately over the rest of the *empire* to the east. The main conclusion that one could draw from all this is that for non-Russian peoples, the struggle against tsarism was often indistinguishable from the struggle against Russian rule and Russian settlers in their country. This expansion was fundamental to the history of Russian Empire, and pointing to these features and saying that they have some relevance to the Russian Revolution is itself an incontestable historiographical service. Yet so many historians are concerned only with Moscow and Petrograd.[9]

What were the relations between these phenomena and the Russian Revolution, or rather, what do historians say was the relation and how do their interpretations differ? As I suggested at the outset, the bourgeois presentation is hostile to the Soviets on this as on virtually every other subject. Soviet historiography has itself shown contradictions in characterizing the struggle of the minorities, beginning in the tsarist period—was it a national struggle or a class struggle or both? What was the nature of tsarist rule over these minorities? Western historians like Frederick Barghoorn and Richard Pierce point out that Soviet historians have been changing their minds on this issue.[10] After the revolution, Soviet historians described Russian conquest of Central Asia as having resulted in a double oppression—a national-colonial oppression based on the bayonets of the Russian military's feudal imperialism, and the feudal oppression of the upper classes. In Central Asia and elsewhere, tsarist policy delayed the cultural growth of non-Russians. Tsarist Russia was "a prison of nations."[11] Consequently, only revolt offered the promise of improving what was clearly an intolerable state of affairs. The uprisings of the toilers, striking back at the system of colonial oppression imposed upon them by tsarism and at the feudal oppression of their own upper classes, were therefore portrayed sympathetically as national liberation movements.

In the 1930s and '40s, Soviet historians underwent a change. The object was to stress national unity and patriotism, and it was essential to underplay the former exploitation carried out by Russian peoples over non-Russians. In fact, the pendulum swung so far that no praise was found to be too abundant for the Great Russian people, thus inaugurating an official policy of Great Russian chauvinism. The party agreed that more attention should be paid to the history of the non-Russian peoples of the Soviet Union, but also that the critique of tsarist plunder and exploitation of non-Russians be mollified. Tsarism was portrayed as a lesser evil than the straightforward continuation of native rule. Association with Russia accelerated bourgeois and capitalist relations in Central Asia and the Far East. Russians and non-Russians were sharing a common historical fate. Soviet historians began to stress that along with the tsarist soldiers and officials came Russian workers, scientists, doctors and teachers who played a great cultural and revolutionary role in the life of the peoples of Asia. By 1951, the Russian "annexation" became a positive good. Uprisings could no longer be portrayed indiscriminately as national liberation movements. Instead, a fine distinction was drawn between uprisings directed against Russians—which were invariably "reactionary," either fostered by feudal elements in native society or instigated and supported by foreign elements (the period of civil war)—and those directed solely against the native exploiter class.[12]

Barghoorn's criticism is that the Soviets were trying to deny the validity of sentiments such as nationalism, but that they themselves, while ostensibly internationalists, were actually urging patriotism and nationalism at the broader level. Most of his remarks are about Stalin's period.[13] Pierce is more relevant. He says that both the imperial government and the Russians as people had failed to win the "friendship and trust of peoples of Central Asia." Indeed, he takes the side of the imperial regime by insisting on the benefits of colonialism and the development of a new middle class of modernizers in the provinces. He is part of the school suggesting that things were improving in Russia until the war intervened. He also sees the Bolsheviks as a determined minority—"small but resolute dissident groups"[14]—reminiscent of early colonial talk about "seditious handfuls" and "agitators," of Southern Rhodesian and Portuguese propaganda that everything would be fine were it not for a minority of "terrorists," and of President Lyndon Johnson's explanation for the black revolt in the United States. Pierce's work comes close to being an apologia for tsarist imperialism, and to explaining the revolution in terms other than the exploitation of the tsarist system.

Richard Pipes wrote the major work on the subject of nationalities and the Russian Revolution.[15] He contends that the nationality question deserves treatment as an extremely important facet of the revolution. A section of Arthur Adams's anthology *The Russian Revolution and Bolshevik Victory* asks the question, "Why did Russia Seek Ever more Radical Solutions" between March and October? Pipes's answer, enshrined in the title of his essay, is that "national minorities sought autonomy and independence."[16] This was crucial. Pipes, therefore, is concerned with the period after March 1917, but he does deal with tsarist policies, and one of his major contributions is to link colonial policy with the revolution. He points out that the era of Russification under Alexander III coincided with the period of greatest governmental reaction, during which the Great Russian population itself lost many of the rights it had acquired during the reforms of Alexander II. The national movement among minorities represented one of the many forms assumed by intellectual and social ferment. It was also part of the general populist movement. The growth of the national movements in Russia during 1917, and especially the unexpected rapid development of political aspirations on the part of the minorities, was caused largely by the same factors that, in Russia proper, made possible the triumph of Bolshevism: popular restlessness, the demand for land and peace, and the inability of the democratic government to provide firm authority.[17]

Bourgeois scholarship on the nationality question treats national governments in 1917 as particularly weak, succumbing to Bolshevik armed forces without much resistance. Accordingly, the rupture between nationalists and Bolsheviks would probably have been permanent had it not been for the White Russians who drove the nationalities into the hands of the Bolsheviks. The Bolshevik program was designed to win nationalist sympathies by generous offers of national self-determination wherever possible. They made alliances with the most reactionary groups among the minorities. After overcoming the enemy, Bolsheviks could not honor their promises, especially since they were hindered by ideological preconceptions.[18]

Bourgeois writers place a halo around the concept of nationalism and either imply or claim explicitly that it was more important than class in 1917 and after. But wherever classes developed—a process involving the vast proportion of the population—the class struggle went on. To this extent the Soviet writers are correct. Wherever the proletariat was—in Ukraine, in Georgia, the Urals, Central Asia or the Pacific, they generally supported left parties, and as the revolution unfolded favored the Bolsheviks. The peasantry reacted as peasantry all over the empire—all the poor peasants gravitated toward the Socialist Revolutionaries, heirs of the Narodnik tradition. Maria Spirodnova, one of Russia's most popular revolutionaries who had spent eleven years in a Siberian prison for assassinating a police official, led the left SRs into an alliance with the Bolsheviks. In effect, the basic and crucial responses of the peasantry were all alike; they were not based on language, nationality or religion, but on class interests, and this continued to be so during the New Economic Policy and throughout Stalin's rule.

Likewise, the landlord class, whether it was European or Asian or kulak, or from the Black Sea region or Siberia, operated according to its interests. And the same could be said about the bourgeoisie, whether from Poland (in Russia) or Turkestan, Catholic or Muslim ("clink, clink" in any language[19]). Civil war displayed the international nature of class phenomena: capitalist powers plus rulers in each locality versus workers and peasants.

All parties had support in most regions in 1917—the Cadets, SRs, Mensheviks and Bolsheviks. Local grievances were registered through the major parties rather than through the locally based, nationalist-oriented parties. For the Constituent Assembly, nationalist parties received few votes, and in some areas, like Belorussia, there was no nationalist party at all. Certainly, ethnic feelings at no time erased the class struggle. Yet, as Pipes writes, "to admit that under some circumstances the economic interests of a society could correspond with its cultural divisions was essentially contrary to Marx's entire system."[20] Marx said precisely the opposite: that different economic systems would produce different cultures, as was true of the Russian empire. Pipes also supports Luxemburg's critique of the Bolsheviks on the national question as "the strict Marxian approach."[21] But as we have seen in the previous chapter, her interpretation that nationalism was a bourgeois phenomenon was dogmatic. It happened to be so in Western Europe. Lenin's support was much more realistic and relevant to conditions in the world at the time.

From the viewpoint of the national question, the world could be divided into three areas: (1) the West, where the problem of nationalism appears to have been solved because each nationality had its own state under bourgeois rule; (2) Eastern Europe, where the process of capitalist development and the national state were only in their formative stage; and (3) the colonial and semi-colonial areas where capitalism and nationalism had barely penetrated. Lenin saw that nationalism was always associated with capitalist development, but was not always favorable to the bourgeoisie. On the contrary, the struggle in the colonies could be expected to assume national forms, which would challenge the bourgeoisie of the imperialist countries. He called the colonies a vast reservoir of potential allies of socialism against imperialism and was particularly interested in the national democratic revolution in Asia.[22] Lenin was right because he applied Marxist analysis to the relevant facts, but few Marxists are consistent with this, and it is significant that the black revolt has been treated similarly (see Richard Wright, Aimé Césaire, and George Padmore).[23] Then reactionaries turn around and say it is *race, not class*. Another criticism is that Bolsheviks used national sentiment in the same way that they used grievances of bread, land, and peace for their own ends.

The right to self-determination is the crucial thing here. For Pipes, the question that confronted Lenin after he had come to power was how to balance the right of national self-determination with the need for preserving the unity of the Soviet state. The Bolshevik program was designed to win nationalist sympathies by generous offers of national self-determination. Wherever possible, they made alliances with even the most reactionary groups among the minorities (generally deemed opportunism, although Mao would see this as a democratic front to overcome the principal contradiction). But when national self-determination threatened efforts to consolidate the Soviet state, Lenin used local Bolshevik organs and the army to overthrow, wherever possible, newly formed national republics. This was regarded as a complete violation of the principle of national self-determination. Besides Pipes's work, these claims are raised in particular with regard to the Ukraine, Georgia, and Soviet Central Asia.[24]

In rebutting these criticisms, one should bear two things in mind. First, that the right of secession was granted and respected as the ultimate right of a Soviet republic. But it had to have borders on the outside to avoid the anomaly of an independent country surrounded by another. Hence, it was granted to the Baltic republics but never to Georgia. As a corollary to the above, each group had to accept the full authority of the central government so long as it did not secede. There could be no half in and half out. Second, class struggle was ongoing in each region. The Soviets granted independence to the Baltic and Finnish states, for example, and the workers crushed it. In Ukraine, on the other hand, where workers were engaged in a bitter struggle, Lenin did not propose to give them up to the bourgeoisie aided by Germany. Ukraine was the basic example of counterrevolution trying to hide behind the bush of nationalism. Pipes argued that the Soviets, in spreading their authority, were inclined to use forces hostile to minority interests. In Ukraine, therefore, the Soviets favored the industrial proletariat, which was by ethnic origin and sympathy oriented toward Russia and inimical to the strivings of the local peasantry, which had wanted to resolve their land problem independently of Russia. A large number of colonists went over to the Bolsheviks when it became clear that the proletarian slogans could be turned against the local peasants.[25]

In June, the Ukrainians got a semi-autonomous constitution from the Provisional Government (Rada). "The four months separating the June agreement from the October Revolution was a period of progressive disintegration of the Ukrainian national movement, marked by indecision, by internal quarrels, by unprincipled opportunism, above all, by an ever-widening gulf between the masses of the population and the politicians who aspired to represent them." Pipes continues,

> In mid-July, the First All-Ukrainian Workers' Congress convened in Kiev by the Rada proved to be very critical of the existing Ukrainian institutions and condemned the Rada for displaying bourgeois tendencies. In general, its whole temper was closer to that of the Bolsheviks than to the spirit fostered by the Ukrainian national parties to which most of the delegates belonged.[26]

It is in this context that Lenin and the Bolsheviks decided to support the workers in Ukraine, bearing in mind the examples of the Baltic states. The Ukraine became an independent workers' republic associated as part of the federation.

With respect to Jews, while they were subjected to pogroms and suffered great restrictions and liabilities, they reacted according to their class—merchants on the one hand, the Jewish bund on the other. Martov, Trotsky, Marx and Engels all noted the perpetual contradictions of the Jewish position. Some historians challenged the achievements of the Soviets and argued that European Russians continued to exploit Soviet Asia. From the viewpoint of self-rule, according to Pipes, the Communist government was even less generous to minorities than was the tsar. It destroyed independent parties, tribal self-rule, and cultural institutions. But most parties represented landowners' interests, and "self-rule" was really indirect rule under the tsar, and thus reactionary and unpopular.

What is needed is an analysis of social formations in the context of uneven development: nomadic pastoralists of Central Asia, mountain peoples of the Caucasus and Urals, and the extent of their isolationism, individualism, and anti-plains mentality. Indeed, we witness something akin to the Soviet approach in Tanzania—drawing people into a money economy; stopping groups from starving; extension of the market economy with furs and fishing, milk and meat.[27] (Consider the quiet revolution taking place on Lake Victoria with motor boats and refrigeration.) From our point of view, this aspect of historiography could be more developed, as opposed to either analysis of class conflict or the emphasis on industrial transformation, hydroelectric plants, new railways, and huge chemical industries.

Ultimately, Marxists have to take the subject of nationalism seriously. Marxist internationalists see nationalism as bourgeois and reactionary based on a narrow interpretation of what Marx said. For Lenin, the role of nationalism depends on objective conditions, and his analysis is still relevant.

9

The Critique of Stalinism

Another criticism that stems from the claim that the outbreak of the Russian Revolution contradicted Marxism by occurring in a backward country is the assertion that, in transforming Russian society, ideology and leadership took the dominant role. Marx said that ideology and political leadership were part of a society's superstructure and were dependent upon its base—that is, upon the mode of production. Bourgeois critics argue that under Stalin the roles were reversed: instead of the base affecting the superstructure it was the superstructure that transformed the base. Consciousness had preceded material reality and had thereby disproved dialectical materialism.

Once more, this criticism can be met at two levels. Firstly, what did Marx and Engels say? And secondly, how would a Marxist apply their analysis? Marx and Engels undoubtedly stressed the economic or material base as the major determining force in human history, but this does not mean that there was a one-way relationship between matter and consciousness. Marx indicates this when he says that consciousness at any given time is a reflection of the mode of production plus those ideas inherited from the past. Consciousness at any given moment is more than a passive reflection of the *current* mode of production. Furthermore, ideas (from wherever derived) interact with the material base.[1]

Marx and Engels explicitly warned against using the materialist conception in any crude way that was to suggest that the dialectic was only one-sided—with matter affecting consciousness and not the other way around. After Marx died, Engels had cause to caution other people who called themselves Marxists against applying the dialectic mechanically. In a letter to Joseph Bloch written in 1890, Engels wrote,

> According to the materialist conception of history, the ultimately determining element in history is the production and reproduction of real life. More than this neither Marx nor I have ever asserted. Hence if somebody twists this into saying that the economic development is the only determining one, he transforms that proposition into a meaningless, abstract, senseless phrase. The economic situation is the basis, but the various elements of the superstructure: political forms of the class struggle and its results ... also exercise their influence upon the course of the historical struggles and in many cases preponderate in determining their form. We make history ourselves, but, in the first place, under very definite assumptions and conditions. Among these the economic ones are ultimately decisive. But the political ones, etc., and indeed even the traditions which haunt human minds also play a part, although not the decisive one.[2]

A few years later, Engels wrote a letter to Heinz Starkenburg (1894) in which he makes this same point.[3] Therefore, individuals who fail to take these specific clarifications into effect are either incapable of understanding, or deliberately trying to portray Marxism as a crude form of economic determinism. Yet, a large number of commentators simply assert that the use of political initiative to transform society is un-Marxist.[4]

Let us turn to the second question: How would a Marxist apply theory to practice? China presented a situation very similar to that of Russia. Indeed, China was even more backward, so that there, too, revolution depended on a conscious party leading in transforming the economic base. Mao Zedong explained the course of action by pointing once more to the two-sidedness of dialectics. There are two opposites involved and each influences the other; sometimes one predominates and sometimes the other. The one that predominates Mao Zedong calls the "principal aspect of the contradiction." He explains in terms similar to Engels that

> while we recognise that in the general development of history the material determines the mental and social being determined social consciousness, we also—and indeed must—recognise the reaction of mental on material things, of social consciousness on social being and of the super-structure on the economic base. This does not go against materialism; on the contrary, it avoids mechanical materialism and firmly upholds dialectical materialism.[5]

To the above, two other observations can be added. Firstly, bourgeois writers fail to raise the question "from whence did the consciousness of the party derive?" The answer is that it derived from the mode of production *inside and outside* of Russia. The fact that imperialism made the world into a single system definitely facilitated this. It is not possible for consciousness to rise in a vacuum. Marx himself has made it clear that his own ideology was a historical product—it arose at a given point in history when the mode of production permitted it. In other words, Marx could not write about a capitalist society until such a society had appeared. Nor could Lenin say that "Communism is Soviet power plus ... electrification"[6] until after the technique for harnessing electricity for power had been mastered. The Soviets were not creating an economic base out of ideology. They were using the consciousness derived from reality to *transfer* from capitalism techniques that were already in existence. Soviet revolution may have come before industrialization within the imperialist world. Such an understanding exposes the fallacy of arguments advanced by writers like John Plamenatz.[7]

Secondly, in all bourgeois writers, there is a tendency to overlook the role of the masses as though they were the passive victims or the passive beneficiaries of transformation. In fact, the achievements of the revolution were possible only because of the tremendous effort of the people. Soviet historians rightly stress this, although sometimes they, too, fall into lapses where they appear to attribute crucial developments to the work of Lenin or the work of the party or Stalin rather than to the people. Popular participation in the revolution was itself impelled by consciousness arising out of an awareness of being backward and exploited. Those notions were deemed possible because external capitalism had impinged upon the less advanced forms of social organization in tsarist Russia, which is again a reflection on the relevance of placing the discussion in an imperialist context.

In the historical writings on the period of transformation in the USSR, several other points are raised by way of challenging the right of the Soviets to call their achievements "Marxist." Sometimes such charges come from non-Marxists, and other times from Marxists. Of course, the non-Marxists or bourgeoisie often resort to the arguments of other Marxists to obscure the issue and dismiss both Marxism and the Russian Revolution. Invariably, they turn to the Trotskyists for confirmation. As I discussed in chapter 4, Trotsky was forced into exile by Stalin in 1928, and from his perch outside of the country he wrote a number of historical and polemical works concerning the Soviet Union. He also attracted a considerable intellectual following, many members of which wrote pamphlets and books. Most outstanding of all from a historical viewpoint are the works of Trotsky himself—notably, *The Revolution Betrayed*—and the works of Isaac Deutscher, which include biographies of both Stalin and Trotsky.[8]

Out of the writings of Trotsky and Deutscher, four different but closely related points emerge: (1) Stalin encouraged "socialism in one country" instead of international socialism; (2) the state did not wither away but became more oppressive and bureaucratic; (3) social and economic inequalities were fostered; and (4) there was an inadmissible element of force in building socialism. I will take up each of these assertions in order.

Socialism in One Country

Marx and Engels envisioned that ultimately the nation-state would disappear, since it functioned as a vehicle for expressing the interest of a particular class. This was their idea behind the world-famous statement in the *Communist Manifesto*: "Proletariat of the world unite."[9] It was this sense of internationalism that motivated Lenin to oppose workers' participation in the First World War; and all the Bolshevik leaders in 1917 felt that revolution was imminent in the more developed countries of the West. That would have allowed them to make socialism a worldwide, or at least European-wide, phenomenon.

Trotsky accused Stalin of having had a national chauvinist mentality that induced him to think of building "socialism in one country"—namely, in the Soviet Union, abandoning workers elsewhere. In *The Revolution Betrayed* there is an appendix entitled "Socialism in One Country." There and elsewhere, Trotsky attacked Stalin for promoting this erroneous notion as opposed to genuine Marxist internationalism. Trotsky alleges that it was a distortion of Marxism to put forward the theory that backward Russia on its own was capable of building socialism. It was more than just a theoretical debate, however. Trotsky analyzes the policy of the Comintern (which was the foreign policy branch of the Soviet Union), and he suggests that through the Comintern Stalin betrayed the Chinese Communists by giving support to Chiang Kai-shek.[10]

Trotsky and Deutscher see most of the distortions of Stalin's period as stemming from his attempt to build socialism in backward Russia alone, instead of the building of socialism in Russia proceeding simultaneously with the building of socialism in more advanced countries, so that the latter could help Russia out. As a matter of fact, it can hardly be denied that the attempt to build socialism in Russia alone has had certain unfortunate consequences, which Trotsky and Deutscher point out. But as criticism of Stalin and the party under Stalin, the attack on "socialism in one country" is very hollow. To be effective, the argument must show that Stalin betrayed certain revolutions, but that is a very ineffectual line of approach because genuine social revolutions have their roots in the locality in which they take place. The failure of revolutions to take place in Western Europe was a function of imperialism, which strengthened their bourgeoisie and disarmed the workers. Stalin and the Russian Communist Party and the Comintern had no control over that.[11]

If one agrees that Stalin was not to blame for the absence of revolutions elsewhere, then it is entirely logical that he should have proceeded on his own. That is, unless the inference is that Russia should have abandoned its social transformation until the workers revolted in Britain! Even Trotsky himself had no intention of doing so, and his comments as a historian conflict with this policy when in power, for in 1925 he was one of the leaders of the "super-industrialization faction" in the Soviet Union. At that time, Trotsky was urging that Russia should rapidly industrialize.[12] Since he criticizes Stalin for what he himself advised, one can only conclude that Trotsky's stand is conditioned by bitterness through having been defeated in the struggle for power. To put it bluntly, personal considerations clouded Trotsky's judgment and it becomes difficult to draw any distinction between Trotsky the political antagonist and Trotsky the historian.

Bureaucracy

Marx makes a very significant prediction that under communism the state, as we know it, will begin to wither away and ultimately disappear. The state as defined by Marx is an instrument of coercion in the hands of a given class, so it follows that if and when a classless society is produced, the state will disappear. Marx never discussed the timing of this disappearance in any detail, and it has therefore been a matter of debate as to exactly at what point this is envisaged.

Trotsky argues that "the dying away of the state begins . . . on the very day after the expropriation of the expropriators"— that is, after bourgeois property has been seized.[13] In Soviet Russia, the bourgeoisie were expropriated and eliminated as a class, but a new bureaucratic state began to appear and rose to great strength under Stalin. Here again, the problem is to determine whether the growth of the bureaucracy was Stalin's responsibility. If so, then one could agree with Trotsky that by fostering bureaucracy Stalin betrayed the revolution. However, on close scrutiny, one finds that Trotsky and Deutscher themselves explain why the bureaucratic state was an inevitable consequence of Russia's historical situation. The growth of the bureaucracy, they concede, started under Lenin. He was aware that bureaucratic control threatened genuine worker democracy, and he fought to keep the bureaucracy under control, but it grew nevertheless—both in numbers and influence. Trotsky explains that the demobilization of the Red Army of 5 million played a major role in the formation of the bureaucracy. The victorious commanders assumed leading posts in the local soviets, in the economy, and in the administration, excluding the masses from actual participation in leadership. This was in 1922, when both Trotsky and Lenin were key figures in the political leadership.[14] The origins of Soviet bureaucracy can hardly be attributed to Stalin.

There were three areas in which the bureaucracy was needed: the administration, the economy (which of course was all public), and inside the Communist Party itself. Trotsky lays greatest emphasis on the latter: bureaucrats replaced and swamped genuine political activists and revolutionaries, causing the party to degenerate. One of the major aspects of Deutscher's *Stalin: A Political Biography* is its account of how Stalin accumulated power through developing and controlling the bureaucratic machinery of the party. Stalin held certain key posts in the political administration, such as commissar for nationalities and the commissar of the Workers' and Peasants' Inspectorate (a kind of ombudsman machinery). By the time he became general secretary, Stalin had filled numerous offices with his own henchmen and "yes men." Deutscher explains that in the absence of a strong working class and of a high general level of culture, the bureaucracy was able to take over as a stratum exercising power on behalf of the workers and peasants. But since there was no workers' control over them, they established a bureaucratic dictatorship.[15]

Here we might recall Marx's important distinction between mental and manual labor. Those with education belong to the first category, and they would inevitably dominate the latter. Only general education could abolish this division. Soviet Russia started out with a minority of the population in the category of mental laborers. That minority constituted the bureaucracy (for the most part), and they dominated the majority. In effect, therefore, the rise of the bureaucratic state was itself a consequence of Russian backwardness rather than the fault of Stalin or the party under Stalin. At most, the bureaucracy might have been limited by a lack of conscious leadership such as that which Lenin was capable of giving, but even that was not certain. Trotsky quotes Lenin's wife, Krupskaya, saying of the Left Opposition in 1926: "If Ilych [Lenin] were alive, he would probably already be in prison."[16] The bureaucrats were so powerful and so interested in running the show themselves that, as Trotsky implies, they chose Stalin rather than the other way around. Although this conflicts with Deutscher's views, it is more logically consistent. In any case, Deutscher himself believed that the phenomenon of Stalinist bureaucratic rule was a direct product of Russia's backwardness.

Trotskyite criticisms sound extremely hollow because they were criticizing things that they admit could not have been avoided. It therefore turns out to be criticism for criticism's sake. The same characteristic is to be found in their statements on the rise of inequalities.

The Dictatorial Element in Soviet Transformation

As indicated above, another major feature of the negative portrayal of Soviet history is the charge of dictatorship. Because the Bolshevik party outlawed all other parties, it was deemed dictatorial; and because Stalin eliminated his own rivals in the Communist Party, he was able to establish a personal dictatorship. Many of the attacks against Stalin are well-grounded in facts and thereby provide an unchallengeable basis on which to use emotive language to deride socialism as a whole. Critics, above all, refer to the great political purges of 1936–8, during which Stalin imprisoned, exiled, or executed a large number of Central Committee members and extended his elimination campaigns to administrators, managers and technicians in industry. The officer class of the Soviet army was particularly hard hit.

Leonard Schapiro talks of the purges as "the national blood-bath into which Russia was to be plunged."[17] He says that critics were called counterrevolutionaries. People who failed to achieve the impossible were called saboteurs. The concentration camps were filled with innocent people. And the secret police (Cheka) came to dominate the whole state under Stalin's supervision. All of the charges Stalin brought to deport people to Siberia or to execute them were false, even when the people "confessed."[18] A comparison with Hitler is always lurking somewhere in the background of bourgeois writings on Stalin.[19] During the Second World War, the Soviet people fought a major part of the struggle against Hitler, and the capitalists in Britain, France and the United States were only too willing to have the Soviets as an ally against Hitler. But, once the war was over, it was possible to return to the interpretation that the rise of fascism in the 1930s was a phenomenon comparable to communism. The particular way in which Schapiro evokes the comparison with Hitler in his book on Soviet government is quite subtle. He says that, to the Russian people, "Hitler seemed to surpass even Stalin in his inhumanity."[20] Thus, he gives Stalin the benefit of the doubt, but at the same time, he projects essentially the same image of two inhuman beings—one representative of German fascism, the other of Russian communism.

The bourgeois historical interpretation of Stalin was very effective within the large part of the world that was until recently politically subjugated to Western Europe, and that until now is culturally colonized by the bourgeoisie of North America and Europe. One did not need to read a history book to know that Stalin was a terrible monster. This "fact" was assumed in every publication from an encyclopedia to a comic strip. In colonial territories, it was part of the warning used against independence movements, which were invariably described as "communist" or "communist-inspired," and many a sermon has been preached in our part of the world against the dangers and evils of Godless Communism—as exemplified under Stalin's rule in the 1930s in particular.

Soviet historians made, at one time, a blank denial of the charges raised by the West against Stalin, or they defended Stalin's reputation without admitting that anything was fundamentally wrong. As discussed in chapter 7, it was not until after Stalin's death that Soviet officials began to offer new explanations for his policies, or for the regime more generally. To be precise, it was after the Twentieth Congress of the Communist Party of the Soviet Union in 1956 that it became the official policy to criticize Stalin. Some writers refer to the years after 1956, when many of Stalin's policies were rejected or modified, as a period of "de-Stalinization." Volume 2 of *A Short History of the USSR* includes a section devoted to "the historic impact of the twentieth Party Congress" in which it reports having "examined the question of the Stalin cult and its consequences" and exposed its errors:

> The cult of an individual is foreign to the spirit of Marxism-Leninism. It is the people who are the true makers of history. Marxism Leninism does not deny the important role played by the leaders of the working class, but condemns any magnification of personalities, because such magnification inevitably relegates the people and the Party to the background and belittles their role in history.[21]

These are the terms in which Soviet historians usually assess the discreditable events of the purges and other things carried out by Stalin.

There is in fact another important section, entitled the "Stalin Personality Cult." According to Soviet historians, things were going well under Stalin up to the early 1930s. By 1934, however, Stalin began assuming credit for all that was done in transforming Soviet Russia to that date. He usurped the functions of the party congress and he abolished the Workers' and Peasants' Inspectorate, which was established as a control on the leadership. Stalin then went on to violate the principles of collective leadership laid down by the party, and the worst elements of his own character came to the fore. "Stalin had come to believe that he was infallible and began departing more and more from the Leninist standards and principles of party life, violating the principle of collective leadership and abusing his position. The negative features of his personality—incivility, disloyalty to leading party workers, intolerance of criticism, administration by injunction—came to the fore."[22] Soviet historians admit that Stalin flagrantly infringed upon socialist legality and engaged in personal victimization against honest people in the party and outside with the help of henchmen like Lavrentiy Beria, Vyacheslav M. Molotov, and Georgi Malenkov. This was possible because ordinary people had come to trust and believe Stalin, unaware of his numerous abuses until after his death. Soviet writers conclude, however, that the cult of the personality could neither change the nature of Soviet society nor stop its onward development.

By facing up to some of the atrocities of the Stalin era, Soviet historiography has come a considerable way toward making itself more credible. It is easier to counter the distorted implications of bourgeois writings if one recognizes where major errors were committed in the process of Soviet transformation. But the Soviet denunciation of Stalin is not entirely convincing. It is impossible to blame Stalin and a few other individuals, while concluding that the Communist Party was all the while correctly leading the Soviet people. This contradiction is blatantly brought out in the pages of *A Short History of the USSR*. On page 178, the authors explain that socialism had triumphed in Russia by 1938, "ensured by the correct leadership given by the Communist Party, which organized and inspired all the victories of socialism." They advance the view that the Constitution of 1936 recorded "the triumph of socialism and provided the foundations for broad socialist democracy." Two pages later, they denounce Stalin for having "flagrantly infringed upon socialist legality" by removing party authority over the People's Commissariat for Internal Affairs and "placing it under his own control." (The People's Commissariat for Internal Affairs, or the NKVD, became Stalin's secret police force.) He continued to do so in spite of the Constitution of 1936.[23] If Stalin could so easily and undemocratically undermine the party's authority, how could the party have been offering correct leadership from 1934 to 1938?

To reiterate, both the achievements and the failures of the Stalin epoch have to be attributed to the Soviet people as a whole and to the Communist Party, in particular. Whatever tragic consequences befell the party under Stalin's leadership must be counted as a serious distortion in the whole society. Because bourgeois scholarship has simply been interested in manufacturing hostile propaganda and Soviet writers have either turned a blind eye or offered apologies, the phenomena of social and political violence under Stalin has not been subject to a profound sociohistorical analysis.[24] Bourgeois historians find it convenient to say that the weaknesses under Stalin were an inherent part of the Marxist position or at least of Marxism under Lenin and the Bolsheviks. Therefore, there is no need to give any serious historical explanation for why profound distortions appeared in Soviet society in the 1930s. To them, Stalin was merely manifesting more fully the dictatorial and tyrannical tendencies of Lenin himself, and the whole process can be traced back to when the Bolsheviks took power in October 1917. That was the beginning of the dictatorship.

Even in the absence of a serious socioeconomic study, one can discern some evidence of a real decline after Lenin's death. Ideological standards dropped, accelerated by the elimination of the Bolshevik old guard of the pre-1917 era. By 1936, Stalin was the only one left in Russia from that original group. Committed and mature Marxists were replaced by a genera-tion of opportunists and sycophants who often made up for their lack of socialist insights by their zeal in persecuting people whom they defined as enemies of the people. Lenin had warned against such types and had kept them under control.[25] But under Stalin they were appointed to the very highest positions. One such ideological illiterate was Beria, who became the powerful chief of police.[26]

It is not accurate to say that the Stalin cult did not change the nature of Soviet society. To a great extent, the political problem in the Soviet Union after 1956 was how to remodel Soviet soci-ety and break from the mold into which it had been cast under Stalin's rule. Quite clearly, there had been a considerable distor-tion of socialism in the previous epoch. Soviet historians have tried to mitigate the unfortunate trends of the Stalin period, mainly by taking into account the intensity of internal and exter-nal counterrevolutionary activity. While it is true that certain critics were suppressed without regard to their rights, it is equally true that many critics were hostile to the regime and were engaged in undermining the state. The Soviet experience demonstrated the various ways in which counterrevolution could manifest itself in modern socialist society. It was not just the person who aimed at killing a party official who was dangerous, but also the economic saboteur, who tried to undermine economic administration by black market practices or by deliberately slowing down production. To root out such individuals required an extension of the secret police machinery. It was certainly abused, but it was a necessity in a period when the internal enemy had not yet been crushed and was receiving aid from the capitalist powers and external organizations. Numerous "White Russians," Mensheviks and SRs had organizations in capitalist countries that the Western governments encouraged in their attempts to undermine the Soviet state.[27]

Every time that a socialist state comes into existence, it is likely to find that its survival comes into conflict with some of the principles of justice it would ideally like to espouse. Who can guarantee that every citizen's rights will be fully protected when the security forces take justifiable action in the interests of the state and citizens as a whole? It is well to recognize that the Soviet state was operating in a real world and had first to guarantee its existence. In the final analysis, however, while Soviet transformation departed from the socialist norms in many ways, it remains a superior alternative to capitalism and bourgeois democracy from the viewpoint of workers and peasants. Moreover, it was at no point equivalent to fascism.

Fascism is a product of capitalism in crisis. It was an attempt to rescue the essence of the capitalist exploitative system while pretending to be representative of all interests, such as those of the working class, the bourgeoisie, and the church. The biggest capitalists in Germany initially went along with Hitler's party because he promised to improve their positions relative to the capitalists of the United States, Britain and France. At the same time, Germans of the lower middle class and the working class were encouraged to believe that their lot would be better by subjugating peoples of all other races and religions—Latin peoples, Slavs, Jews and Africans. After being fed with the supremacist racist doctrines, a large number of Germans voluntarily relinquished their own power into the hands of the small clique who were to carry out the enslavement of non-German people. In the process, a dictatorship arose—that is, a government that ruled by no sanction other than the principle of force—such as was never remotely true of the Soviet regime.[28]

An excellent contemporary example of a fascist system is South Africa. Whites of all classes have been convinced that the only way their own well-being can be protected is through the permanent suppression and exploitation of Africans. They have accepted the doctrine of white racial superiority just as the Germans accepted the doctrine of Aryan racial superiority. The majority of the whites have voluntarily relinquished their own rights to a police state for the purpose of dominating Africans within and without South Africa. At the same time, South Africa remains a capitalist state. Its fascist policies are a result of fear of change, so they are prepared to preserve capitalism so long as it preserves white supremacy.[29]

Fascism is compatible with capitalism in Portugal, Greece and South Africa, because fascism is only a more reactionary version of capitalism. Undoubtedly, the liberal middle class dislike fascism because it threatens privileges and rights for which they fought since the eighteenth century, but the real capital-owning class prefer it to socialism because it does not threaten capitalist property. And they liken communism to fascism because they would like some of the bitterness against fascism to be transferred to the Soviet state, China and any others who seek to construct socialism.

Socialism is based upon equality, not domination. Socialists can obviously fail to live up to expectations, as in the Soviet Union under Stalin, but this does not bring them anywhere near the war-mongering fascists. The comparison between Hitler and Stalin is a crude propaganda device. The comparison also displays the extreme of subjectivism, which concentrates on the individual ruler and not on the structure of society as a whole. In this respect, we already drew attention to the work of Francis Randall. Having decided that everything that was done in the Soviet Union from 1925 to 1953 was an expression of Stalin's will, Randall becomes preoccupied with Stalin as a person and proceeds to psychoanalyze him to understand why he was one of the worst men in history. He concentrates on such facts as Stalin having been wrapped in swaddling clothes, his short stature, his drunken peasant father, and the likelihood that Stalin witnessed the sexual relations of his parents.[30]

A ruler in the final analysis is as good or as bad as the society he represents. Two contemporary examples will illustrate this. When South African prime minister Hendrik F. Verwoerd was assassinated, John Voerster took his place.[31] It is a complete waste of time to try and determine how Verwoerd's personal life varied from that of Voerster's. The two are carrying on essentially the same policy because the structure of society and the state did not change with Verwoerd's assassination. They both must be assessed, not by Freudian theory, but by an analysis of the vicious society in which they lived and ruled. In the United States, John F. Kennedy is regarded as one of the best presidents in modern times. Yet it was he who escalated the war in Vietnam and launched the invasion of Cuba while blatantly lying to the American people. He was no less a spokesman for US imperialism than Lyndon B. Johnson or Richard Nixon. They are all the chief representatives of a social system that is the most exploitative the world has ever known. It is quite irrelevant to discuss whether they were ever wrapped in swaddling clothes, whether they have inferiority complexes, or whether their fathers abused their mothers.

From a socialist perspective, much can be said by way of adverse criticism of the political process of building socialism in the Soviet Union. But in the end, the balance is in favor of the positive elements. There was an enlargement of freedom in the Soviet Union after 1917 because real freedom is a function of cultural and economic equality. Because of economic and cultural inequality, capitalist society is full of fictitious freedoms. A poor man is as free to buy a helicopter as a capitalist playboy. A worker may have freedom of expression, but the means of expression are owned by the capitalist. An illiterate peasant is free to enjoy written literature, and so forth. Soviet society went a long way toward economic equality guaranteed by education. In this way, it proved itself superior to capitalism and fascism, which are premised on inequality.

And yet, we ought to be skeptical of the Soviet claims of having fully achieved Socialism in 1937–8 and that they are now building Communism. That they can pin down a precise date is immediately suspicious because in history one epoch gradually merges into another. Communism, after all, is the highest stage of socialism; one in which goods and services are produced in such super-abundance that they can be given to all citizens according to need. It is also the epoch in which the state withers away in the sense that a state machine of class oppression ceases to exist. Neither of these conditions obtain in the Soviet Union nor are they likely to obtain in the immediate future.

Thus, while the Soviet Union has solved the problem of poverty and is moving to raise the general level of consumption, it is far from super-abundance. If this were so, why are the Soviets carrying on trade with underdeveloped countries and demanding their pound of flesh? Why would they invite Ford and Fiat to build cars and trucks in the USSR if their own level of production was approximating the stage of communist abundance? It is entirely understandable that the Soviet state is not withering away, because socialism has not yet become an international phenomenon. Caught up in contradictions with capitalist powers, the Soviet Union has to strengthen its state apparatus. And in doing so, it is behaving so much like a capitalist state that it is demanding from China land areas once held by the former tsarist state and it is invading other countries, as in Czechoslovakia.

Much of the humbug in Soviet historiography is not really necessary. It is enough to say that they have constructed Socialism. Trotskyite critics like Deutscher and even the capitalists are willing to concede this point. Having accepted this major achievement, however, socialists have to be concerned with the factors limiting further development and with eliminating weaknesses in the system. Making unjustifiable claims to greatness will not address these problems and advance the struggle toward Communism.

We have examined bourgeois interpretations of the Russian Revolution and found no fundamental disagreements among them. Our study of various Marxist interpretations revealed no real unity. Indeed, their positions range widely, from Kautsky and the Mensheviks who echo bourgeois scholarship, the Soviets, the Trotskyites, to those Marxists who forgot to be radical (Social Democrats) and those who forgot to be humanists (Stalinists).

But where do *we* stand? We cannot say that we are in between, neutral, or any more objective. We have our own historical stand and must define our position relative to our own history. By "we" I mean the colonized and formerly colonized, black Africans, workers and peasants or intellectuals with roots in said classes. Because we were colonial inside capitalism, we were taught that the varieties of bourgeois thought encompassed the truth (just like people in the developed capitalist countries). The materialist worldview is excluded or mentioned as one among many alternative views. The result is a Marxist view through a distorted bourgeois lens. Ours clearly could not be that of the bourgeoisie. Is it that of Soviets? They have their national and international interests, and their historiography reflects this. While we share much with the Soviets because of the similarity of our present and past with their past in the period under study, current political and economic developments mentioned above complicate our position vis-à-vis the Soviets.

Essentially, what we need to do is define our own stand first and see where it coincides. Assuming a view springing from some Socialist variant not necessarily Marxist but anti-capitalist, assuming a view that is at least radical humanist—then the Soviet Revolution of 1917 and the subsequent construction of Socialism emerges as a very positive historical experience from which we ourselves can derive a great deal as we move to confront similar problems.

Acknowledgements

This book provides an "African Perspective" for understanding the Russian Revolution. Brilliant as it may be, the work was in development as a series of lecture notes. It is imperfect and certainly will not be without its critics. Readers are reminded that this work needs to be examined in the context of the world as it existed at that time and in the context of who Rodney was at that time, a twenty-eight-year-old enigmatic historian and scholar-activist, engaging, learning, and earning his stripes.

Acknowledgement is defined as the acceptance of the truth or existence of something and the action of expressing or displaying gratitude or appreciation for something. In essence, how we are able to read this book is what is to be acknowledged.

To his parents and siblings and to his education and experiences, that shaped his young life. To where Rodney was situated at the time, having lived and worked in the Caribbean, UK and Africa, and the many people and places that touched him. To the students at the University of Dar es Salaam, for whom the lectures were prepared. To those who cared enough to help the family prevent the destruction of his work, to remove and store its possessions outside of Guyana, and to preserve his intellectual property along the way. To those who stored and engaged with his work at University of California, Los Angeles (UCLA).

To Robin Kelley, who from a young and dedicated intern to his current renowned status has meticulously transformed the lecture notes into this book and whose scholarship on the Russian Revolution is masterful. To Jesse Benjamin, whose tremendous and methodical work on this book is important, particularly with respect to the theoretical framing of Rodney's works, and arguably second only to his passion and tireless efforts helping preserve and promote Rodney's legacy. To Vijay Prashad, whose work is inimitable, whose insight into Rodney is palpable, and who introduced the Rodney family to Verso Books. To Verso, for its belief in Rodney's works and commitment to publish a series of his works that will introduce them to a new and broader audience. To the WRF Board and Committees and the Atlanta University Center Robert W. Woodruff Library's leadership and staff, whose dedication to the preservation and promotion of his legacy is immeasurable.

To our understanding of him, his life, and his works, that is constantly evolving as we grasp the breadth and depth of his works and their usefulness and timelessness both as historical tools and in contemporary debate and discourse.

And finally, to Patricia, his wife and life partner and our mother, whose dedication to his living memory and determination for justice for Walter Rodney makes everything possible and meaningful.

Shaka, Kanini and Asha Rodney

First and foremost, I want to thank the Rodney family, especially Pat and Asha, for giving me the opportunity to complete the work I had begun thirty-three years ago. I discovered Walter Rodney during my first year of college and his work, along with my embrace of Marxism, set me on the path to History. I entered graduate school at UCLA as an Africanist solely because of *How Europe Underdeveloped Africa*. So imagine what it meant for me, a young Marxist, to work on Rodney's lectures on the Russian Revolution in my second year of graduate school. For that, I owe my greatest debt to Edward A. Alpers, my professor and advisor who trusted a green twenty-three-year-old kid to take on the daunting task of digitizing, editing, and sourcing these lectures. I also enjoyed the encouragement of Robert A. Hill, who not only knew Rodney quite well but was one of my mentors in graduate school.

Thanks, of course, to Jesse Benjamin for not only helping me complete the work but for inviting me to Atlanta to speak on Rodney and Russia in 2015. That was the beginning of our collaboration. To my dear comrade, Vijay Prashad, who, as a scholar, a revolutionary, and founding editor of LeftWord Books, immediately saw the value of these lectures and worked tirelessly to make the publication happen. And if that wasn't enough, he contributed a foreword that beautifully captures Rodney's restless revolutionary imagination and abiding commitment to a better world. To Dave Roediger for putting the pieces together that inspired all of us to resurrect this project and finally bring it to fruition. To my wonderful research assistants, Kela Caldwell, Shamell Bell, Kristen Glasgow and Amber Withers, for their valuable help in re-digitizing the lectures—which involved a lot more than scanning pages! To Verso Books, especially our editor Ben Mabie for shepherding this project from the beginning, and our production editor Duncan Ranslem for smoothing the road, as it were.

Several friends and colleagues either shared insights on

Rodney or Russian history, extended invitations for me to think out loud about the book, or were just invaluable interlocutors. They include Robert A. Hill, Horace Campbell, David Austin, Peter Linebaugh, S. Ani Mukherji, Bill Mullen, Tithi Bhattacharya, Christina Heatherton, Jordan Camp, Howard Brick, Ronald G. Suny, Geoff Eley, Kathleen Canning, Geneviève Zubrzycki, and, as always, my intellectual hero Elleza Kelley.

Finally, much gratitude to LisaGay Hamilton for having to endure my long absences and sleepless nights in pursuit of elusive citations, reading Russian and Tanzanian histories, revisiting Marxist classics, and above all, for giving me permission to work for free.

Robin D. G. Kelley

It has been a singular honor to be entrusted by the Rodney family with the immense responsibility of co-editing this book, and with all the work of the Walter Rodney Foundation (WRF). Pat and Asha Rodney have been consistent allies, sources, and contributors as we developed the broader publishing plan for Rodney's works, and from start to finish while producing this book, in great detail and always with precision. Collaborating with Robin D. G. Kelley is an honor and a pleasure. I thank him for embracing my early suggestion that we co-write one of his substantive introductions, which I hold as exemplars of the craft. Vijay Prashad's contributions and guidance, especially at a pivotal phase of this work, were instrumental and deeply appreciated; as was Dave Roediger's generosity and integrity. At Verso, it has been a true pleasure to build the relationship with WRF, and to work on this book with Andy Hsiao and Ben Mabie, whose guidance and acumen were instrumental and invaluable from start to finish. Duncan Ranslem and his team did incredible, complex and quick work that made the final text shine. Deep thanks also to Firoze Manji and Roger van Zwanenberg, for their extensive and committed guidance. Sincere gratitude to Aajay Murphy, my student turned colleague, whose work is consistently excellent, often in the trenches with impossible deadlines.

I am also indebted for the inspiration, mentoring and friendship over many years of Sylvia Wynter, Carole Boyce Davies, Babacar M'bow, Beverly Guy-Sheftall, Chapurukha Kusimba, Maghan Keita, Atieno-Odhiambo, Jesus "Chucho" Garcia, Ismail Khalidi, Natsu Saito, Ward Churchill, Satya Mohanty, Robert A. Hill, Ngugi wa Thiong'o, Howard Dodson, Bill Fletcher, and Aljosie Harding. My work on this project directly benefitted from my work with Nicole N. Yearwood, Akinyele Umoja, Derrick White, Seth Markle, Seneca Vaught, and too many other incredible students, friends, and volunteers over the years to fully enumerate.

Far and away, my work on this project has been most influenced, grounded and improved by my ongoing dialogue with

Sharana B about all aspects of this project. I am grateful for the benefits her skills and wisdom brought at every stage. She has provided the greatest support at every level, and is the truest of personal and intellectual partners, a friend across the many late nights and zombie-like states that my work on this book, and the broader work that led to it, entailed.

Jesse J. Benjamin

Notes

Foreword

1. *Walter Rodney Speaks: The Making of an African Intellectual*, ed. Robert Hill (Trenton, NJ: Africa World Press, 1990), 17, original emphasis.
2. "The Arusha Declaration: Socialism and Self-Reliance," Julius Nyerere, *Freedom and Socialism* (Dar es Salaam: Oxford University Press, 1968), 234–5.
3. Yoweri Museveni, "Activism at the Hill," *Cheche* 2, reprinted in *Cheche: Reminiscences of a Radical Magazine*, ed. Karim F. Hirji (Dar es Salaam: Mkuki na Nyota, 2010), 14.
4. Walter Rodney, Kapepwa Tambila and Laurent Sago, *Migrant Labour in Tanzania During the Colonial Period: Case Studies of Recruitment and Conditions of Labour in the Sisal Industry* (Hamburg: Institut für Afrika-Kunde im Verbund der Stiftung Deutsche Übersee-Institut, 1983).
5. Walter Rodney, "Marxism in Africa," *Solidarity* 7 (1981), 34–41.
6. Hirji, "Tribulations of an Independent Magazine," *Cheche: Reminiscences of a Radical Magazine*, 38–9.
7. Walter Rodney, "Tanzanian Ujamaa and Scientific Socialism," *African Review* 1, no. 4 (1972), 61–72.
8. "One must understand the specific contextual nature of the discussions that were going on in Russia at that time. This comes to my mind because I feel that a lot of the debates that do go on about

Marxism are definitely out of context." *Walter Rodney Speaks*, 28.

9. C. L. R. James, *Note on Dialectics. Hegel-Marx-Lenin* (London: Allison and Busby, 1980), 138, original emphasis.

Introduction

1. A copy of Rodney's syllabus "Historians and Revolution," is located in box 9 of the Walter Rodney Papers, Atlanta University Center Robert W. Woodruff Library. See also Seth M. Markle, *A Motorcycle on Hell Run: Tanzania, Black Power, and the Uncertain Future of Pan-Africanism, 1964–1974* (East Lansing: Michigan State University Press, 2017).

2. Walter Rodney to Ewart Thomas, 1971, box 4, Walter Rodney Papers; also quoted in Rupert Charles Lewis, *Walter Rodney's Intellectual and Political Thought* (Kingston: The University of the West Indies Press, 1998), 168.

3. See the editors' note for an explanation of the origins and construction of the book.

4. Patricia Rodney interviewed by Jesse Benjamin, at her home in Atlanta, July 26, 2017. Asha T. Rodney, Rodney's youngest child, also participated.

5. Walter Rodney, *How Europe Underdeveloped Africa* (Washington, DC: Howard University Press, 1974), 176. The first edition was published in 1972 by Bogle-L'Ouverture Publications in London, and Tanzania Publishing House in Dar es Salaam.

6. Issa G. Shivji, "Remembering Walter Rodney," *Monthly Review* 64, no. 7 (December 2012), monthlyreview.org. On Rodney and the political culture of the University of Dar es Salaam, see Seth M. Markle, *A Motorcycle on Hell Run*, chapter 3; Kiluba L. Nkulu, *Serving the Common Good: A Postcolonial African Perspective on Higher Education* (New York: Peter Lang, 2005), 91–115; Lewis, *Walter Rodney's Intellectual and Political Thought*, 124–66.

7. P. Rodney interview.

8. Vijay Prashad's *The Poorer Nations: A Possible History of the Global South* (New York and London: Verso, 2013) is the best treatment of this historical conjuncture and the future possibilities, had the Third World project succeeded in stopping neoliberalism in its tracks.

9. An earlier version of portions of this section appears as the entry

for "Walter Rodney" in *Black Power Encyclopedia: From "Black is Beautiful" to Urban Uprisings*, Akinyele Umoja, ed., ABC-CLIO, expected 2018. See also Markle, *A Motorcycle on Hell Run*, chapter 3; Lewis, *Walter Rodney's Intellectual and Political Thought*.

10. Rodney visited Russia while a student at the University of the West Indies, Mona Jamaica during August and September 1962 and met Richard Small in Leningrad at the International Union of Students conference. A Jamaican student studying law in England, Small was later active in the Campaign Against Racial Discrimination and the Caribbean Artists Movement. Walter was representing UWI students in the West Indies and Richard was representing the Federation of West Indian Students Unions in Britain and Northern Ireland. According to Richard, "they right away agreed to have a joint delegation and speak as one, and it worked out very well." They had never met before, but learned of each other's attendance at the conference and arranged to meet. They subsequently became good friends; Richard wrote an introduction for an early edition of *The Groundings with My Brothers* and was Walter's lawyer in Guyana when he and comrades were falsely charged with arson during the height of WPA activities there.

11. Rodney was somewhat disillusioned with the academy for a while and seriously considered leaving it altogether—especially after Jamaica—when he spent a few months in Cuba writing and reflecting. During his brief stay in London he was offered an attractive position at SOAS, but he declined because he wanted the benefits of community and friendships for himself and his family, which Tanzania provided. P. Rodney interview.

12. In an incredibly insightful essay on Rodney's intellectual development, Horace Campbell recounts the impact of the journal and, in particular, his essay on the Ujamaa villages. "Rodney drew on the correspondence between Karl Marx and Vera Zasulich to point to the importance of peasant struggles in the context of a wider revolutionary struggle on the world stage. This article was debated while it was in draft form by the members of USARF and exposed the ways in which Walter Rodney wanted to draw out the most positive aspects of the Tanzanian politics at that time. Walter Rodney was aware of the constraints on transformation and sought to engage the best scholars in the world in the debates on socialist transformation in Africa. With hindsight, many of those

who were sharply critical of the idealism of Julius Nyerere now recognize the important contribution that was made by Nyerere and the Tanzanian people at that historical moment." Horace G. Campbell, "Philosophy and Praxis: The Life and Work of Walter Rodney," unpublished paper presented at the AAAPS Biennial Congress, Cairo, 2005, quoted with permission by author.

13. Lewis, *Walter Rodney's Intellectual and Political Thought*, 124–153.

14. In 1980, Walter Rodney was working on the *History of the Guyanese Working People*, vol. II. On the day he was assassinated, the death squad searched the house, and Patricia Rodney reports that the papers, which he had been actively working on and finalizing, disappeared.

15. See, for example, Huw Beynon, Lionel Cliffe, Michael Craton et al., "The Walter Rodney Affair," *New York Review of Books*, May 14, 1981, nybooks.com.

16. "Report of the Commission of Inquiry Appointed to Enquire and Report on the Circumstances Surrounding the Death of the Late Dr. Walter Rodney on Thirteenth Day of June, One Thousand Nine Hundred and Eighty at Georgetown [Guyana]," report issued February 8, 2016, copy maintained at the Atlanta University Center Robert W. Woodruff Library, digitalcommons.auctr.edu/wrcoi.

17. The synopsis presented here is drawn from several recent syntheses of the Russian Revolution, notably S. A. Smith, *Russia in Revolution: An Empire in Crisis, 1890–1928* (New York and Oxford: Oxford University Press, 2017); Orlando Figes, *Revolutionary Russia, 1891-1991: A History* (New York: Henry Holt and Co., 2017); China Mieville, *October: The Story of the Russian Revolution* (New York and London: Verso, 2017); Sheila Fitzpatrick, *The Russian Revolution* (New York and Oxford: Oxford University Press, 2008, updated ed.); Aaron B. Retish, *Russia's Peasants in Revolution and Civil War: Citizenship, Identity, and the Creation of the Soviet State, 1914–1922* (New York: Cambridge University Press, 2008); Alexander Rabinowitch, *The Bolsheviks Come to Power: The Revolution of 1917 in Petrograd* (Chicago: Haymarket, 2004); Tamas Krausz, *Reconstructing Lenin: An Intellectual Biography*, trans. Bálint Bethlenfalvy with Mario Fenyo (New York: Monthly Review Press, 2015); Robert J. Service, *Lenin: A Biography* (Basingstoke: Macmillan, 2000). On new developments in Russian Revolution historiography since the fall of the Soviet Union, see

Ronald Grigor Suny, *Red Flag Unfurled: History, Historians, and the Russian Revolution* (New York and London: Verso, 2017); Michael Confino, "The New Russian Historiography, and the Old—Some Considerations," *History and Memory* 21, no. 2 (Fall/Winter 2009), 7–33; Boris Kolonitskii and Yisrael Elliot Cohen, "Russian Historiography of the 1917 Revolution: New Challenges to Old Paradigms?" *History and Memory* 21, no. 2 (Fall/Winter 2009), 34–59; Sheila Fitzpatrick, "Revisionism in Soviet History," *History and Theory* 46, no. 4 (December 2007), 77–91.

18. Figes, *Revolutionary Russia*, 17–18.

19. Georgii Plekhanov, "Speech at the International Workers' Socialist Congress in Paris (14–21 July, 1889)," available at marxists.org.

20. Rosa Luxemburg, *Social Reform or Revolution* (1900), available at marxists.org; see also Rosa Luxemburg, *The Essential Rosa Luxemburg: Reform or Revolution and The Mass Strike*, ed. Helen Scott (Chicago: Haymarket Books, 2008).

21. For the purposes of consistency, all of the dates to which we refer are based on the Julian calendar. Until 1918, Russia continued to use the Julian calendar, which was about thirteen days behind. Thus, the events of Bloody Sunday according to the Gregorian calendar would have been recorded as January 17. Likewise, the February Revolution of 1917 begins on February 23 according to the Julian calendar, but March 8 according to the Gregorian calendar (which, incidentally, is the official date of International Women's Day).

22. Not all of the anti-Jewish pogroms were the result of the Black Hundreds or the Union of the Russian People. There is a long history of anti-Semitism in Russia, particularly in the Ukraine, where the worst incidence of anti-Jewish violence occurred in Odessa by unruly supporters of the battleship *Potemkin* mutineers. However, during the 1905 Revolution Jews were often singled out as the source, and beneficiaries, of liberal reform. When the tsar issued the October Manifesto in 1905, extending some constitutional rights to the populace, it also directed right-wing mobs to attack Jews in over 600 cities and towns. These mobs asserted that Jews were the source of the undermining of the true autocracy, but recent evidence reveals that these pogroms were a state strategy to suppress the Left. See Victoria Khiterer, "The October 1905 Pogroms and the Russian Authorities," *Nationalities Papers* 43, no. 5 (2015), 788–803; George Gilbert, *The Radical Right in Imperial*

Russia (London: Routledge, 2015).

23. S. A. Smith, *Russia in Revolution*, 76–7.

24. Vladimir Ilyich Lenin, "The Tasks of the Proletariat in the Present Revolution [a.k.a. The April Theses]," published in *Pravda* 26 (April 7, 1917), available at marxists.org.

25. V. I. Lenin, "Report on Peace," (October 26, 1917), available at marxists.org.

26. In *The State and Revolution*, written between August and September of 1917, Lenin wrote, "The dictatorship of the proletariat … as the ruling class for the purpose of suppressing the oppressors, cannot result merely in an expansion of democracy. Simultaneously with an immense expansion of democracy, which for the first time becomes democracy for the poor, democracy for the people, and not democracy for the moneybags, the dictatorship of the proletariat imposes a series of restrictions on the freedom of the oppressors, the exploiters, the capitalists. We must suppress them in order to free humanity from wage slavery, their resistance must be crushed by force; it is clear that there is no freedom and no democracy where there is suppression and where there is violence." V. I. Lenin, *The State and Revolution* (1917), available at marxists. org.

27. These figures come from S. A. Smith, *Russia in Revolution*, 155.

28. V. I. Lenin, "Report on Peace," (October 26, 1917), available at marxists.org.

29. Quoted in Victor Serge, "Year One of the Russian Revolution: VIII – Left Communism and Inner-Party Conflict," available at marxists.org.

30. "Theses on the National and Colonial Question Adopted by the Second Congress of the Comintern Congress," in Jane Degras, ed., *The Communist International, 1919–1943, Documents*, vol. I (London: Oxford University Press, 1956), 142.

31. Manabendra Nath Roy, *M.N. Roy's Memoirs* (Bombay: Ajanta Publishers, 1964), 378; see also John Haithcox, *Communism and Nationalism in India: M.N. Roy and Comintern Policy, 1920–1939* (Princeton, NJ: Princeton University Press, 1971), 14–15. A copy of Roy's theses is available in V. B. Karnik, *M.N. Roy: A Political Biography* (Bombay: Nav Jagriti Samaj, 1978), 107–10. For Lenin's views on Roy's supplementary theses, see "The Report of the Commission on the National and Colonial Questions, July 26, 1920," in *Lenin on the National and Colonial Questions*, 30–37.

For his part, Rodney followed more closely Roy's position on this question throughout his life, and was a consistently sharp critic of the petty-bourgeoisie.

32. C. L. R. James, *World Revolution, 1917-1936: The Rise and Fall of the Communist International* (Durham, NC: Duke University Press, 2017, orig. 1937)

33. Of course, one obvious exception is Vijay Prashad, ed., *Communist Histories: Volume 1* (New Dehli: LeftWord Books, 2016).

34. See chapter 3. Here Rodney anticipates some of the more recent scholarship that revisits Marx's later writings on the peasantry, colonialism, and capitalist agriculture. See, for example, Kevin B. Anderson, *Marx at the Margins: On Nationalism, Ethnicity, and Non-Western Societies* (Chicago: University of Chicago Press, 2010), 223–36.

35. Walter Rodney, "Tanzanian *Ujamaa* and Scientific Socialism," *African Review* 1, no. 4 (1972), 61–76.

36. C. L. R. James, *State Capitalism and World Revolution*, written in collaboration with Raya Dunayevskaya, and Grace Lee Boggs (Chicago: Charles H. Kerr, 1986, orig. 1950). *State Capitalism and World Revolution* represented the collective position of the Johnson-Forest Tendency, former Trotskyists who broke from the Workers' Party whose principal members included the authors of this book. James and his colleagues broke with Trotsky over his analysis that the Soviet Union under Stalin had become a "degenerated workers' state." In response, the Johnson-Forest Tendency developed the theory of state capitalism to explain the character of the USSR. They write, "The Stalinists are not class-collaborationists, fools, cowards, idiots, men with 'supple spines,' but conscious clear-sighted aspirants for world-power. They are deadly enemies of private property capitalism. They aim to seize the power and take the place of the bourgeoisie . . . But the Stalinists are not proletarian revolutionists. They aim to get power by help, direct or indirect, of the Red Army and the protection of Russia and the Russian state . . . Theirs is a last desperate attempt under the guise of 'socialism' and 'planned economy' to reorganize the means of production without releasing the proletariat from wage-slavery. Historical viability they have none; for state-ownership multiplies every contradiction of capitalism."

37. C. L. R. James, *Notes on Dialectics* (London: Allison and Busby,

1980, orig. 1950), 350; see also Cedric J. Robinson, *Black Marxism: The Making of the Black Radical Tradition* (Chapel Hill, NC: University of North Carolina Press, 2000), 281–2. When James wrote *World Revolution, 1917-1936*, his position was identical with Trotsky's. James conceded that the Third International's fall as a revolutionary force began "when Stalin, in defiance of all the teachings of Marx and Lenin, first produced his theory that it was possible to build Socialism in a single country, that country being Soviet Russia. The present policies have resulted from this first conscious concession to nationalism. The opponents of this theory said at the time that, if it was adopted, then it led straight to the liquidation of the Third International as a revolutionary force"(p. 17).

38. See C. L. R. James, Grace Lee Boggs, and Pierre Chaulieu, *Facing Reality: The New Society—How to Look for It and How to Bring It Closer* (Detroit: Correspondence Publishing Co., 1958).

39. Walter Rodney, "The African Revolution" in *C.L.R. James: His Life and Work*, Paul Buhle, ed., special issue of *Urgent Tasks* 12 (Summer 1981), 13.

40. James proposed Lenin as the model for Kwame Nkrumah and Ghana. See C. L. R. James, "Lenin and the Problem," *The C.L.R. James Reader*, Anna Grimshaw, ed. (Cambridge, MA: Blackwell, 1992), 331–46; Matthew Quest, "C.L.R. James, Direct Democracy, and National Liberation Struggles," (PhD diss., Brown University, 2008), 51–6.

41. For a thoughtful critique of James's selective reading of Lenin, see Quest, "C.L.R. James," 51–5.

42. Lewis, *Walter Rodney's Intellectual and Political Thought*, 169.

43. For example, Ranajit Guha, "The Prose of Counter-Insurgency," in Ranajit Guha and Gayatri Chakravorty Spivak, eds., *Selected Subaltern Studies* (New York: Oxford University Press, 1988); Gayatri Chakravorty Spivak, "Can the Subaltern Speak?," in *Marxism and the Interpretation of Culture*, Cary Nelson and Lawrence Grossberg, eds., (Urbana and Chicago: University of Illinois Press, 1988).

44. For example, Vine Deloria Jr., *Custer Died for Your Sins: An Indian Manifesto* (New York: Avon Books, 1969); Linda Tuhiwai Smith, *Decolonizing Methodologies: Research and Indigenous Peoples* (Boston: Zed, 1999); Steven Salaita, *Inter/Nationalism: Decolonizing Native America and Palestine* (Minneapolis:

University of Minnesota Press, 2016).

45. Craig Steven Wilder, *Ebony and Ivy: Race, Slavery and the Troubled History of America's Universities* (London: Bloomsbury, 2013).

46. Rodney visited, lectured at, and participated in the Institute of the Black World in Atlanta several times in the early 1970s, and embodied the kind of engaged and committed praxis this movement-based academic community was founded on and aspired to maintain. In this volume, we have one additional text in which to see his manifestations of this practice, as both a specific key case study and as a model of this methodology.

47. Michel Foucault, *The Archaeology of Knowledge: And the Discourse on Language* (New York: Vintage, 1969).

48. Edward Said, *Orientalism* (New York: Pantheon, 1978).

49. Angela Davis, "Reflections on the Black Woman's Role in the Community of Slaves," *Black Scholar*, December, 1971; Davis, *Women, Race, and Class* (New York: Random House, 1981); Cedric J. Robinson, *Black Marxism: The Making of the Black Radical Tradition* (Chapel Hill, NC: University of North Carolina Press, 2000, orig. 1983).

50. Ngũgĩ wa Thiong'o, *Petals of Blood* (Nairobi: Heinemann, 1977); Ngũgĩ, *Detained: A Writer's Prison Diary* (London: Heinemann, 1981); Ngũgĩ, *Decolonising the Mind: The Politics of Language in African Literature* (Nairobi: Heinemann, 1981).

51. Sylvia Wynter, "Sambos and Minstrels," *Social Text*, Summer, 1979; Wynter, "After 'Man,' Toward the Human: Rodney and the Rethinking of Intellectual Activism on the Eve of the New Millennium," keynote address at Engaging Walter Rodney's Legacies, conference at SUNY Binghamton, November 6–8, 1998.

52. Decoloniality developed first in Latin America, in texts published mostly in Spanish, and reached English in essays such as Anibal Quijano and Immanuel Wallerstein, "Americanity as a Concept, or the Americas in the Modern World-System," *International Social Science Journal* 134, 1992; and Anibal Quijano, "Modernity, Identity, and Utopia in Latin America," *boundary 2*, 20(3), 1993; Walter Mignolo, *Local Histories/Global Designs: Coloniality, Subaltern Knowledges and Border Thinking* (Princeton, NJ: Princeton University Press, 2000).

1 The Two World Views of the Russian Revolution

1. From *Selected Works of Mao Tse-Tung*, vol. 1 (Oxford: Pergamon Press, 1965), 311.

2. Of course, Walter Rodney had explored the relationship of this experience and the impact of imperialism on the continent of Africa in his classic text, *How Europe Underdeveloped Africa* (Washington, DC: Howard University Press, 1981, orig. 1972). He acknowledges as critical precursors in this regard V. I. Lenin, *Imperialism: The Highest Stage of Capitalism* (New York: International Publishers, 1969, orig. 1917), and Kwame Nkrumah, *Neo-Colonialism: The Last Stage of Imperialism* (New York: International Publishers, 1966, orig. 1965).

3. See, especially, Alfred Cobban, *Historians and the Causes of the French Revolution* (London: Routledge & Kegan Paul, 1958 rev., orig. 1946); Geoffrey Ellis, "The Marxist Interpretation of the French Revolution," *English Historical Review* 93 (April 1978), 353–76. Some of the more prominent Marxist interpretations of the French Revolution are Albert Soboul, *The Sans-culottes: The Popular Movement and Revolutionary Government, 1793–1794*, trans. Remy Inglis Hall (Princeton, NJ: Princeton University Press, 1980, orig. 1964), Soboul, *The French Revolution 1787–1799*, trans. Alan Forrest and Colin Jones (New York: Random House, 1975); Georges Lefebvre, *The Coming of the French Revolution, 1789*, trans. R. R. Palmer (New York: Vintage, 1947, orig. 1939); Lefebvre, *The French Revolution: From its Origins to 1793,* trans. Elizabeth Moss Evanson (London: Routledge & Kegan Paul, 1962, orig. 1957); and Jean Jaurès's classic eight-volume *Histoire Socialiste De la Revolution Francaise* (1901–1907), which has since been translated and drastically abridged in the one-volume *A Socialist History of the French Revolution*, ed. and trans. Mitchell Abidor (London: Pluto Press, 2015).

4. See Christopher Hill, "Recent Interpretations of the Civil War," *History* 41 (1956), 67–87. Rodney highly regarded Hill's work (see Walter Rodney Papers, "notes on comparative revolutions," as well as his comments in this text on Hill's biography of Lenin). Other works by Hill on the English Civil War include *The English Revolution* (London: Lawrence & Wishart Ltd, 1955); and "The English Civil War Interpreted by Marx and Engels," *Science and Society* 12, no. 1 (Winter 1948), 130–56.

5. Of course, Rodney is writing from the vantage point of the late 1960s and 1970s, so he would not be privy to the latest historiography of the French Revolution. His characterizations are confirmed by his contemporaries, such as J. Cavanaugh, "The Present State of French Revolutionary Historiography: Alfred Cobban and Beyond," *French Historical Studies* 7, no. 4 (Fall 1972), 587–606; John Stewart Hall, *The French Revolution: Some Trends in Historical Writing* (Washington, DC: American Historical Association, 1967).

6. James H. Billington, "Six Views of the Russian Revolution," *World Politics* 18, no. 3 (April 1966), 452–73.

7. The works to which Rodney is referring include, for example, P. N. Sobolev, *The Great October Socialist Revolution*, trans. D. Skvirsky (Moscow: Progress Publishers, 1976); Joseph Stalin, *The October Revolution* (New York: International Pub., 1934); A. Bryusov, A. Sakharov, A. Fadeyev et al., *Outline History of the USSR*, trans. by George Hanna (Moscow: Progress Publishers, 1960); A. M. Pankratova et. al., *A History of the USSR* (Moscow: Foreign Language Pub.,1947). See also John L. H. Keep, "The Great October Revolution," in *Windows on the Russian Past: Essays on Soviet Historiography Since Stalin*, ed. S. Baron and N. Heer (Columbus, OH: Ohio State University Press, 1976) for a more detailed overview of Soviet works on the Russian Revolution published before the collapse of the Soviet Union. Of course, as we discuss in the introduction, the historiography of the USSR underwent a veritable revolution with perestroika and the subsequent collapse of the Soviet Union. The shift has been subject to a mountain of books and articles too numerous to list here. For a sampling, see P. V. Volobuev and Kurt S. Schultz, "Perestroika and the October Revolution in Soviet Historiography," *Russian Review* 51, no. 4 (October 1992), 566–76; Volobuev and Schultz, "Perestroika, History, and Historians: A Roundtable," *Journal of Modern History* 62, no. 4 (December 1990), 782–830; Steve Smith, "Writing the History of the Russian Revolution after the Fall of Communism," *Europe-Asia Studies* 46, no. 4 (1994), 563–78; Ronald Grigor Suny, "Revision and Retreat in the Historiography of 1917: Social History and Its Critics," *Russian Review* 53, no. 2 (April 1994), 165–82; Michael Confino, "The New Russian Historiography, and the Old—Some Considerations," *History and Memory* 21, no. 2 (Fall/Winter 2009), 7–33; Boris Kolonitskii and Yisrael Elliot

Cohen, "Russian Historiography of the 1917 Revolution: *New Challenges to Old Paradigms?*," *History and Memory* 21, no. 2 (Fall/Winter 2009), 34–59; Sheila Fitzpatrick, "Revisionism in Soviet History," *History and Theory* 46, no. 4 (December 2007), 77–91.

8. John Reed, *Ten Days that Shook the World* (New York: New American Library, 1967, orig. 1919).

9. William Z. Foster, *The Russian Revolution* (Chicago: Trade Union Educational League, 1922).

10. Christopher Hill, *Lenin and the Russian Revolution* (Middlesex, England: Penguin Books, 1971, orig. 1947). Of course, since the 1970s and especially after the fall of the Soviet Union and the opening of the archives, there has been a wide range of new scholarship on the Russian Revolution sympathetic to the Bolsheviks and, especially, to the other worker-based movements such as the Socialist Revolutionaries. See Alex Rabinowitch, *Prelude to Revolution: The Petrograd Bolsheviks and the July 1917 Uprising* (Bloomington, IN: Indiana University Press, 1968); *The Bolsheviks Come to Power: The Revolution of 1917 in Petrograd* (New York: Norton, 1976); Ronald Grigor Suny, *The Baku Commune, 1917–1918: Class and Nationality in the Russian Revolution* (Princeton, NJ: Princeton University Press, 1972); William G. Rosenberg, *Liberals in Russian Revolution* (Princeton, NJ: Princeton University Press, 1974); Diane Koenker, *Moscow Workers and the 1917 Revolution* (Princeton, NJ: Princeton University Press, 1981); Steve A. Smith, *Red Petrograd: Revolution in the Factories 1917–1918* (Cambridge, UK: Cambridge University Press, 1983), as well as citations at the end of footnote 7.

11. Maurice Dobb, *Russian Economic Development Since the Revolution* (London: Routledge, 1928) and *Soviet Economic Development Since 1917* (New York: International Publishers, 1966, orig. 1948).

12. Raphael Ambramovitch, *The Soviet Revolution, 1917–1939* (New York: International Universities Press, 1962).

13. Karl Kautsky, *The Dictatorship of the Proletariat* (Ann Arbor, MI: University of Michigan Press, 1964, orig. 1919); Rosa Luxemburg, *The Russian Revolution and Marxism or Leninism?* (Ann Arbor: University of Michigan Press, 1961).

14. Some of Trotsky's essential pre-exile works include *Our Political Tasks* (1904); *Results and Prospects* (1906); *1905* (1907); *The Bolsheviks and World Peace*, also published as *War and the*

International (1914); *History of the Russian Revolution to Brest-Litovsk* (1918); and *The New Course* (1923). All of these writings are available at marxists.org.

15. In 1929, Stalin had Trotsky expelled from the Communist Party and subsequently exiled. 1934, he founded the Fourth International to counter Stalinism and what he called the "degeneration of the workers' state." Trotsky never considered the Soviet Union and the Third International enemies of socialism or capitalist. In fact, he consistently called for the defense of the Soviet Union after the Fourth International was founded. See Leon Trotsky, "War and the Fourth International," June 10, 1934, available at marxists.org; Trotsky, "Once Again: The USSR and Its Defense (November 1937)," available at marxists.org. For more on Trotsky s life and the history of the Fourth International, see Isaac Deutscher's three-volume biography recently gathered into a single volume, *The Prophet: The Life of Leon Trotsky* (London and New York: Verso, 2015).

16. Richard Crossman, ed., *The God That Failed* (New York: Harper & Brothers, 1950).

17. The works to which Rodney refers are mainly collections edited by Arthur E. Adams: *Imperial Russia after 1861: Peaceful Modernization or Revolution?* (Boston: D.C. Heath Co., 1965); *The Russian Revolution and Bolshevik Victory: Why and How?* (Boston: D.C. Heath Co., 1960); *The Russian Revolution and Bolshevik Victory: Causes and Processes* (Boston: D.C. Heath Co., 1960).

18. Hugh Seton-Watson, *The Pattern of Communist Revolution: A Historical Analysis* (London: Methuen & Co., 1953), vii.

19. This is the case in all of his works. See *The Russian Empire, 1801–1914* (Oxford: Clarendon Press, 1967); *The Decline of Imperial Russia, 1855–1914* (London: Methuen & Co., 1952); in addition to *The Pattern of Communist Revolution*.

20. Jacob Walkin, *The Rise of Democracy in Pre-Revolutionary Russia: Political and Social Institutions Under the Last Three Czars* (New York: Praeger, 1962), 206.

21. Ibid., 206.

22. Ibid., 235.

23. Ibid., 239.

24. R. N. Carew Hunt, *A Guide to Communist Jargon* (New York: Macmillan, 1957). Another popular work by Hunt is *The Theory*

and Practice of Communism (New York: Macmillan, 1950).

25. Francis B. Randall, *Stalin's Russia: An Historical Reconsideration* (New York: The Free Press, 1965), 1–2, 6, 8, 9.

26. Bernard Pares, *The Fall of the Russian Monarchy: A Study of the Evidence* (New York: Alfred Knopf, 1930).

27. Ibid, 82.

28. G. William Domhoff, *Who Rules America?* (Engelwood Cliffs, NJ: Prentice-Hall, 1967), 77.

29. Professor Rodney is speaking here from his own experience. In February 1968, Rodney left a teaching position at the University of Dar es Salaam, Tanzania to take a similar position at the University of the West Indies in Jamaica. Due to his political activities and perspective, he was banned from returning to Jamaica in October 1968. In 1974, after a six-year teaching stint at Dar es Salaam, he returned to his place of birth to head the history department at the University of Guyana. Unfortunately, his appointment was withdrawn as a result of intervention by Guyana's ruling regime. Edward A. Alpers and Pierre Michel Fontaine, eds., *Walter Rodney: Revolutionary and Scholar – A Tribute* (Los Angeles: Center for Afro-American Studies, 1982), 187.

30. Michael Karpovich, *Imperial Russia, 1801–1917* (New York: Henry Holt, 1932); George Vernadsky, *The Russian Revolution, 1917–1931* (New York: Henry Holt, 1932); Vernadsky, *A History of Russia* (New Haven, CT: Yale University Press, 1930); Vernadsky, *Lenin: Red Dictator* (New Haven, CT: Yale University Press, 1931); Michael Florinsky, *Russia: A History and Interpretation* (New York: Macmillan, 1953); Florinsky, *Russia: A Short History* (London: Macmillan, 1969).

31. Leonard Schapiro, *The Origins of the Communist Autocracy: Political Opposition in the Soviet State – First Phase, 1917–1922* (Cambridge, MA: Harvard University Press, 1977, orig. 1955), xi.

32. Adam B. Ulam, *The Unfinished Revolution: An Essay on the Sources of Influence of Marxism and Socialism* (New York: Random House, 1960), i.

33. Even the bourgeois scholars readily admit this connection. Philip Mosely writes, "An important by-product of the development of Russian Soviet studies has been the strengthening of the research function within government. This has been accomplished in large part by younger scholars who have gone from the area centers into government research posts; within government their reputation stands high

and they have made valuable contributions to the background of policy, some also in the formulation and execution of policy. Government agencies have come to feel that they can benefit a great deal in meeting their responsibilities through sending selected officers to the major centers for advanced training in research, and they have done so on a substantial scale." Mosely, "The Growth of Russian Studies," in Harold H. Fisher, ed., *American Research on Russia* (Bloomington, IN: Indiana University Press, 1959), 20. See also Robert F. Byrnes, "USA: Work at the Universities," in Walter Laqueur and L. Labedz, eds., *The State of Soviet Studies* (Cambridge, MA: MIT Press, 1965).

34. Harold H. Fisher, *The Communist Revolution: An Outline of Strategy and Tactics* (Palo Alto, CA: Stanford University Press, 1955), iii.

35. See E. H. Carr, *What is History?* (New York: Vintage, 1961).

36. Carr's numerous works on Russian history include his massive fourteen-volume *A History of Soviet Russia* (London: Macmillan, 1950–1978); *The October Revolution Before and After* (New York: Knopf, 1969); *The Russian Revolution: From Lenin to Stalin, 1917–1929* (London: Macmillan, 1979).

37. Schapiro, *The Origins of the Communist Autocracy*, xiv.

38. *Outline History of the USSR* (Moscow: Foreign Languages Publishing House, 1960), 142–5; V. I. Lenin, *The Development of Capitalism in Russia, Collected Works*, vol. 3, 228–35, 431–5, 496–507; A. M. Pankratova et. al., *A History of the USSR* (Moscow: Foreign Languages Publishing House, 1947), part II, 231–4.

39. Pankratova et. al., *A History of the USSR*, part II, 230–7; Lenin, *The Development of Capitalism in Russia*, 191–3; 369–78.

40. Pankratova et. al., *A History of the USSR*, part II, 240–3.

41. *Outline History of the USSR*, 155–67; Pankratova et. al., *A History of the USSR*, part III, 13–18; Lenin, *Imperialism: The Highest Stage of Capitalism*, in *Collected Works*, vol. 22.

42. This view is furthest developed in P. N. Sobolez et al., *The Great October Socialist Revolution* (Moscow: Progress Pub., 1977), 19–56. See also Pankratova et. al., *A History of the USSR*, part III, 199–54; N. Popov, *Outline History of the Communist Party of the Soviet Union* (Moscow: Cooperative Publishing Society of Foreign Workers, 1934), part I, 306–44.

2 The Russian Regime and the Soviet Revolution

1. See debate between George Vernadsky and L. V. Cherepin in Thomas Riha, ed., *Readings in Russian Civilization* (Chicago and London: University of Chicago Press, 1964), vol. I, 75–91. Cherepin convincingly argues that one must distinguish between varieties in form and real similarities in substance–between superstructural relations and the fundamental contradictions of social life. [note by WR]

2. Ibid., 88–91. See also Jerome Blum, "Land and Peasant in Russia," ibid., 157–72; Lazar Volin, "The Russian Peasant and Serfdom," *Agricultural History* 17, no. 1 (1943), 41–61.

3. See V. I. Lenin, *The Development of Capitalism in Russia*, *Collected Works*, vol. 3, 384–6; 468–83; 541–51.

4. Between 1914 and 1916, 2,512 strikes involving an estimated 1,674,210 workers took place in Russia. About 20 percent of these strikes were considered "political' according to official documentation from the Duma. Golder, ed., *Documents of Russian History, 1914–1917*, 186.

5. These events are described in greater detail in George Katkov, *Russia, 1917: The February Revolution* (New York: Harper and Row Publishers, 1967), 306–52.

6. See N. Popov, *Outline History of the Communist Party of the Soviet Union*, 343–75; P. N. Sobolev, *The Great October Socialist Revolution*, 19–28; Pankratova et. al., *A History of the USSR*, part III, 142–51.

7. See Katkov, *Russia, 1917*, 388–99; R. P. Browder and A. F. Kerensky, eds., *The Russian Provisional Government, 1917: Documents*, vol. I (Stanford, CA: Stanford University Press, 1961), 127–8.

8. Quoted in Katkov, *Russia, 1917*, 376.

9. Ibid., 377.

10. Ibid., 394.

11. Ibid., 377–87.

12. Kerensky's writings have made a substantial impact on America historiography of the Russian Revolution. See *The Catastrophe: Kerensky's Own Story of the Russian Revolution* (New York: D. Appleton, 1927); *The Prelude to Bolshevism: The Kornilov Rising* (New York: Dodd, Mead and Co., 1919); *The Crucifixion of Liberty* (New York: John Day, 1934); *Russia and History's Turning Point* (New York: Duell, Sloan and Pearce, 1965).

13. See V. I. Lenin, *Imperialism: The Highest Stage of Capitalism Collected Works*, vol. 22; N. Popov, *Outline History of the CPSU*, part I, 306–11; 322–4; Pankratova et. al., *A History of the USSR*, part III, 119–34.

14. Hugh Seton-Watson, *The Pattern of Communist Revolution*, 34.

15. Katkov, *Russia, 1917*, 101–5.

16. Ibid., 104.

17. Quoted in Leon Trotsky, *History of the Russian Revolution*, trans. Max Eastman (Chicago: Haymarket Books, 2008), 105.

18. William Chamberlin, "The March Revolution was Spontaneous," in *The Russian Revolution and Bolshevik Victory*, Arthur E. Adams, ed. (Boston, MA: D.C. Heath Co., 1960), taken from William Chamberlin, *The Russian Revolution, 1917–1921*, vol. I (New York: Macmillian, 1935), 73–80.

19. Leon Trotsky, *History of the Russian Revolution*, 109.

20. In a marginal note, Rodney refers to a story Trotsky relates in his *History of the Russian Revolution* in which a tram car conductor took his own initiative in the February Revolution. On February 24 in St. Petersburg, the conductor stopped the car and demanded that all his passengers get out after discovering a Russian official riding in the car. Trotsky wrote, "It was just such conductors who stopped the car of the monarchy and with practically the same words—this car does not go any farther!—and who ushered out the bureaucracy, making no distinction in the rush of business between a general of gendarmes and a liberal sector. The conductor on the Liteiny Boulevard was a conscious factor of history." Ibid., 149.

21. Ibid.

22. Ibid. 152.

23. Oliver Radkey, *The Agrarian Foes of Bolshevism: Promise and Default of the Russian Socialist Revolutionaries, February and October, 1917* (New York: Columbia University Press, 1958), 127.

24. Ibid., 53–64, 455–6.

25. Katkov, *Russia, 1917*, 418–27.

26. Ibid., 370–71.

27. Ibid., 251.

28. See especially P. N. Sobolev et. al., *The Great October Socialist Revolution* (Moscow: Progress Publishers, 1977).

29. Radkey, *The Agrarian Foes of Bolshevism*, ix.

30. George Vernadsky, *A History of Russia* (New York: Bantam Books., 1967), 317.

31. Ivar Spector, *Russia: New History* (Portland: Metropolitan Press, 1935), 171–2.
32. Leonard Schapiro, *The Origins of the Communist Autocracy*, 53ff.
33. Radkey, *The Agrarian Foes of Bolshevism*, xii.
34. A. M. Andreyev, *The Soviets and Workers' Deputies on the Eve of the October Revolution* (Moscow: Progress Publishers, 1971), 52, 163, 171, 257, and 267; and also Andreyev, *Soldiers in the Russian Army Garrisons in the October Revolution* (Moscow: Progress Publishers, 1975).
35. Christopher Hill, *Lenin and the Russian Revolution*, 117.
36. On April 4, 1917, Lenin attended a meeting of the Bolshevik Party where he delivered a report under the heading "On the Tasks of the Proletariat in the Present Revolution." In his presentation, he explicitly stated that the Soviet form of government "is the only possible revolutionary government, which directly expresses the mind and will of the majority of the workers and peasants. Humanity has not yet evolved and we do not as yet know a type of government superior to and better than the Soviets of Workers', Agricultural Labourers', Peasants' and Soldiers' Deputies." V. I. Lenin, *Collected Works*, vol. 24, 22.
37. See S. N. Sobolev et. al., *The Great October Socialist Revolution*, 48–56.
38. Melvin C. Wren, *The Course of Russian History* (New York: Macmillan Co., 1958, first ed.), 554. It should be noted that this very statement is missing from the text of the second edition (1963) and the third edition (1968) of this volume. A reading of the later editions gives the impression that there was opposition to the dissolution from the Constituent Assembly, although Wren provides no additional evidence.
39. J. P. Nettl, *The Soviet Achievement* (London: Thames & Hudson Ltd., 1967).
40. Stanley W. Page, ed., *Russia in Revolution: Selected Readings in Russian Domestic History Since 1855* (Princeton, NJ: Van Nostrand, 1965), 114.
41. Rheta Chiled Dorr, *Inside the Russian Revolution* (New York: Arno Press, 1970, reprint), 22.
42. Ibid. 18.
43. Hugh Seton-Watson, *The Pattern of Communist Revolution*, 29.
44. Ibid., 37.
45. Schapiro, *The Origins of the Communist Autocracy*, 359.

46. Arthur E. Adams, ed., *The Russian Revolution and Bolshevik Victory: Why and How?* (Boston: D.C. Heath, 1960). Fainsod's works include *How Russia is Ruled* (Cambridge, MA: Harvard University Press, 1954); and "Censorship in the USSR," *Problems of Communism 5*, no. 2 (March–April, 1956), 12–19.
47. Although Rodney does not name him, he is clearly referring to John W. Gardner, who was assigned chief of the Latin American section of Foreign Broadcast Intelligence during World War II and then assigned to Italy and Austria as an OSS operative. After the war he joined the Carnegie Corporation and drafted the proposal for funding the Center for Russian Studies at Harvard University. See Ellen Condliffe Lagemann, *The Politics of Knowledge: The Carnegie Corporation, Philanthropy, and Public Policy* (Chicago: University of Chicago Press, 1989), 170–3.

3 Marx, Marxism and the Russian Left

1. H. R. Trevor-Roper, "Karl Marx and the Study of History," in Trevor-Roper, *Men and Events: Historical Essays* (New York: Harper & Brothers, 1957), 285–98.
2. Klaus Mehnert, *Stalin Versus Marx: The Stalinist Historical Doctrine* (London: George Allen and Unwin Ltd., 1952), 15.
3. David Mitrany, *Marx Against the Peasant: A Study of Social Dogmatism* (London: Weidenfeld & Nicolson, 1951), ix.
4. Ibid., 63.
5. Kermit E. McKenzie, "Lenin's 'Revolutionary Democratic Dictatorship of the Proletariat and the Peasantry,'" in *Essays in Russian and Soviet History: In Honor of Geroid Tanquary Robinson*, ed. John Shelton Curtiss (Leiden, Netherlands: E. J. Brill, 1963), 150.
6. Frederick Engels, "On Social Relations in Russia," *Karl Marx and Frederick Engels Collected Works: Marx and Engels, 1874–1883*, vol. 24, (London: Lawrence and Wishart, 1986), 39–50.
7. Ibid., 43.
8. "Karl Marx, "Letter to Otechestvenniye Zapiski," in ibid., 199.
9. Ibid., 200. Editor's note: some of the quotes from Marx and Engels are slightly different than what Rodney had in his lecture notes, in part because the translations are different (since we could not source every single edition, we chose to use the latest translations)

and because of errors in his transcriptions. Note, too, that this particular letter was written by Marx—a German native—in French, which was then translated into English.

10. Ibid., 199.

11. Engels, "On Social Relations in Russia," 44–8.

12. Karl Marx, letter to Vera Zasulich, in *Karl Marx and Frederick Engels Collected Works*, vol. 24, 370–1.

13. The text of the 1882 Russian edition of the Communist Manifesto is available at marxists.org.

14. "Engels to Nikolai Danielson in St. Petersburg, October 17, 1893," available at marxists.org.

15. Mitrany, *Marx Against the Peasant*, 41.

16. Avrahm Yarmolinsky, *Road to Revolution: A Century of Russian Radicalism* (New York: Collier Books, 1962), 5.

17. Karl Marx and Frederick Engels, "Address of the Central Authority to the League," in *The Collected Works of Karl Marx and Frederick Engels: Marx and Engels, 1849–1851*, vol. 10 (London: Lawrence and Wishart, 1976), 281. See also chapter 4, on Trotsky, for an elaboration of the concept of permanent revolution.

18. These works include Yarmolinsky, *Road to Revolution*; Nicolas Berdyaev, *The Origins of Russian Communism* (London: Geoffery Books, 1937); Berdyaev, *The Russian Idea* (Boston: Beacon Press, 1962); Franco Venturi, *Roots of Revolution: A History of Populist and Socialist Movements in Nineteenth Century Russia* (Chicago and London: University of Chicago Press, 1960); E. Lampert, *Studies in Rebellion* (London: Routledge and Kegan Paul, 1957); *Sons Against Fathers: Studies in Russian Radicalism and Revolution* (Oxford: Clarendon Press, 1965); David M. Lang, *The First Russian Radical: Alexander Radischev 1749-1802* (London: George Allen & Unwin, 1959). In the text of the original lecture, Rodney adds, "There is a sixth publication which *is* marginally relevant—A. Mazour, *The First Russian Revolution, 1825* [*The Decembrist Movement, Its Origins, Development and Significance*]. Besides, there are large numbers of articles in journals or compilations. Then general books like Florinsky and Vernadsky. Finally, the Soviets themselves deal with the *issue*, though from a different perspective."

19. Yarmolinsky, *Road to Revolution*, 10.

20. Berdyaev, *The Origins of Russian Communism*, 7, emphasis WR.

21. Ibid., 8–12; 19–21. The last point is stressed in *The Russian Idea*,

193–8.

22. Berdyaev, *The Origins of Russian Communism*, 22–3; Lang, *The First Russian* Radical, 14–15.
23. Berdyaev, *The Origins of Russian Communism*, 7, 24, 42.
24. Ibid., 42.
25. Ibid., 38.
26. Ibid., 50–3.
27. Ibid., 67.
28. Ibid.
29. Ibid., 63–4.
30. Ibid., 72.
31. Ibid., 115.
32. Ibid., 104.
33. Ibid., 106.
34. Ibid., 63.
35. Ibid., 63.
36. See, for example, Michael Adas, *Prophets of Rebellion: Millenarian Protest Movements Against the European Colonial Order* (Chapel Hill, NC: University of North Carolina Press, 1979); James Giblin and Jamie Monson, eds., *Maji Maji: Lifting the Fog of War* (Leiden and Boston: Brill, 2010).
37. For more on Pyotr Struve and the "Legal Marxists," see Richard Kindersley, *The First Russian Revisionists: A Study of Legal Marxism in Russia* (Oxford: Oxford University Press, 1962); M. C. Howard and J. E. King, "Russian Revisionism and the Development of Marxian Political Economy in the Early Twentieth Century," *Studies in Soviet Thought* 37, no. 2 (February 1989), 95–117.
38. Louis Fischer, *The Life of Lenin*, (New York: Harper & Row, 1964), 45.
39. Frederick Engels, "Karl Marx, *A Contribution to the Critique of Political Economy* (1859)," *Collected Works*, vol. 16, 465.
40. Ivar Spector, *An Introduction to Russian History and Culture* (New York: Van Nostrand, 1961, 3rd ed.), vi.
41. G. A. Kursanov, *Fundamentals of Dialectical Materialism* (Moscow: Progress Publishers, 1967), 33.
42. This was the Russian Social-Democratic Labour Party, founded in 1898. It had its roots in such movements as the Union of Struggle for the Emancipation of the Working Class and the Union of Russian Social Democrats Abroad, both of which Plekhanov worked closely with.

43. One should see, in particular, Jonathan Frankel's introduction to *Vladimir Akimov on the Dilemmas of Russian Marxism* (Cambridge, UK: Cambridge University Press, 1969), 60ff. Other workers which illuminate the Menshevik position are Abraham Ascher, *The Mensheviks in the Russian Revolution* (Ithaca and London: Cornell University Press, 1976); Ascher, *Pavel Axelrod and The Development of Menshevism* (Cambridge, MA: Harvard University Press, 1972); Geoffrey A. Hosking, *The Russian Constitutional Experiment: Government and Duma, 1907–1914* (Cambridge, UK: Cambridge University Press, 1973).

44. In a pamphlet denouncing the July Uprising entitled "To All Men and Women Workers," the Mensheviks exposed their enthusiastic support for the Provisional Government: "It should be our immediate aim to help the state in its struggle against the economic chaos by means of regulation and control of industry." It also proclaimed its support for the war. Frank Alfred Golder, ed., *Documents of Russian History, 1914–1917* (Gloucester, MA: Peter Smith, 1964), 459.

45. Raphael Abramovitch, *The Soviet Revolution, 1917–1939* (New York: International Universities Press, ,1962). 129.

46. Ibid., 313.

47. See for instance, *Outline History of the USSR* (Moscow, Progress Publishers, 1960); *History of the October Revolution* (Moscow: Progress Publishers, 1977).

48. For his reply, directed to the editor of *The Otecestvenniye Zapisky*, see David McLellan, ed., *Karl Marx: Selected Writings* (Oxford: Oxford University Press, 1977), 571.

49. Mao Tse-Tung, "On Contradiction," in *Selected Readings from the Works of Mao TseTung* (Peking: Foreign Languages Press, 1971), 91–109.

50. Mao writes, "In studying the particularity and relativity of contradiction, we must give attention to the distinction between the principal contradiction and the non-principal contradictions and to the distinction between the principal aspect and the non-principal aspect of a contradiction; in studying the universality of contradictions and the struggle of opposites in contradiction, we must give attention to the distinction between the different forms of struggle. Otherwise we shall make mistakes. If, through study we achieve a real understanding of the essentials explained above, we shall be able to demolish dogmatist ideas which are contrary to the basic

principles of Marxism-Leninism and detrimental to our revolutionary cause, and our comrades with practical experience will be able to organize their experience into principles and avoid repeating empiricist errors." Ibid., 128–9.

51. Karl Marx, "The Bourgeoisie and the Counter Revolution," *Collected Works*, vol. 8, 161.

52. Frederick Engels, "Introduction" (1895) to Karl Marx, *The Class Struggles in France, 1848–1850*, in *Karl Marx: Selected Works*, ed. C. Palme Dutt (New York: International Publishers, 1936), 175. This quote also appeared in Engels's essay, "Tactics of Social Democracy," published that same year (1895). In Rodney's lectures, he placed in quotes what was really a close paraphrase, and he attributed to Marx himself the original text, which was actually Engels. We've adjusted the prose and corrected the quote accordingly.

53. Pavel N. Miliukov, *Russia and its Crisis* (Chicago: University of Chicago Press, 2015,, orig. 1905).

4 Trotsky as Historian of the Russian Revolution

1. "Introduction," Irving Howe, ed., *The Basic Writings of Trotsky* (New York: Vintage, 1965), 5.

2. There is a substantial literature on the life and work of Leon Trotsky. The most comprehensive biography to date is Isaac Deutscher's three-volume study, recently gathered into a single volume, *The Prophet: The Life of Leon Trotsky* (London and New York: Verso, 2015). See also, Paul Le Blanc, *Leon Trotsky* (London: Reaktion Books, 2015); Victor and Natalia Sedova Trotsky, *The Life and Death of Leon Trotsky* (Chicago: Haymarket Books, 2016); Joshua Rubenstein, *Leon Trotsky* (New Haven, CT: Yale University Press, 2011); Irving Howe, *Leon Trotsky* (New York: Viking Press, 1978); and Trotsky's own memoir, *My Life: An Attempt at an Autobiography* (New York: Charles Scribner's Sons, 1930). It appears from Rodney's own notes that he often used Howe, ed., *The Basic Writings of Trotsky*.

3. Trotsky, "The Motive Forces of the Russian Revolution," in Howe, ed., *The Basic Writings of Trotsky*, esp. 50–52. On George Vernadsky's interpretation, see chapter 2 as well as his book *The Russian Revolution, 1917–1931* (New York: Henry Holt and Co., 1932).

4. Trotsky, "The Motive Forces of the Russian Revolution," 47. A slightly different version of this passage appears in Trotsky's book *1905*, trans. Anya Bostock (Chicago: Haymarket Books, 2017, orig. published in 1907): "European capital, in preventing the development of Russian artisanal trade, thereby snatched the ground from under the feet of Russia's bourgeois democracy. Can the Petersburg or Moscow of today be compared with the Berlin or Vienna of 1848, or with the Paris of 1789, which had not yet begun to dream of railways or the telegraph and regarded a workshop employing 300 men as the largest imaginable? We have never had even a trace of that sturdy middle class which first lived through centuries of schooling in self-government and political struggle and then, hand in hand with a young, as yet unformed proletariat, stormed the Bastilles of feudalism." (34–5)

5. Trotsky, "The Motive Forces of the Russian Revolution," 47.

6. Ibid., 49.

7. Leon Trotsky, *History of the Russian Revolution*, trans. Max Eastman (Chicago: Haymarket Books, 2008), xv. Although it is not clear which edition Rodney had read, we chose to source his quotes and references from the Haymarket edition, the most authoritative, complete English-language edition. The book was originally published in three volumes, but because the Haymarket edition combines the entire text in a single volume, we cite only page numbers.

8. Ibid., 5.

9. Ibid., 6.

10. As quoted in ibid., 7. Trotsky invoked him to counter his claim, arguing instead that "in reality the possibility of this swift growth was determined by that very backwardness which, alas, continued not only up to the moment of liquidation of the old Russia, but as her legacy up to the present day." (Ibid., 7).

11. See Christopher Hill, *Lenin and the Russian Revolution* (London: English Universities Press, 1947); Irving Howe, ed., *The Basic Writings of Trotsky* (New York: Vintage Books, 1965), 16–17.

12. Hill, *Lenin and the Russian Revolution*, 20.

13. Karl Marx and Frederick Engels, "Address of the Central Authority to the League," in *The Collected Works of Karl Marx and Frederick Engels: Marx and Engels, 1849–1851*, vol. 10 (London: Lawrence and Wishart, 1976), 281.

14. Kermit E. McKenzie, "Lenin's 'Revolutionary Democratic

Dictatorship of the Proletariat and the Peasantry,'" in *Essays in Russian and Soviet History: In Honor of Geroid Tanquary Robinson*, ed. John Shelton Curtiss (Leiden: E. J. Brill, 1963), 151; George Lichtheim, *Marxism: An Historical and Critical Study* (New York: Praeger, 1961), 122–7, 222–32. Lichtheim does document Marx's hostility toward anarchism, as well, while showing that the concept of permanent revolution has its origins in the post-1848 revolutions.

15. Trotsky, *History of the Russian Revolution*, 10.
16. Leon Trotsky, "The Events in St. Petersburg," *Our Revolution* (January 1905), www.marxist.org
17. Trotsky, *History of the Russian Revolution*, , 25–6; see also Leon Trotsky, *1905*.
18. Trotsky, *History of the Russian Revolution*, 19.
19. Ibid., 28.
20. Ibid., 28.
21. Ibid., 6.
22. Ibid., 7–12.
23. Ibid, 49.
24. Ibid., 40, 71.
25. Ibid., 88.
26. Ibid., 111.
27. Ibid., 157.
28. Ibid., 124–5, 135.

5 On the "Inevitability" of the Russian Revolution

1. Michael Karpovich, *Imperial Russia, 1801–1917* (New York: Henry Holt and Co., 1932), 22.
2. What Rodney is referring to is the existence of "state peasants." In 1858, the Russian tsarist state had over 12 million registered male peasants, whereas private serfs comprised over 10 million. G. T. Robinson, *Rural Russia Under the Old Regime* (Berkeley and Los Angeles: University of California Press, 1967, orig., 1932), 63.
3. Karpovich, *Imperial Russia*, 36.
4. See, *Outline History of the USSR* (Moscow: Progress Publishers, 1960), 137 ff.
5. Michael T. Florinsky, *Russia: A Short History* (London: Macmillan, 1969, 2nd ed.), 301–4; Karpovich, *Imperial Russia*, 94–100.

Rodney appears to be referring to both authors' analysis of the effects of the Emancipation Act of 1861 in terms of the relationship between the produces and the means of production. "Under the existing conditions of farming," writes Florinsky, "the allotment were inadequate to occupy fully the members of the household of to provide proper maintenance for the owners' family." (Ibid., 303) Because the redemption payments were too high, it contributed to the creation of an urban proletariat, although limitations and restrictions on internal migration and the slow growth of industry immobilized the Russian peasantry for some time until the late nineteenth century. For an even more "Marxist-sounding account," see Michael Florinsky, *Russia: A History and Interpretation*, vol. II, New York: Macmillan, 1953), 921–8.

6. George Verdanksy, *A History of Russia* (New Haven, CT: Yale University Press, 1930), 154–5; Ivar Spector, *Russia: A New History* (Portland, OR: Metropolitan Press, 1935, 3rd ed.), 108–11.

7. Geroid T. Robinson, *Rural Russia Under the Old Regime* (Berkeley: University of California Press, 1969); George P. Pavlovsky, *Agricultural Russia on the Eve of the Revolution* (New York: Howard Fertig, 1968). For a more recent accounts of Stolypin and his reforms, see Abraham Ascher, *P. A. Stolypin: The Search for Stability in Late Imperial Russia* (Stanford, CA: Stanford University Press, 2002); David A. J. Macey, *Government and Peasant in Russia, 1881–1906: The Prehistory of the Stolypin Reforms* (DeKalb, IL: Northern Illinois University Press, 1987).

8. In his 1908 book, *The Agrarian Programme of Social-Democracy in the First Russian Revolution, 1905–1907,* Lenin wrote, "Let us take the Stolypin programme, which is supported by the Right landlords and the Octobrists. It is avowedly a landlords' programme. But can it be said that it is reactionary in the economic sense, i. e., that it precludes, or seeks to preclude, the development of capitalism, to prevent a bourgeois agrarian evolution? Not at all. On the contrary, the famous agrarian legislation introduced by Stolypin . . . is permeated through and through with the purely bourgeois spirit. There can be no doubt that it follows the line of capitalist evolution, facilitates and pushes forward that evolution, hastens the expropriation of the peasantry, the break-up of the village commune, and the creation of a peasant bourgeoisie. Without a doubt, that legislation is progressive in the scientific-economic sense. But does that mean that Social-Democrats should 'support' it? It does not. Only vulgar

Marxism can reason in that way, a Marxism whose seeds Plekhanov and the Mensheviks are so persistently sowing when they sing, shout, plead, and proclaim: we must support the bourgeoisie in its struggle against the old order of things." Lenin *Collected Works*, vol. 13 (Moscow: Progress Publishers, 1972), 243, available at marxists.org.

Although it is common for historians to emphasize Lenin's grudging respect for the Stolypin reforms, the truth is that he wrote far more viciously attacking Stolypin than praising him. Immediately after his assassination in 1911, he published a scathing denunciation of him, his brutal policies of repression, and the liberals who supported him. See V. I. Lenin, "Stolypin and the Revolution," Lenin Collected Works, vol. 17 (Moscow: Progress Publishers, 1974, orig. 1911), 247-256, available at marxists.org.

9. Karpovich, *Imperial Russia*, 94; also, Florinsky writes that it was a "move in the right direction. Coupled with a firm policy that [could] meet the unmistakable longing of the peasantry for more land, it might have had a profound effect upon the future course of Russian history, and might have saved the upper class from the tragic fate that befell them in 1917"(*Russia: A History and an Interpretation*, 1224).

10. John C. Dewdney, *A Geography of the Soviet Union* (Oxford: Pergamon Press, 1965), 79.

11. See Howard D. Mehlinger and John M. Thompson, *Count Witte and the Tsarist Government in the 1905 Revolution* (Bloomington: Indiana University Press, 1972); Theodore H. von Laue, "Russian Peasants in the Factory, 1892–1904," *Journal of Economic History* 21(March 1961), 61–80; von Laue, "Tsarist Labor Policy, 1895–1903," *Journal of Modern History* 34, vol. 2 (June 1962), 135–45.

12. See Leon Trotsky, *1905* (New York: Random House, 1971), 75–7, 131–9, 140–56.

13. George Vernadsky, *The Russian Revolution 1917–1931* (New York: Henry Holt and Co., 1932), 10–22; Vernadsky, *A History of Russia* (New Haven, CT: Yale University Press, 4th ed.), 241–73; Michael T. Florinsky, *Russia: A History and an Interpretation*, vol. II (New York: Macmillan, 1953), 1184–257; Florinsky, *Russia: A Short History* (London: Macmillan, 1969, 2nd ed.), 343–56.

14. See especially Michael Karpovich, "After 1905: Revolution or Cooperation with Government," in Arthur Adams, ed., *Imperial Russia After 1861*, 38–41.

15. Florinsky, *Russia: A Short History*, 409.
16. Anna M. Pankratova et. al., *A History of the USSR*, vol. II, chapter 1; *Outline History of the USSR*, 199; P. N. Sobolev et. al., *The Great October Socialist Revolution*, 7–14.
17. Konstantin Petrovich Pobedonostsev, *Reflections of a Russian Statesman*, trans. Robert Crozier Long (London: Grant Richards, 1898), 26, 32.
18. Baron Boris Vladimirovich Stürmer (July 27, 1848–September 9, 1917) was a lawyer who served as a district governor, member of the Russian Assembly, prime minister, and both minister of internal affairs and foreign minister under Tsar Nicholas II. He proved incompetent both as minister of internal affairs and foreign minister, and was forced to resign in disgrace; he was ultimately arrested after the February Revolution. Stürmer was accused of secret negotiations with Germany—and his German surname certainly gave credence to the rumors. Alexander Dmitriyevich Protopopov (December 18, 1866–October 27, 1918) was a member of the Octobrist party who had been elected to the third and fourth Dumas and later served as minister of the interior from September 1916 to February 1917. He became a disciple of Rasputin and showed signs of delusional behavior. See Christopher Hill, *Lenin and the Russian Revolution* (London: Hodder and Stoughton, 1947), 20–3; Simon Sebag Montefiore, *The Romanovs: 1613–1918* (New York: Knopf, 2016), 594–8.
19. Michael Karpovich, *Imperial Russia, 1801–1917* (New York: Henry Holt & Company, 1950), 95.
20. Benedict H. Sumner, *Survey of Russian History* (Edinburgh: Riverside Press, 1944), 70.

6 On Democracy: Lenin, Kautsky and Luxemburg

1. V. I. Lenin, *The Proletarian Revolution and the Renegade Kautsky* (Peking: Foreign Languages Press, 1965), 7.

Rodney had much more to say about Lenin. At the very end of what he had identified as lecture 11, Rodney jotted down a very bare outline assessing Lenin's essential role in the revolution and contributions to Marxist theory; we thought it was important to include it here. Because of its very schematic form, we decided not to try and turn it into prose and insert it in the chapter (and some of it is repetitive). Below is the outline as he wrote it:

Lenin in Action

Various ways in which his name comes up—take Gorky's sketch found in Riha and Berdyaev's chapter VI—Bertram Wolfe—political theorists like Plamenatz.

How do we make a historical assessment of a man? There are a number of Marxist writings on the whole question of man and history, but we shan't go into that now. What were the concrete historical events with which he was associated? What was his impact on those events and hence his contribution to Russia and humanity?

Born 1871—rapid rise to maturity—at 23 he was a Marxist intellectual organizing St. Petersburg and when he organized the Union for the Liberation of Working Class in 1895 he was exiled to Siberia. (All the leaders went to school in Siberia)—Plekhanov was since 1883, however, and he gets short sighted.

(a) 1905 and March 1917 [redacted]. However, he held the party together, got funds by any means etc.

(b) October 1917—April Theses, calling for land and peace, persuading the whole party—get credit for [redacted] is not solely his, and as he himself would admit they made mistakes in the intervening months. This is generally held—see [redacted]

(c) Brest-Litovsk and the Red Army

(d) N.E.P.—Perhaps his greatest victory, a strategic retreat, holding the reins of power.

Lenin and Theory

(1) His contribution to the Peasant question—The Development of Capitalism in Russia, (1889) and The Agrarian Question in Russia (1908).

(2) Questions of the nature of the party—The Iskra board (Plekhanov, Axelrod [redacted]

(3) The question of the two-stage revolution

(4) Imperialism, the highest stage of capitalism

(5) The Nature of the State (The State and Revolution [redacted])

(6) Nationalities question

(7) According to Soviets—peaceful co-existence (undoubtedly

internationalism was not immediate after 1920, but peaceful co-existence was a lie)
(8) Materialism and Empirio-criticism.

What was his overall contribution to Marxism?
(a) Russian conditions
(b) The Revolutionary Marx

2. Kautsky himself admits his support for the Bolsheviks. See Karl Kautsky, "Die Aussichten der Funfjahresplanes," *Die Gesellschaft* 8, no. 3 (March, 1931), 255–64. For an English translation, see the preface of Kautsky, *Bolshevism at a Deadlock* (London: George Allen and Unwin, 1931), 7–23.

3. Karl Kautsky, *The Dictatorship of the Proletariat,* (Ann Arbor, MI: University of Michigan Press, 1964, orig. 1919), 42–6.

4. Ibid., 140.

5. Kautsky, *The Dictatorship of the Proletariat*, 42–58. His discussion of the dismissal of the Constituent Assembly is treated on pages 65–9. Kautsky never actually attempts to apply his arguments directly to the historical process in which the Bolsheviks seized power. Rather, he outlines what he sees as Marx's and Engels's definition of the dictatorship of the proletariat, using examples from the Paris Commune (1871) and the French Revolution. For an elaboration of his concept, see Kautsky, *Von der Demokratie zur Staatssklaverei: Eine Ausieinandersetzung mit Trotzki* (Berlin: Freiheit, 1921), 38–43, 83–84; *The Labour Revolution* (New York: Dial Press, 1925), 59–89; *Democracy versus Communism* (New York: Rand School Press, 1946), 29–47.

6. Lenin, *The Proletarian Revolution and the Renegade Kautsky* (Moscow: Kommunist Publishers, October–November 1918), 16. Available in *Lenin's Collected Works*, vol. 28 (Moscow: Progress Publishers, 1974) 227–325, trans., ed., Jim Riordan.

7. Vladimir Lenin, "Two Tactics of Social Democracy," in *V. I. Lenin: Selected Works* (New York: International Publishers, 1971), 99–107; 139–147; "State and Revolution," in *Selected Works,* 279–288; "The Immediate Tasks of the Soviet Government," in *Selected Works,* 401–31.

8. Lenin discusses the distinction between bourgeois and worker democracy in "The Proletarian Revolution and the Renegade Kautsky," 19–29.

9. In addition to the statement by Seton-Watson cited above, many other bourgeois historians admitted the lack of public reaction to the dismissal of the Constituent Assembly. See George Vernadsky, *Lenin: Red Dictator* (New Haven, CT: Yale University Press, 1931), 192–5; and Adam Ulam, *The Bolsheviks: The Intellectual and Political History of The Triumph of Communism in Russia* (New York: Collier Books, 1968). Ulam writes, "The lack of violent public reaction to the dissolution of the Assembly shows that the 'masses' in general did not care about its fate." (397)

10. Lenin, "The State and Revolution," in *Selected Works*, 293–5, where he discusses the failure of the Paris Commune and the need to destroy the existing state.

11. Marx's view of the peasantry has been a major point of controversy. The best-known work on the subject is David Mitrany, *Marx Against the Peasant: A Study of Social Dogmatism* (London: Weidenfeld & Nicolson, 1951), Unfortunately, the controversy only focuses on whether Marx's view was correct or not—very little discussion takes place on what actually is Marx's view. Marx's later writings, especially in reference to Russia, indicate that he was not as dogmatic on the "peasant question" as many commentators have portrayed him. In Marx's notes on Bakunin's *Statism and Anarchy*, he wrote, "Where the mass of the peasants are still owners of private property, where they even form a more or less important majority of the population, as they do in the states of the Western European continent, where they have not yet disappeared and been replaced by agricultural wage labourers, as in England; in these cases the following situation arises: either the peasantry hinders every workers' revolution and causes it to fail, as it has done in France up to now; or the proletariat ... must as a government inaugurate measures which directly improve the situation of the peasant and which thus win him for the revolution; measures which in essence facilitate the transition from private to collective property in land so that the peasant himself is converted for economic reasons; the proletariat must not, however, come into open collision with peasantry by, for example, proclaiming the abolition of inheritance or the abolition of property; this latter is only possible when the capitalist landlord has expropriated the peasant and the real worker of the land is just as much a proletarian wage labourer as the city worker, and thus has directly the same interests." In David McLellan, ed., *Karl Marx: Selected Writings* (Oxford and New York: Oxford University Press, 1977), 561.

12. Kautsky, *Dictatorship*, xxxi. In a draft of a letter to renowned Russian revolutionary Vera Zasulich, Marx wrote in reference to Russian conditions, "In every instance, the Western precedent would prove nothing at all about the 'historical inevitability' of this process." In the same draft, Marx explicitly stated that for a proper understanding of Russian conditions, "we must come down from pure theory to Russian reality." In McLelland, ed., *Karl Marx: Selected Writings*, 577–8.

13. Lenin, "The Development of Capitalism in Russia," in *Collected Works*, vol. 3 (Moscow: Progress Publishers, 1960), 172–87, 310–30; "Theory of the Agrarian Question," in *Selected Works*, vol. 8 (New York: International, 1938). There are numerous examples of Lenin's discussions on the role of the peasantry in the revolution. See part 4 of "From Bourgeois Revolution to Proletarian Revolution," in *Selected Works*, vol. 6 (New York: International, 1938), 339–96; and part 2 of "The Period of War Communism (1918–1920) in *Selected Works*, vol. 8 (New York: International, 1938), 105–210.

14. Lenin, "Speech Delivered at the First All-Russian Congress of Land Department, Committees of Poor Peasants and Communes, December 11, 1918,". in *Collected Works*, vol. 28 (Moscow: Progress Publishers, 1972, 4th Ed.), 338–448. He writes, "We know very well that in countries where small peasant economy prevails the transition to socialism cannot be effected except by a series of gradual preliminary stages. We fully realise that such vast upheavals in the lives of tens of millions of people as the transition from small individual peasant production to the social cultivation of the land, affecting as they do the most profound roots of life and habits, can be accomplished only when necessity compels people to reshape their whole lives." (pp. 339–40)

15. The Socialist Revolutionary Party, formed between 1899 and 1901, was a pseudo-anarchist organization made up of the middle peasantry and some revolutionary intellectuals. Their program called for the socialization of land and greater decentralization of the state. G. T. Robinson, *Rural Russia*, 140.

16. Kautsky writes, "A minority dictatorship always finds its most powerful support in an obedient army, but the more it substitutes this for majority support, the more it drives the opposition to seek a remedy by an appeal to the bayonet, instead of an appeal to that vote which is denied them. Civil war becomes the method of

adjusting political and social antagonisms." Kautsky, *Dictatorship*, 51–2.

17. Ironically, even the Mensheviks recognized the primacy of the struggle against counter-revolution. In a pamphlet denouncing the July Uprisings, the organizing Committee of the Russian Social Democratic Labor Party (Mensheviks) proclaimed that what "endangers our revolution and our freedom is the union of all dark forces of all secret and open counterrevolutionists." In Alfred Golder Frank, ed., *Documents of Russian History, 1914–1917* (Gloucester, MA: Peter Smith, 1964, orig., 1927), 459.

18. Karl Marx, "Civil War in France"; Frederick Engels, "On Authority," in *Marx and Engels: Selected Works*, vol. 1 (Moscow: Progress Publishers, 1951).

19. Engels, "On Authority," 578; also quoted in Lenin, *The Proletarian Revolution and the Renegade Kautsky*, 16.

20. Rodney here is referring to Marx's eleventh thesis on Feuerbach: "The philosophers have only interpreted the world in various ways; the point, however, is to change it." Karl Marx and Frederick Engels, *Collected Works*, vol. 5 (New York: International, 1976), 8.

21. For more on the history of the Second International, see G. D. H. Cole, *The Second International: 1889–1914*, vol. 3 of *The History of Socialist Thought* (London: Macmillan, 1956); James Joll, *The Second International* (London: Weidenfeld & Nicolson, 1955); Gerhart Niemeyer, "The Second International: 1889–1914," in M. M. Drachkovitch, ed., *The Revolutionary Internationals* (Stanford, CA: Stanford University Press, 1964).

22. Eduard Bernstein, son of a Berlin railroad engineer, joined the German Social Democratic Party in 1872. In the face of anti-socialist measures implemented by the state, Bernstein was forced into exile to England, where he subsequently developed the gist of his political ideas. He eventually revised Marxism, creating the notion of "evolutionary socialism." According to Bernstein, socialism could evolve within the state's political structure of parliamentarianism. His most famous work is *Evolutionary Socialism: Criticism and Affirmation* (New York: Shocken, 1961, orig., 1899). See also Peter Gay, *The Dilemma of Democratic Socialism: Edward Bernstein's Challenge to Marx* (New York: Columbia University Press 1952).

23. For more on Jean Juarès, see Harvey Goldberg's definitive biography, *The Life of Jean Juarès* (Madison, WI: University of Wisconsin

Press, 2003, orig. 1966).

24. Rosa Luxemburg, *The Russian Revolution and Leninism or Marxism* (Ann Arbor, MI: University of Michigan Press: 1961), 25.

25. Ibid., 31.

26. Luxemburg, *The Russian Revolution*, 35. Her critique of Kautsky dots the first chapter, especially 26–39.

27. One need only look at Bertram Wolfe's introduction to Luxemburg's *Russian Revolution*.

28. Luxemburg, *Russian Revolution*, 49.

29. Ibid., 42–4.

30. Ibid., 57–62.

31. For Luxemburg's position on the national question, see Luxemburg, *Russian Revolution*, 47–56. See also Horace B. Davis, ed., *The National Question: Selected Writings by Rosa Luxemburg* (New York: International Publishers, 1976), and for a critique, see Mary-Alice Waters, ed., *Rosa Luxemburg Speaks* (New York: Pathfinder Press, 1970), 12–17.

32. In an abortive rising of Berlin's workers, Luxemburg was arrested. During her removal to prison she was attacked and fatally beaten by soldiers. Her body was recovered days later from a canal.

33. Luxemburg, *Russian Revolution*, 72.

7 Building the Socialist State

1. Naum Jasny, *The Socialized Agriculture of the USSR: Plans and Performance* (Stanford, CA: Stanford University Press, 1949). A little over a decade later, Jasny revised his estimate dramatically, from 5.5 million deaths to "hundreds of thousands, perhaps a million," who died during the winter of 1932–3. See his *Essays on the Soviet economy* (New York: F. A. Praeger, 1962), 106.

2. William H. Hinton, *Fanshen: A Documentary of Revolution in a Chinese Village* (New York: Monthly Review Press, 1966).

3. This very famous and popular quote appears in hundreds, if not thousands of sources. It derives originally from Stalin's speech, "Concerning Questions of Agrarian Policy in the U.S.S.R. Speech Delivered at a Conference of Marxist Students of Agrarian Questions," December 27, 1929, *Collected Works of Stalin*, vol. 12 (April 1929–June 1930) (Moscow: Foreign Languages Publishing House, 1954), 147–78, available at marxists.org.

The problem is that in the English edition of the speech, which many scholars and journalists translated as "liquidate" is translated here as "eliminate." We don't know exactly where Rodney took this quote from, since the lectures cite few sources.

4. See Merle Fainsod, "Collectivization: The Method," in Robert V. Daniels, ed., *The Stalin Revolution: Fulfillment or Betrayal of Communism?* (Boston: D. C. Heath, 1965), 38.

5. Ibid., 38.

6. Quotes from Fainsod, *Smolensk Under Soviet Rule*, 245–6.

7. Rodney inserted a parenthetical note here to "see Maynard." He is referring to Sir John Maynard's classic study, *The Russian Peasant and Other Studies* (London: V. Gollancz Ltd, 1942). Rodney most likely identified Maynard because he was a Fabian socialist who spent considerable time in the Soviet Union, and his book is both critical of Stalin's policies but sympathetic to the Soviet experiment and, especially, to the plight of the peasantry. He does point out in his book that part of what attracted some of the poorer peasants and intellectuals to collectivization wasn't just settling accounts, but the introduction of new technologies—tractors and combines—to end the most back-breaking labor involved in ploughing and harvesting. But overall, Maynard concluded that collectivization was generally a failure. On Sir John Maynard, see E. John Russell, "Sir John Maynard and His Studies of the Russian Peasant (12 July, 1865–6 December, 1943)," *The Slavonic and East European Review* 24, no. 63 (January 1946), 56–65.

8. Academy of Sciences of the USSR, *A Short History of the USSR*, vol. II (Moscow: Progress Publishers, 1965), 168–71.

9. Lenin said this in a speech to the Eighth Party Congress on March 23, 1919, titled "Report On Work In The Countryside," available at marxists.org. The quote from Frederick Engels comes from his essay "The Peasant Question in France and Germany," Marx and Engels, *Selected Works*, vol. II (Moscow: Progress Publishers, 1962), 436–9. Rodney identifies Lenin's "Report" as well as his "Preliminary Draft Theses on the Agrarian Question," prepared for the Second Congress of the Communist International in 1920, as important statements on the peasantry that ultimately prepared the way for Lenin's New Economic Policy. A copy of the latter can be found in V. I. Lenin, *Collected Works*, vol. 31, 4th English ed. (Progress Publishers, Moscow, 1965), 152–64, available at marxists.org.

10. Maurice Dobb, *Soviet Economic Development Since 1917* (New York: International Publishers, 1966, orig. 1948), 222–30.

11. Leonard Schapiro, *The Origins of the Communist Autocracy: Political Opposition in the Soviet State – First Phase, 1917–1922* (Cambridge, MA.: Harvard University Press, 1977, orig. 1955), 43.

12. This is a massive subject and the results have been uneven and complicated by transformations in the global economy. Of course, during Rodney's tenure at the University of Dar es Salaam, the state was attempting to collectivize the peasantry through the creation of Ujamaa Villages. Rodney had written on the concept of Ujamaa and scientific socialism, but he did not drill down on the experiences of the peasantry. Others did, including some of his comrades at the university. See, for example, Issa G. Shivji, *Class Struggles in Tanzania* (New York: New York University Press, 1976); Michaela von Freyhold, *Ujamaa Villages in Tanzania: Analysis of a Social Experiment* (New York: Monthly Review Press, 1980); Göran Hydén, *Beyond Ujamaa in Tanzania: Underdevelopment and an Uncaptured Peasantry* (Berkeley and Los Angeles: University of California Press, 1980); Jannik Boesen, Birgit Storgaard Madsen, and Tony Moody, *Ujamaa: Socialism from Above* (Uppsala, Sweden: Scandinavian Institute of African Studies, 1977).

    For other efforts, see Merle L. Bowen, *The State Against the Peasantry: Rural Struggles in Colonial and Postcolonial Mozambique* (Charlottesville, VA: University Press of Virginia, 2000); Peter Dwyer and Leo Zeilig, *African Struggles Today: Social Movements Since Independence* (Chicago: Haymarket Books, 2012), esp. 66–71. Of course, Rodney's remark about the satisfaction of peasants in China, Vietnam, and Cuba must be taken in context, and should not be accepted as fact. Especially as these societies moved deeper into the neoliberal order and away from socialism, the conditions of agricultural production shifted significantly. The transformation of the peasantry under global neoliberalism is beyond the scope of this work, but it is worth reading D. A. Low's skeptical lectures on the subject of the peasantry from the era of independence to the onset of globalization. D. A. Low, *The Egalitarian Moment: Asia and Africa, 1950–1980* (New York: Cambridge University Press, 1996).

13. Rodney included a parenthetical note: "For a picture of the old regime see G.T. Robinson, *Rural Russia under the Old Regime*. The

full citation is Geroid T. Robinson, *Rural Russia under the Old Régime: A History of the Landlord-Peasant World and a Prologue to the Peasant Revolution of 1917* (New York: MacMillan, 1961).

14. Much of the scholarship on "settler colonialism" takes off long after Rodney's death, but there was work during the 1970s on Africa, in particular, that would have caught Rodney's attention, notably Arghiri Emmanuel, "White-Settler Colonialism and the Myth of Investment Imperialism," *New Left Review*, May 1, 1972, 35–57; Kenneth Good, "Settler Colonialism in Rhodesia," *African Affairs* 73, no. 290 (1974), 10–36; Good, "Settler Colonialism: Economic Development and Class Formation," *Journal of Modern African Studies* 14, no. 4 (1976), 597–620.

15. Regarding Soviet periodization, Rodney made a note to see Aleksandr Podkolzin, *A Short Economic History of the USSR*, trans. David Fidlon, ed. G. Ivanov-Mumjiev (Moscow: Progress, 1968).

16. Dobb, *Soviet Economic Development Since 1917*, 400.

17. Here Rodney is drawing on Podkolzin, *A Short Economic History of the USSR*, 150–7.

18. Podkolzin, *A Short Economic History of the USSR*, 145–6.

19. Both quotes from Ibid., 150.

20. Ibid., 151–3.

21. Ibid., 167–8.

22. Eugene Varga, *Two Systems: Socialist Economy and Capitalist Economy*, trans. R. Page Arnot (New York: International Publishers, 1939), 30–2, 169, 172.

23. Varga, *Two Systems*, 72.

24. Ibid., 23.

25. Benjamin E. Lippincott, "Introduction," in *On the Economic Theory of Socialism: Papers by Oskar Lange and Fred M. Taylor*, Lippincott, ed., (Minneapolis, MI: University of Minnesota Press, 1938), 1. This was originally Rodney's reference, an incomplete citation in parentheses.

26. Harry G. Shaffer, ed., *The Soviet Economy: A Collection of Western and Soviet Views* (London: Methuen & Co., Ltd., 1964), vii.

27. E. H. Carr, *1917: Before and After* (London: Macmillan, 1969), 7–8.

28. Alec Nove, *Communist Economic Strategy: Soviet Growth and Capabilities* (Washington, DC: National Planning Association, 1959), 4. WR emphasis.

29. Harry Schwartz, *Russia's Soviet Economy*, 2nd ed. (New York: Prentice Hall, 1954), 216.

30. John C. Dewdney, *A Geography of the Soviet Union* (Oxford: Pergamon, 1964), 89. It should be noted that Dewdney never altered this passage and that it still appears in the 2013 edition of the book (3rd ed., Oxford and New York: Pergamon Press, 2013), 86.

31. Ibid., 89.

32. Jasny, *Essays on the Soviet economy*, 18–25, 65, 76.

33. Alec Nove, *The Soviet Economy: An Introduction* (London: George Allen and Unwin, Ltd, 1961), 308.

34. See Shaffer, *The Soviet Economy*.

35. Naum Jasny, *Soviet Industrialization* (Chicago: University of Chicago Press, 1961). In his memoir, Jasny talks about the controversy surrounding that chapter title but concludes that it nevertheless was becoming a standard way of thinking about periodization. See Jasny, *To Live Long Enough: The Memoirs of Naum Jasny* (Lawrence, KS: University of Kansas Press, 1976), 132.

36. Schwartz, *Russia's Soviet Economy*, 115–17.

37. The incident to which Rodney refers occurred in January 1968, the context being the Vietnam War. For more, see Jack Cheevers, *Act of War: Lyndon Johnson, North Korea, and the Capture of the Spy Ship Pueblo* (New York: Penguin, 2013).

38. Dobb, *Soviet Economic Development Since 1917*.

39. See especially, Naum Jasny, *The Soviet Economy During the Plan Era* (Stanford, CA: Stanford University Press, 1951); and Jasny, *The Soviet Price System* (Stanford, CA: Stanford University Press, 1951).

40. It is beyond the scope of this project, but we should note that Varga was a brilliant economist who came to the Soviet Union to work on the national and colonial question in the Communist International. He initially endorsed Stalin's positions on the world economy, though it was clear he had reservations. The book to which Rodney refers, *Two Systems: Socialist Economy and Capitalist Economy*, while reflecting sound scholarship, fell squarely within the Stalinist framework. However, in 1946, he broke with the prevailing wisdom and published *The Economic Transformation of Capitalism at the End of the Second World War*. His argument that capitalism was actually more stable than Marxists had previously believed was regarded as sacrilege in the Soviet Union. He was roundly attacked

and forced to make a public self-criticism. After Stalin's death, however, he retracted his critique and in 1964 published what fellow Soviet economists and other Marxists dismissed as a "revisionist" work titled *Politico-Economic Problems of Capitalism* (Moscow: Progress, 1968) (The English translation appeared in 1968.) He argues, among many other things, that state economic planning was possible under modern capitalism, that wars are no longer inevitable under imperialism, that the national bourgeoisies in postcolonial states are not inherently reactionary, and that the capitalist state not only act in the interests of monopolists but the bourgeoisie as a whole, while making concessions to elements of the working class in order to retain its allegiance.

Evidently, Rodney was unaware of the book when he put together his lectures, which is unfortunate because Varga addressed several themes related to the Third World. For a thorough treatment of Varga's work, see André Mommen, *Stalin's Economist: The Economic Contributions of Jenö Varga* (New York: Routledge, 2011).

41. Here Rodney is clearly referencing Julius Nyerere's philosophy of "self-reliance," a pillar of the Tanganyika African National Union (TANU) Arusha Declaration of February 5,1967. The policy emphasized building a socialist society while becoming self-sufficient. In his March 1967 address "Education for Self-Reliance," and later issued as a pamphlet, Nyerere concludes with an impassioned plea for an education that encourages "socialist values," a "free citizenry which relies upon itself for its own development," and the cultivation of "members and servants of the kind of just and egalitarian future to which this country aspires." See the Arusha Declaration, available at marxists.org. "Education for Self-Reliance" is available at swaraj.org/shikshantar/resources_nyerere.html.

42. Given the overwhelming evidence of the use of forced labor under Stalin, Rodney is surprisingly cavalier with his skepticism about the numbers of people sent to the gulag and forced to labor in prison camps. Of course, he was writing in the midst of the Cold War, when defenders and detractors of the Soviet Union tended to exaggerate the numbers in both directions. Moreover, he did not have access to the Soviet archives, which have made possible a more accurate assessment of forced labor. And the figures are still inconclusive, but what we can determine is still staggering—by

some estimates, between 15 and 18 million people passed through between 1929 and 1953. An excellent account is Stephen A. Barnes, *Death and Redemption: The Gulag and the Shaping of Soviet Society* (Princeton, NJ: Princeton University Press, 2011).

43. Schwartz, *Russia's Soviet Economy*, 448–9.

44. Rodney is likely referring to the 1966 measure requiring all graduating university students to serve two years in the National Service before they could work in the Civil Service. They were to spend two months working in the rural areas and eighteen months as teachers or civil servants at a pay rate of 40 percent of the regular salary. Ironically, the students revolted against this measure, calling it "forced labor" and a form of colonialism. President Nyerere, not surprisingly, was incensed and regarded the students as elitists. See Seth M. Markle, *A Motorcycle on Hell Run: Tanzania, Black Power, and the Uncertain Future of Pan-Africanism, 1964-1974* (East Lansing, MI: Michigan State University Press, 2017), chapter 3; Ronald Aminzade, *Race, Nation, and Citizenship in Post-Colonial Africa: The Case of Tanzania* (New York: Cambridge University Press, 2013), 153.

45. Schwartz, *Russia's Soviet Economy*, 487.

46. The history of slavery in the United States challenges Rodney's assertion here, since a substantial portion of skilled labor in the antebellum South was enslaved. There are too many examples to cite here, but see Frederick C. Knight, *Working Diaspora: The Impact of African Labor on the Anglo-American World, 1650–1850* (New York: New York University Press, 2010), 111–30; and Martin Ruef, *Between Slavery and Capitalism: The Legacy of Emancipation in the American South* (Princeton, NJ: Princeton University Press, 2014), 67–8.

47. Nove, *Communist Economic Strategy*, 5.

48. Jasny, *The Soviet Economy During the Plan Era*, 97–107.

49. Nove, *Communist Economic Strategy*, 12.

50. Italy's uneven regional development has long been a subject of Italian Marxists, most famously Antonio Gramsci and Giuseppe Prezzolini. Gramsci's unfinished essay on the "Southern Question" (1926) has been widely cited on the challenges of building an alliance between the industrial proletariat in the North and the Southern peasantry. See Gramsci's "Some Aspects of the Southern Question," in *Antonio Gramsci: Pre-Prison Writings*, ed. Richard Bellamy (New York: Cambridge University Press, 1994), 313–37.

51. Nove, *The Soviet Economic System*, 85–105.

52. Nove, *Communist Economic Strategy*, 19. Jasny also echoes these criticisms in *Essays on the Soviet Economy*.

53. Jasny, *The Soviet 1956 Statistical Handbook: A Commentary* (East Lansing, MI: Michigan State University Press, 1957), 77.

54. Alexis de Tocqueville, *The Old Regime and the French Revolution*, trans. John Bonner (New York: Harper & Brothers, 1856); Alfred Cobban, *The Social Interpretation of the French Revolution* (New York: Cambridge University Press, 1964).

55. W. W. Rostow, *The Stages of Economic Growth*, 7th ed. (Cambridge, UK: Cambridge University Press, 1969), 93–105.

56. Nove, *Communist Economic Strategy*, 4.

57. S. Zagorsky, *State Control of Industry in Russia During the War* (New Haven, CT: Yale University Press, 1928), 145–9.

58. Nove, *Communist Economic Strategy*, 4.

59. Ibid., 4.

60. Immediately following this paragraph, Rodney included a long passage that he crossed out. It is not clear why he deleted it, but it is worth reproducing here: "In the historiography of the Soviet Revolution and in several other contexts, bourgeois writers are guilty of treating industrialization and modernization as though [they] were independent of ideology and the notion of social equality. They are also guilty of treating the way Britain and Germany developed industrially as colonial powers in the same way that Russia, China and Korea developed in spite of being victims of foreign capitalism. E. H. Carr, to some extent, reveals that such an approach is unhistorical. He perceived that 'in Great Britain foreign trade and the international division of labour was thought of as an integral part of the economy and an instrument of progress, in Russia it was a badge of inferiority and backwardness, of a situation in which Russia was an "agrarian colony of the industrial west."' Here Carr is coming close to an appreciation of the fact that in the 20th century, any development of the colonized area must be development in spite of imperialism and the international division of labour established during the capitalist epoch. He does not go far enough." The Carr quote is from "Some Random Reflections on Soviet Industrialization," in *Socialism, Capitalism, and Economic Growth: Essays Presented to Maurice Dobb*, ed. C. H. Feinstein (Cambridge, UK: Cambridge University Press, 1967), 283.

61. Klaus Mehnert, *Stalin vs Marx: The Stalinist Historical Doctrine*

(London: George Allen and Unwin, 1952).

62. Hugh Trevor-Roper, "Karl Marx and the Study of History," *Problems of Communism* 5 (September–October 1956), 36–42; the essay also appears in Trevor-Roper's collection *Men and Events: Historical Essays* (New York: Harper & Brothers, 1957), 285–98.

8 The Transformation of Empire

1. Between the Tsarist Empire's first census in 1897 and the Revolution of 1917, the numbers of nationalities/ethnic groups in Russia fluctuate between 170 and 200. An accurate "count" is impossible since the 1905 Revolution opened a path for more demands for national recognition, rights, and even sovereignty. It is a complicated issue, which is precisely Rodney's point: the nationality question is in flux at this moment and no matter how we count, the numbers are massive. Since Rodney delivered these lectures, there has been an explosion of work on nationalities and the shift from empire to a socialist regime committed to national self-determination. See, for example, Ronald Grigor Suny, "Nationalities in the Russian Empire," *Russian Review* 59 (October 2000), 487–92; Juliette Cadiot, "Searching for Nationality: Statistics and National Categories at the End of the Russian Empire (1897–1917)," *Russian Review* 64 (July 2005), 440–55; Theodore R. Weeks, *Nation and State in Late Imperial Russia: Nationalism and Russification on the Western Frontier, 1863–1914* (DeKalb, IL: Northern Illinois University Press, 1996); Willard Sunderland, *Taming the Wild Field: Colonization and Empire on the Russian Steppe* (Ithaca, NY: Cornell University Press, 2004); Jeffrey Sahadeo, *Russian Colonial Empire in Tashkent, 1865–1923* (Bloomington, IN: Indiana University Press, 2007); and the cutting edge essays in these edited collections: Jane Burbank, Mark Von Hagen, and Anatolyi Remnev, eds., *Russian Empire: Space, People, Power, 1700–1930* (Bloomington, IN: Indiana University Press, 2007); Ronald Suny and Terry Martin, eds., *A State of Nations: Empire and Nation-Making in the Age of Lenin and Stalin* (New York: Oxford University Press, 2001).

2. The question of dual colonial legal systems has been further explored since Rodney's engagements with the subject, in particular the recent work of Mahmood Mamdani, a student and comrade

of Rodney's in Dar, *Define and Rule: Native as Political Identity (The W. E. B. Du Bois Lectures)* (Cambridge, MA: Harvard University Press, 2012).

3. Beneath this section Rodney wrote, "Note Lenin's preface to his *Imperialism*." We believe he is referring to the original preface rather than the preface to the French and German editions. The original preface is a very short apologia for having to mask his indictment of Russian imperialism in order to get past the censors. Thus, we can reasonably speculate that he is referring to the following passage: "In order to show how shamelessly they *screen* the annexations of *their* capitalists, I was forced to quote as an example—Japan! The careful reader will easily substitute Russia for Japan, and Finland, Poland, Courland, the Ukraine, Khiva, Bokhara, Estonia or other regions peopled by non–Great Russians, for Korea." Lenin, "Preface," *Imperialism: The Highest Stage of Capitalism* (1916), available at marxists.org.

4. Here Rodney is probably drawing his impressions from reading Frederick C. Barghoorn, *Soviet Russian Nationalism* (New York: Oxford University Press, 1956); Richard A. Pierce, *Russian Central Asia 1867–1917: A Study in Colonial Rule* (Berkeley, CA: University of California Press, 1960); and possibly George J. Demko, *The Russian Colonisation of Kazakhstan 1896-1916* (Bloomington, IN: Indiana University Press, 1969), works with which he disagrees. But he is groping for a deeper analysis, one that anticipates much of the current work on settler colonialism. Indeed, his thoughts here, though incomplete, reveal an affinity with the recent excellent work by Alexander Morrison, especially "Russian Settler Colonialism," in *The Routledge Handbook of the History of Settler Colonialism*, eds. Lorenzo Veracini and Ed Cavanagh (Abingdon, VA: Routledge, 2017), 313–26, and "Peasant Settlers and the 'Civilizing Mission' in Russian Turkestan, 1865–1917," *Journal of Imperial and Commonwealth History* 43, No. 3 (2015), 387–417.

5. In the original lecture notes, Rodney places in parentheses: "Examples from Britain and the USA—Civil Rights legislation." By this we can assume that he is referring to legislation such as the Civil Rights Act (1964) and Voting Rights Act (1965) in the United States; and in the case of Britain, where there is no parallel body of civil rights laws per se, perhaps he was referring to their signing of the European Convention on Human Rights in 1950, the advent of

decolonization in the '50s and '60s, and the adoption of anti-discrimination legislation in the '70s, modeled on US civil rights law.

6. V. I. Lenin, *The State and Revolution: The Marxist Theory of the State and the Tasks of the Proletariat in the Revolution* (1918), in *Lenin: Collected Works*, vol. 25 (Moscow: Progress Publishers, 1964), 385–499, available at marxists.org.

7. Oblasts were administrative units—a province or region in the Russian Empire that the Soviets repurposed as administrative divisions of the union republics.

8. Georges Jorré, *The Soviet Union: The Land and its People*, trans. E. D. Laborde, rev. C. A. Halstead (London: Longmans, 1967, third ed.), 90.

9. On the almost-singular focus on Moscow and Petrograd, Rodney cited Arthur E. Adams, *The Russian Revolution and Bolshevik Victory: Causes and Processes* (Boston: D. C. Heath, 1960), 64. Judging from partial citations listed in this text, his descriptions of the peopling of Russia come from his reading of Jorré, *The Soviet Union*; Paul E. Lydolph, *Geography of the USSR* (New York: John Wiley and Sons, 1964); Roy E. H. Mellor, *Geography of the USSR* (London: Macmillan, 1964); Erich Thiel, *The Soviet Far East: A Survey of its Physical and Economic Geography* (New York: Praeger, 1957).

10. Barghoorn, *Soviet Russian Nationalism*; Richard A. Pierce, *Russian Central Asia 1867–1917*. There is yet a third book published in 1969 that addressed the shift in Soviet historiography on nationalities and national liberation movements very directly: Lowell Tillett, *The Great Friendship: Soviet Historians on the Non-Russian Nationalities* (Chapel Hill, NC: University of North Carolina Press, 1969), 171–93. It should be noted that this first generation of Soviet historians also included Kazakhs or other non-Russians.

11. In the original text, Rodney wrote "a prison of nationalities," which is a fairly common translation of Lenin from the Russian, but going back to his own writings and the source of the phrase, it is translated as "prison of nations." We decided to correct it since we could not find any citation for "prison of nationalities"—it was quoted frequently without attribution. For the original quote, see, V. I. Lenin, "On the Question of National Policy" (April 1914), *Collected Works*, vol. 20, (Moscow: Progress Publishers, 1972), 218, available at marxists.org.

12. See Tillett, *The Great Friendship: Soviet Historians on the Non-Russian Nationalities*, 331–81.

13. Barghoorn, *Soviet Russian Nationalism*, 28–34, chapter 2.

14. Pierce, *Russian Central Asia 1867–1917*, 248.

15. Richard Pipes, *The Formation of the Soviet Union: Communism and Nationalism, 1917–1924* (Cambridge, MA: Harvard University Press, 1964, 2nd ed.). Rodney most likely had access to the revised edition, which we cite here. Pipes's text was first published in 1954.

15 Richard Pipes, "National Minorities Sought Autonomy and Independence," in Adams, ed., *The Russian revolution and Bolshevik Victory*, 64.

16. Pipes, *The Formation of the Soviet Union*, 1–20.

17. Rodney's prime target is Pipes, *The Formation of the Soviet Union*, which is also considered to this day the best account by a Cold War historian. His work has since come under scrutiny not only by Marxist historians but many non-Marxists. The result has been a more sympathetic treatment of Bolshevik national policy and Lenin's concept of self-determination, portraying him as neither a "chauvinist," an "imperialist," nor a Machiavellian manipulating national sentiments to build Bolshevik power. See Helene Carrère d'Encausse, *The Great Challenge: Nationalities and the Bolshevik State, 1917–1930* (New York: Holmes & Meier, 1992, French ed. 1987); Yuri Slezkine, "The USSR as a Communal Apartment, or How a Socialist State Promoted Ethnic Particularism," *Slavic Review* 53, no. 2 (1994), 414–52; Terry Martin, *The Affirmative Action Empire: Nations and Nationalism in the Soviet Union, 1923–1929* (Ithaca, NY: Cornell University Press, 2001).

18. This is an old parochial phrase with which most young readers might not be familiar. For some it refers to the sound of glasses striking, evoking the bourgeoisie toasting with champagne or expensive wine. Or it is the sound of coins or a cash register. We considered deleting it for clarity but chose to keep it in since it reveals something of Rodney's wicked sense of humor.

19. Pipes, *The Formation of the Soviet Union*, 22.

20. Ibid., 23.

21. Lenin, *Imperialism: The Highest Stage of Capitalism*; Lenin, "The Revolutionary Proletariat and the Right of Nations to Self-Determination," (1915), Lenin Collected Works, vol. 21 (Moscow: Progress Publishers, 1974), 407–14, available at marxists.org. Rodney's summary of Lenin's position here is echoed by Pipes, who

writes that the colonies represent "a vast reservoir of potential allies of socialism in its struggle against Imperialism. This struggle could be effectively undertaken only on a world-wide scale and socialism had to take advantage of the forces of popular dissatisfaction by allying itself with the liberation movements in the colonies." *The Formation of the Soviet Union*, 48.

22. Rodney here is clearly referring to Richard Wright, *Black Power: An American Negro Views the African Gold Coast* (New York: Harper, 1954); Aimé Césaire, *Discourse on Colonialism* (New York: Monthly Review Press, 2000, orig. 1950); and George Padmore, *Pan-Africanism or Communism: The Coming Struggle for Africa* (London: Dennis Dobson, 1956). Although he did no more than jot down the names of these three authors in parentheses, it should be evident that he is sympathetic to their arguments despite their respective breaks with the Soviet Union. What they all had in common was a radical critique of colonialism that recognized class divisions among the colonized, warned of the potential betrayal of the black elites, and characterized Soviet meddling as a new form of imperialism. National liberation did not mean the end of class struggle, nor should one conclude that Wright, Césaire, or Padmore placed race *over* class. This is the kind of sophisticated analysis Rodney not only appreciated but applied to all of his work, notably *How Europe Underdeveloped Africa* (1972).

23. In parentheses, Rodney jotted down three last names: Reshetar, Lang, Wheeler. Here are the sources to which he is likely referring: John S. Reshetar, Jr., *The Ukrainian Revolution, 1917–20: A Study in Nationalism* (Princeton, NJ: Princeton University Press, 1952); David Marshall Lang, *A Modern History of Georgia* (London: Weidenfeld and Nicolson, 1962) and *The Georgians* (New York: Praeger, 1966); Geoffrey Wheeler, *The Modern History of Soviet Central Asia* (London: Weidenfeld and Nicolson, 1964) and *The Peoples of Soviet Central Asia: A Background Book* (London: Bodley Head, 1966).

24. Pipes, *The Formation of the Soviet Union*, 53–74.

25. Ibid., 61 and 67, respectively.

26. See, for example, Leander Schneider, *Government of Development: Peasants and Politicians in Postcolonial Tanzania* (Bloomington, IN: Indiana University Press, 2014).

9 The Critique of Stalinism

1. See Karl Marx, "Preface," *A Contribution to the Critique of Political Economy* (New York: International Publishers, 1970), 21.
2. "Engels to J. Bloch, September 21, 22, 1890," in *Karl Marx and Friedrich Engels: Selected Works,* vol. 2 (Moscow: Foreign Languages Publishing House, 1962), 488.
3. "Engels to H. Starkenburg, January 25, 1894," Ibid., 503.
4. Following this passage, Rodney added in parentheses "Abramovitch, Mehnert, Trevor-Roper, Plamenatz, Schapiro." The specific citations to which he is referring are most likely these: Raphael Abramovitch, *The Soviet Revolution, 1917–1939* (New York: International Universities Press, 1962); Klaus Mehnert, *Stalin versus Marx* (London: George Allen & Unwin, 1952); H. R. Trevor-Roper, "Karl Marx and the Study of History," in Trevor-Roper, *Men and Events: Historical Essays* (New York: Harper & Brothers, 1957), 285–98; John Plamenatz, *From Marx to Stalin* (London: Batchworth Press, 1953); Plamenatz, *German Marxism and Russian Communism* (London: Longmans, 1954); Leonard Schapiro, *The Origins of Communist Autocracy: Opposition in the Soviet State, 1922–1938* (Cambridge, MA: Harvard University Press, 1955).
5. Mao Tse Tung, "On Contradiction," (August 1937), *The Selected Works of Mao Tse Tung,* vol. I (Peking: Foreign Languages Press, 1967), 336.
6. V. I. Lenin, "Our Foreign and Domestic Position and Party Tasks Speech Delivered To the Moscow Gubernia Conference Of The R.C.P.(B.), November 21, 1920," *Lenin Collected Works,* vol. 31 (Moscow: Progress Publishers, 1965), 419. Rodney most likely found the quote in Adam Ulam, *The Bolsheviks: The Intellectual and Political History of the Triumph of Communism in Russia* (New York: Macmillan, 1965), 481.
7. See John Plamenatz, *German Marxism and Russian Communism,* especially chapter 10. Rodney, it seems, was taking issue with Plamenatz's argument that the Marxism was the product of the revolutionary traditions of eighteenth-century Western Europe, and for all of its limitations emerged in an environment the cherished freedom, civil liberties, and democracy. Marx was essentially a democrat. But once Lenin and the Bolsheviks got a hold of Marxism, they distorted it for their own pragmatic means, laying the foundations for a dictatorship based on violent state repression

as early as 1902. Russia simply wasn't prepared for revolution, materially or ideologically. As Plamenatz put it, "Bolshevism is the distorted Marxism of a backward society exposed to the impact of the West." (318)

8. Leon Trotsky, *The Revolution Betrayed: What is the Soviet Union and Where is it Going*, trans. Max Eastman (London: Faber & Faber, Ltd., 1937); Isaac Deutscher, *The Prophet: The Life of Leon Trotsky* (London and New York: Verso, 2015); Isaac Deutscher, *Stalin: A Political Biography* (New York: Vintage, 1960, orig. 1949).

9. Often translated at "Proletarians of the world unite" or, more frequently, "Workers of the world unite." There are literally hundreds of editions of the *Communist Manifesto* (1848).

10. Trotsky, *The Revolution Betrayed*, 91–2, 275–84.

11. Surprisingly, Rodney glosses over the international consequences of Stalin's theory of "socialism in one country." While in theory, the direction of "genuine social revolutions" may be governed by local conditions, the Communist International imposed a discipline on Communist parties all over the world geared toward defending Soviet interests—often at the expense of their own revolutionary movements. The example Trotsky gives is of Stalin and Bukharin directing the Chinese Communist Party to maintain an alliance with Chiang Kai-shek and the nationalists, who ultimately used the Communists to organize workers to wage battles on behalf of the nationalists, both to take over cities such as Shanghai and to fight the warlords in the North. Then in 1927, Chiang turned on the Communists, arresting them en masse and slaughtering as many as 200,000. Despite the massacre, the Comintern still forced the Chinese Communist Party to maintain a united front with the nationalists. The united front collapsed only when Chiang began to reject Soviet assistance and turn to Chinese business interests. At this point the Comintern finally changed course, but it was too late. There are other examples to which we can point: the "third period" when Communists were directed to attack the Left inside the social democratic parties and the trade unions; the popular front, when Communists were asked to build alliances with liberals to fight fascism and defend the USSR at the expense of the proletarian revolution; the period of the Nazi-Soviet Pact (1939–1941), when Communists were instructed to support a non-aggression pact that cleared the way for the Nazi invasion of Poland and simultaneously enabled Russia to invade Finland. One could

argue that local parties could simply choose to operate independently of the Soviets, but there are too many examples of "local" party leaders having to face disciplinary action, expulsion, or worse, for "deviating" from the party line. See Elliot Liu, *Maoism and the Chinese Revolution: A Critical Introduction* (Oakland, CA: PM Press, 2016); C. L. R. James, *World Revolution, 1917–1936: The Rise and Fall of the Communist International* (Durham, NC: Duke University Press, 2017, orig. 1937); E. H. Carr, *The Comintern and the Spanish Civil War* (New York: Pantheon, 1984).

12. Again, Rodney's treatment of Trotsky and the Left Opposition's support for what had been called "super-industrialization" is a little disingenuous. First, the Left Opposition argued that the socialist state could not advance as long as it was forced to trade agricultural produce for imported manufactured goods. Such a policy would have only enriched the kulak rather than connected socialist industries with the peasant economy. They proposed accelerating industrialization in part by taxing the kulaks. Stalin and Bukharin vehemently rejected "super-industrialization" as well as their proposal for a Five-Year Plan. Moreover, the Left Opposition were labeled Trotskyists and ultimately condemned to state repression or exile. A few years later, Stalin adopted the Five-Year Plan as a model for development as well as a version of super-industrialization as if it were his own. But Trotsky maintains that what transpired in the name of speeding up the tempo of industrialization occurred "under impulses from without, with a crude smashing of all calculations and an extraordinary increase of overhead expenses." Trotsky, *The Revolution Betrayed*, 33–6; Martin Abern, "Vindicating the Trotsky Platform," *The Militant* 2, no. 1 (January 1, 1929), 6; Ruth Fischer, *Stalin and German Communism: A Study in the Origins of the State Party* (New Brunswick and London: Transaction Publishers, 1948), 567; Richard B. Day, *Leon Trotsky and the Politics of Economic Isolation* (Cambridge, UK: Cambridge University Press, 1973), 165.

13. Trotsky, *The Revolution Betrayed*, 105.

14. Ibid., 90–1.

15. Deutscher, *Stalin: A Political Biography* (New York: Vintage, 1960, orig. 1949), 256–60; he writes quite a bit about bureaucratization and its consequences in *The Prophet Armed*, especially chapters 4 and 5 of volume 2.

16. Trotsky, *The Revolution Betrayed*, 94.

17. Leonard Schapiro, *The Government and Politics of the Soviet*

Union (London: Hutchinson University Library, 1967), 50.

18. Ibid., 44–55.

19. Following this sentence, Rodney wrote in parentheses, "Koestler & others on the intellectuals—Carr, Labin on Secret Police—anti-religion." He is probably referencing Arthur Koestler, *Darkness at Noon* (New York: Macmillan, 1941); Victor Kravchenko, *I Chose Freedom: The Personal and Political Life of a Soviet Official* (New York: Charles Scribner's Sons, 1946); Richard Krebs [Jan Valtin], *Out of the Night* (New York: Alliance Book Corporation, 1941); Suzanne Labin, *Stalin's Russia* (London: Victor Gollancz, 1949); E. H. Carr, "The Origin and Status of the Cheka," *Soviet Studies* 10, no. 1 (July 1958), 1–11. It is worth noting that comparisons between Hitler and Stalin, and Nazi Germany and the Soviet Union, remain a popular subject for historians and journalists in the post–Cold War era, although some of the recent comparative work plays down similarities. See Michael Geyer and Sheila Fitzpatrick, eds., *Beyond Totalitarianism: Stalinism and Nazism Compared* (Cambridge, UK: Cambridge University Press, 2008); Richard Overy, *The Dictators: Hitler's Germany, Stalin's Russia* (New York: W. W. Norton, 2004); Allen Bullock, *Hitler and Stalin: Parallel Lives* (New York: Vintage, 1993); Ian Kershaw and Moshe Lewin, eds., *Stalinism and Nazism: Dictatorships in Comparison* (Cambridge, UK: Cambridge University Press, 1997).

20. Schapiro, *The Government and Politics of the Soviet Union*, 51.

21. Academy of Sciences of the USSR Institute of History, *A Short History of the USSR*, vol. 2 (Moscow: Progress Publishers, 1965), 289.

22. Ibid., 180.

23. Ibid., 178.

24. Writing in 1970–71, Rodney was correct. Following the collapse of the Soviet Union and the opening of the archives, we've witnessed a mountain of new scholarship reassessing the revolution and the Stalinist period. And yet, the kinds of ideological and political constraints Rodney discusses have not completely disappeared; they have taken new forms. Within Russia itself, the state under Vladimir Putin has sought to directly influence the writing of history, pushing both for a more critical assessment of Stalinism as part of a global strategy to reengage the West, and a vindication of Soviet achievements provoked by a resurgence of Russian nationalism. In the United States and the broader neoliberal world of global capital, narratives of the abject failure of the socialist experiment prevail. See Thomas Sherlock, "Russian politics and the Soviet past: Reassessing Stalin and

Stalinism under Vladimir Putin," *Communist and Post-Communist Studies* 49, no. 1 (March 2016), 45–59, and his book, *Historical Narratives in the Soviet Union and Post-Soviet Russia: Destroying the Settled Past, Creating an Uncertain Future* (New York: Palgrave, 2007); Sheila Fitzpatrick, ed., *Stalinism: New Directions* (New York: Routledge, 1999); Ronald Grigor Suny, *Red Flag Unfurled: Historians, the Russian Revolution, and the Soviet Experience* (New York: Verso, 2017). On the other hand, while Rodney's call for a genuine and "profound socio-historical analysis" of Stalinism still eludes us, we've also seen the development of new scholarship that looks at Stalinism "from below," in the practice of authority in everyday life, expressions of art and culture, in social and family relations, among other things. This work partly confirms Rodney's central thesis that the "distortions" of Stalinism do not fall on the shoulders of one man but on the people, the party, and the broad structure of the society. See, for example, Sheila Fitzpatrick, *Everyday Stalinism: Ordinary Life in Extraordinary Times – Soviet Life in the 1930s* (New York: Oxford University Press, 2000, 2nd ed.); J. Arch Getty, *Practicing Stalinism: Bolsheviks, Boyars, and the Persistence of Tradition* (New Haven, CT: Yale University Press, 2013); Boris Groys, *The Total Art of Stalinism: Avant-Garde, Aesthetic Dictatorship, and Beyond*, trans. Charles Rougle (New York: Verso, 2011); Sergei Prozorov, *The Biopolitics of Stalinism: Ideology and Life in Soviet Socialism* (Edinburgh: Edinburgh University Press, 2016).

25. See V. I. Lenin, "'Last Testament' Letters to the Congress," (December 1922–January 1923), *Lenin Collected Works*, vol. 36, 593–611, available at marxists.org; Lenin, "Better Fewer, But Better," (March 2, 1923), *Lenin Collected Works*, vol. 33, 487–502, available at marxists.org.

26. Lavrentiy Beria, a fellow Georgian like Stalin, was appointed head of the People's Commissariat for Internal Affairs (NKVD), which essentially became Stalin's secret police force. He was responsible for carrying out purges and directing the Gestapo tactics of the state. After Stalin's death, he made a bid to take power but was assassinated in 1953 by a faction backing Khrushchev. The most thorough treatment of Beria is Amy Knight, *Beria: Stalin's First Lieutenant* (Princeton, NJ: Princeton University Press, 1993).

27. Today many scholars on the left identify the counterrevolution as Stalinist suppression of workers' power and workers' control and democracy. Of course, this resonates with Trotsky's movement for a

Fourth International, but most of these new historians are not Trotsky acolytes. Perhaps the best account is Kevin Murphy, *Revolution and Counterrevolution: Class Struggle in a Moscow Metal Factory* (New York and Oxford: Berghahn Books, 2005). On ways in which Rodney's defense of the state police as a bulwark against counterrevolution breaks with C. L. R. James, see the introduction to this volume.

28. Rodney further elaborates his analysis of fascism in *How Europe Underdeveloped Africa*, 196.

29. There is a vast literature examining the fascist roots of apartheid, comparing apartheid to the fascist state, and/or situating fascism and apartheid within a larger trajectory of racial capitalism. Some of this work was obvious produced in Rodney's lifetime. See, for example, Pierre L. van den Berghe, "Apartheid, Fascism and the Golden Age," *Cahiers d'Études Africaines* 2, no. 8 (1962), 598–608; Brian Bunting, *The Rise of the South African Reich* (Harmondsworth, UK: Penguin,1964); Harold Wolpe, *Race, Class, and the Apartheid State* (Trenton, NJ: Africa World Press, 1990); Dan O'Meara, *Volkskapitalisme: Class, Capital and Ideology in the Development of Afrikaner Nationalism, 1934–1948* (Johannesburg: Ravan Press, 1983); H. Simson, *The Social Origins of Afrikaner Fascism and Its Apartheid Policy* (Stockholm: Almquist and Wiksell International, 1980); Patrick J. Furlong, *Between Crown and Swastika: The Impact of the Radical Right on the Afrikaner Nationalist Movement in the Fascist Era* (Middletown, CT: Wesleyan University Press, 1991).

30. Francis B. Randall, *Stalin's Russia: An Historical Reconsideration* (New York: The Free Press, 1965).

31. Hendrik F. Verwoerd was South Africa's prime minister from 1958–1966, leader of the Afrikaner National Party, and one of the main architects of the apartheid state. Balthazar Johannes (John) Voerster was also a National Party stalwart who supported the Nazis during the Second World War. He served as minister of justice during the Rivonia Trial that resulted in Nelson Mandela's life sentence for sabotage, and prime minister from 1966–78. He was ultimately forced to resign when it was revealed that he had secretly skimmed from the military budget to finance a secret pro-apartheid propaganda campaign. Voerster accepted a symbolic appointment as president in 1978 but was forced to resign in disgrace after eight months. On Verwoerd, seesahistory.org.za/people/hendrik-frensch-verwoerd; on Voerster, seesahistory.org.za/people/balthazar-johannes-vorster.

Index

Walter Rodney
Foundation

Walter Rodney (1942–1980) was a historian, Africanist, professor, author and scholar-activist. Rodney challenged assumptions of Western historians about African history, provided a framework to address the underdevelopment of the African continent and its people, and proposed new standards for analyzing the history of oppressed peoples. Rodney's works provide a platform to discuss contemporary issues and are comprehensive historical resources.

The Walter Rodney Foundation (WRF) is a 501(c)(3) not-for-profit organization that was formed by the Rodney Family to share the life and works of Dr. Walter Rodney with students, scholars, researchers, activists and communities worldwide. The WRF seeks to advance Rodney's contributions to the praxis of scholarship, political activism and consciousness, and social change. Proceeds from this book support the work of The Walter Rodney Foundation.

CONTACT:
The Walter Rodney Foundation
3645 Marketplace Blvd, Suite 130-353
Atlanta, GA 30344

walterrodneyfoundation.com

Phone: 678.597.8754 | Fax : 404.601.1885
Email: walterrodneyfoundation@gmail.com
Twitter: @RodneyProject
Facebook: facebook.com/thewalterrodneyfoundation

KEY ROLES and ACTIVITIES of
THE WALTER RODNEY FOUNDATION

<u>Walter Rodney Papers</u>: In 2003, the Walter Rodney Papers were donated by the Rodney family to the Atlanta University Center Robert W. Woodruff Library (AUC RWWL) in Atlanta, Georgia. The Collection is the largest and most comprehensive collection of writings, speeches, correspondence, photographs and documents created by or about Walter Rodney anywhere in the world and are available for viewing and research. Travel Awards are available. Contact 404.978.2052 or archives@auctr.edu.

<u>Publications</u>: Rodney authored more than ten books and fifty articles, including *How Europe Underdeveloped Africa* and *A History of the Upper Guinea Coast*. An up-to-date bibliography of all books, papers, journals and articles written by and about Walter Rodney is maintained. The Foundation also publishes the peer-reviewed journal, *Groundings: Development, Pan-Africanism and Critical Theory*.

<u>Walter Rodney Legacy Projects</u>: Ongoing worldwide outreach to collect, record and preserve oral history, information and memories about Dr. Walter Rodney. All materials will become a part of the Walter Rodney Collection at the AUC RWWL.

<u>Walter Rodney Symposium</u>: Since 2004, an annual symposium is held in Atlanta, Georgia, during the week of Walter Rodney's birthday (23 March). The goal is to bring together scholars, researchers, activists, students and the community to discuss contemporary issues from a Rodney perspective and how Rodney's methodology remains relevant today.

<u>Walter Rodney Speaker Series</u>: An annual spring lecture series started in 2013, based on the life and legacy of Dr. Walter Rodney. In collaboration with Atlanta area colleges and universities, undergraduate and graduate students can register for the course component and receive credit towards their degrees.